Four Thousand Bowls of Rice

A PRISONER OF WAR COMES HOME

The Men We Left Behind

The "Lost Battalion" made their stand
On the island of Java, a foreign land,
Waiting for help that did not come
Doing all that could be done.

While in Sunda Strait, in a valiant fight
The Houston vanished in the night,
Carrying most of her crew to a watery grave,
An honored crypt for the lives they gave.

These men first met as prisoners-of-war,
Not knowing what Fate would have in store,
Beaten and starved, tortured and ill,
Months became years as our world stood still.

"Hellships" and jungles, the "Railway of Death",
Forced to work till our dying breath.
The cemeteries filled, the rails bore on,
Still faith remained when strength was gone.

Sixteen thousand men: English, Aussie, Dutch and Yanks
Died waiting for ships, and planes, and tanks,
Now they lie in peace 'neath Eastern soil,
Free from starvation, disease and toil.

Though their bodies remain, the soul departs,
Their names cherished forever in our hearts,
On God's green earth you'll never find,
Better men than those we left behind.

Lloyd V. Willey, died in 2006.

Brick Tower Press
New York

Brick Tower Press
1230 Park Avenue
New York, New York 10128

© Linda Goetz Holmes 2002

Cover design by Mike Stromberg
Typeset by The Great American Art Co.

Library of Congress Cataloging-in-Publication Data

Linda Goetz Holmes
Four Thousand Bowls of Rice
Includes biographical reference and index.
ISBN 1-883283-51-5
1. Holmes, Linda, —

Trade Paperback, Nonfiction, Adult/General, Biography
& Autobiography, Military, World War II

Library of Congress Control Number: 2007937284
First Trade Paper Edition November 2007

Contents

3209

Illustrations

*indicates photo taken secretly in captivity

To All the Members of the 2/2 Australian Pioneer Battalion

Wherever they Draw the Sweet Breath of Freedom

or Wherever They Lie at Rest

Who Taught Us All What Brotherhood Really Means

And to Margaret

Who Loved Her Gallant Lad With All Her Heart

This Book Is Respectfully Dedicated

Colonel J.M. Williams, OBE, ED, Commanding Officer,
2/2 Autralian Pioneer Battalion. This photo was taken in 1941,
when Williams was Second-in-command, 2/17 Autralian Infantry Battalion.
(COURTESY OF J.M. WILLIAMS)

Foreword

Colonel J.M. Williams, OBE, ED
Commanding Officer, 2/2 Australian
Pioneer Battalion, 1941–45

Linda Holmes has written very vividly about her friend Cecil Dickson who was a Staff Sergeant in the 2/2 Pioneer Battalion and of his experiences as a prisoner of war of the Japanese, captured in Java and taken to Burma to work on the Burma Railway.

She has gone to a considerable amount of trouble to tell why the Japanese acted as they did during the building of the Burma Railway, and to explain the treatment they meted out to the prisoners of war in Japan.

There is another period in Sergeant Dickson's army experience which is yet unexplained, and which needs to be told about the action he and his unit took part in, and the part they played in the planned Japanese action.

After serving with distinction in the Syrian Campaign, the 2/2 Pnr Bn returned to Palestine and was brought up to strength and refitted and together with 2/3 MG Bn, 2/6 Fld Coy, 105 Gen. Tpt Coy, it set sail on the HMT *Orcades* on 1 February 1942 for an undisclosed destination.

After a false landing at Oosthaven, the *Orcades* arrived in Java on 16 February 1942. An exchange of cables with Australia resulted in the troops on the *Orcades* being ordered to land and join the American, British and Dutch troops on Java, under the command of Field Marshall Lord Wavell, and to guard five airfields with these troops.

When the Japanese landed on Java they were stopped by Black Force (Brig. A.S. Blackburn) at Llewiliang River, with the 2/2 Pnr Bn defending the bridge. At this stage, orders were received from the Dutch Command to withdraw to the capital and capitulate. We became prisoners of war of the Japanese on 5 March 1942.

During my interrogation by the Japanese Staff in Java, they pressed me for information regarding the whereabouts of the 6th and 7th Australian Divisions. They had assumed that these divisions had already landed in Java and had held up the initial advance of the Japanese. Now the 6th and 7th Divisions had disappeared!

We now know that both the 6th and 7th Divisions were diverted to Columbo, then sent unescorted, via the Indian Ocean, to Australia. These were the troops who stopped the Japanese advance on New Guinea.

The Japanese Task Force that landed in Java via the Sunda Straits, sinking the *HMAS Perth* and the *USS Houston* was at sea heading for Darwin when it heard that the 6th and 7th Divisions had landed in Java. It changed course and eventually landed in Java. The Japanese from this Task Force were trying to exchange their invasion money—Australian pound notes made in Japan—with the Australian prisoners of war for Dutch coins.

Did the landing of the troops from the *Orcades* in Java cause the Task Force heading for Australia to change course?

Over the years since World War II there have been many books telling of the experiences and hardships of those who were prisoners of the war of the Japanese, but Linda Holmes has managed to produce an interesting book written from a totally different aspect.

I know something of the time spent by Les Hall in writing, checking and re-checking details from his oft quoted *Blue Haze*. I can only start to imagine the time, effort and patience it has taken Linda Holmes to produce *Four Thousand Bowls of Rice*. She should be well satisfied.

J.M. Williams
February 1993

Acknowledgements

Permission to quote from their work is gratefully acknowledged:

A.H. Bishop, for permission to use excerpts from his unpublished manuscript, 'A Voyage With the Jap in South East Asia'; Sir Edward Dunlop, for permission to quote from the preface to his *War Diaries;* Benjamin Dunn, for permission to use excerpts from his book, *The Bamboo Express;* The Reverend Dr. Ernest Gordon, for permission to use passages from his book, *Miracle on the River Kwai;* Leslie G. Hall, to quote portions of his book, *The Blue Haze,* and his unpublished manuscript, 'The Queen of Hearts'; Takashi Nagase, for permission to use excerpts from his book, *Crosses and Tigers;* and H. Shigeru Yagake, for permission to use portions of his essay which appeared in an edition of the newspaper *Rafu Shimpo.*

In addition, the author is grateful to artist Ronald Searle for permission to use portions of text from his book, *To The Kwai—And Back,* and to the Australian War Memorial for reproducing the photographs, newspaper clipping and war diary from their archives, as well as the drawings from their exhibit, 'Prisoners of War', which appear in this book.

So many people, in several parts of the globe, helped this book to happen; it is daunting to wonder if I can name them all.

In Australia: Special, heartfelt thanks to Margaret Dickson, whose willingness to share her precious mementos made this work possible; and to members of the Dickson and Dodgshun families: to Cecil's brother, John Dickson who, though bedridden, knew just where to tell his nieces to look for a special photograph; to Celeste Dickson, Jeanette Malone, Barbara and Brian Clements and Maryan Reynolds, for sharing their memories.

To E. H. 'Ted' Hansen, President of the 2/2 Pioneer Battalion Association in Melbourne, for his hospitality; to George Murphy, Secretary of the Association, for endlessly and patiently supplying addresses of Pioneers, and offering so much friendship and technical assistance in other ways; to Lionel 'Snowy'

Anderson for photocopying Walter Summons' book and the entire Battalion History, to send me; to Pioneers Bob Adolphson, Harry Bishop, George Carroll, Jack D'Argaville, Gordon Hamilton, Bill Mayne, Kevin Nolan, Tom O'Brien, and Ron Winning for sharing recollections with such precision and detail; and to Harry Whelan, for his colorful insights about daily camp life among the Pioneers, I owe so much. And I thank the many who dug out personal photographs and sent them half way around the world for me to copy. I am in awe of Jack Hocking, whose carefully crafted and detailed newsletters are a tribute to the brotherhood which so clearly marks this Battalion.

I appreciate the reminiscences of Eileen Mitchell, for sharing what it was like to wait all those years.

Just about in a class by himself is Cal Mitchell, whose early and continued correspondence has been invaluable; and who, by sharing the captivity photographs, has made this book special already; and whose interest, encouragement and friendship are so deeply appreciated.

To the Battalion Commanding Officer, Colonel J.M. Williams, who has taken the time to help me achieve an accuracy which would not otherwise have been possible, my heartfelt thanks.

The kind interest and clarifications rendered by that busy legend, Sir Edward 'Weary' Dunlop, will long be remembered.

I appreciate the assistance rendered by W.H. Schmitt, Federal President, Ex-POW Association of Australia; and to Gordon Jamieson of that organization. To playwright Jill Shearer for her resources and insights, I am much indebted.

Dr. Michael McKernan, Director of the Australian War Memorial, found time to help me despite my choosing the day of their 50th Anniversary for my visit. I appreciate the kindness and accomodation shown to me by AWM staff, especially Pam Ray, Curator of Photographs; Marie Wood, Assistant Curator, Brendan O'Keefe and Janet Reed.

Don Richards, Libraries Manager at the Melbourne *Herald and Weekly Times,* and his staff have rendered the kind of assistance a researcher only dreams about; my thanks for their professionalism.

To Tom Gillespie, of the War Veterans Village in Narrabeen, NSW, for the many ways he found to help me in my research and work, I am grateful.

It is not enough to thank POW author Les Hall for permission to quote from his works; his interest, encouragement and friendship are a most cherished result of this endeavor.

And it's difficult to find adequate words to thank Bruce Merchant, Senior

Vice President, Bozell Jeffress Advertising in New York. A chance conversation at the Australian Consulate in New York has resulted in a steady stream of ideas and enthusiasm, from circulating my manuscript to lists of contacts, to finding the best airline passage. The generosity of Bruce and his wife, Liz, in loaning me the use of their home in Fairlight—still dumbfounds me.

However, the Australian who has truly made this book possible is publisher Mark Tredinnick, whose early interest and perception about my concept, and willingness to take it on, has meant everything to me.

I appreciate so much the willingness of Allen & Unwin/Australia Publishing Director Patrick Gallagher to revert the rights of publication to me in 1996, paving the way for a paperback edition a decade later.

The enthusiasm of John Colby, Publisher of Brick Tower Press, in launching this edition in 2007, has been thrilling. The marketing skill of Mia Amato is very much appreciated.

Special thanks must go to my original editor, Lynne Frolich, for guiding the hardcover work along its way to publication, and to Mike Stromberg for the cover design and computer wizardry as we created this new edition.

In Japan, I am indebted to my Wellesley College classmate, Michiko Hosomi Asano, for sharing her views; and to author Takashi Nagase for understanding the nature of my queries, and for taking the time to answer them so thoughtfully.

In the United States, I owe thanks to members of the Japanese American community, for their perspectives, resources and assistance: to my neighbor, Reiko Uyeshima for finding and translating the essay by Shigeru Yagake, and for putting me in touch with Michi Nishiura Weglyn; and to Michi, whose resources and perceptions have provided my work with such valuable dimension; to The Reverend Yuri Ando, for sharing much insight and history; and to Meredith Judy of the Youth Fellowship at Hitchcock Memorial Church in Scarsdale, NY, for her sharp recollections and assistance in helping me contact Pastor and others; to Yasuko and Ryushi Hara, for their friendship and the continuity which their remembrances allowed me to glean; to Reiko Sassa, Librarian at the Japan Society; and to Judith Harper at the Society as well. My special thanks to Henry Shigeru Yagake, who added further thoughts for inclusion in my work.

Otto Schwarz, founder of the *USS Houston* Survivors Association, was a walking resource library right up until his death in August 2006, for which I am very grateful. Crayton 'Quaty' Gordon of the Lost Battalion Association has been most generous in sharing memories and resources as well, along with author Ben Dunn.

The Reverend Dr. Ernest Gordon has given me several hours of his time and perspective, for which I am especially grateful.

Margaret Dickson's daughter Susan Gross and her husband, Ralph, have provided recollections, resources and travel tips over several years, capped by carrying two manuscripts to Australia; their friendship and guidance have meant much. And many years after the first edition was published, Susan found among her mother's effects the photograph of Cecil and Freda Dickson which I tried so hard to locate for several years, and which finally becomes part of this new edition.

Edith Stark's recollections have been an unexpected treasure; and perhaps no one has illuminated Cecil Dickson's life more than The Reverend Peter D. MacLean, sometimes in ways he did not imagine.

I am indebted to Mary Allen, Librarian at Columbia Grammar School in New York, for her computer skills in tracking down source material; to Jean Lindsay, for her knowledge of the archives at the US Library of Congress; and to Andrew Malone, Librarian at the Australian Consulate in New York, for being such a constant resource.

Helen Fisher at the Australian Overseas Information Service has offered continued assistance from the beginning of this project. And Australian expatriate Joffré Burger has been a constant source of ideas and encouragement.

Perhaps no one has provided more consistent valuable advice than my friend and neighbor, literary agent Perlette Abecassis. And I owe much to another special friend and neighbor, publisher Kenneth Giniger, whose skills and contacts have been so encouraging. I am very grateful for his worldwide knowledge of the business. The expertise of retired publishing executives Strome Lamon (Simon and Schuster) and Robert Scudellari (Random House) has been very much appreciated as well.

Finally, and with a certain pride, I want to thank my sons: Ted, for his steadfast encouragement; and Philip, for his technical assistance, resources, and sense of history.

As I reviewed this list of Acknowledgments in preparation for the 2007 edition, I realized how many people listed here have died since 1993, when the list was first compiled. I have left those thanksgivings in the present tense, however, because my gratitude for their help has not been extinguished, and never will be.

Photo reproductions by Kate's One Hour Studio, Greenport, New York.

Introduction

Sometimes we learn about courage and bravery in the oddest ways. A light remark at the dinner table, thrown out with humor which belies the speaker's thoughts, can summarize unforgettable horror. Such a remark was made by my Australian friend Cecil Dickson one evening in 1979 at the dinner table in his stepdaughter's home on Shelter Island, off New York's peninsula which we call Long Island. Cecil began to chuckle as he passed along the serving dish of rice: "Do you know, heh heh, I once had over 3800 consecutive meals of rice, and do you know [more laughter] *I still enjoy rice!*"

It was easy to share Dickson's obvious mirth—unless one happened to know that those "3800 consecutive meals" were a steadily-diminishing starvation diet, grudgingly provided by Japanese captors, often for a fee demanded, as they brutally forced Dickson and 60,000 other Prisoners of War, including 668 Americans, to build the infamous Burma-Thailand Railway during World War II. 16,000 POWs died in that effort.

Dickson just happened to be the first ex-POW I met who had actually worked on the "Railway of Death", as it is commonly called by those who saw 70 men die for each mile of track laid; and he also happened to be a member of No. 1 Mobile Force, the unit which toiled the hardest of all on that project.

Despite growing up in the home of a newspaper editor with international connections, like many Americans I first learned about 'The Bridge Over the River Kwai' by seeing the classic film based on Pierre Boulle's 1954 book. For many of us, that film provided our first awareness that such horrible brutality really occurred; and even then, the facts were skewed to make a good story. For example, the pride those POW took in sabotaging the many bridges they were forced to build—was lost in the image of glorious engineering achievement projected by the film.

But one thing the movie may have accomplished was to prompt the publication of several genuine accounts of what *really* happened in the jungles of Burma and Thailand: Ernest Gordon's *Miracle on the River Kwai* [1963]; Leslie G. Hall's *The Blue Haze* [1985]; Sir Edward "Weary'" Dunlop's *War Diaries* [1986]; and more recently, Peter N. Davies' *The Man Behind The Bridge: Colonel Toosey and the River Kwai* [1991], to name a few.

According to Leslie Hall, himself a toiler on the Railway, "Of all the forces on the Burma side of the death railway, no one suffered more than the No. 1 Mobile Force." This force consisted primarily of two Australian units: one commanded by Lieutenant Colonel C.G.W. Anderson; and the second, which had as its core nearly an entire Australian unit, the 2/2 Pioneer Battalion, commanded by Lieutenant Colonel J.M. Williams. My friend Cecil Dickson was a Staff Sergeant and Company Quartermaster in the 2/2 Pioneers.

Cecil Dickson was one of the last Australian POWs to be shipped home. He arrived in Melbourne on November 3, 1945 aboard the *Circassia,* which carried the final group of ambulatory POWs to Australia—over two months after Japan's Foreign Minister Mamoru Shigemitsu signed the terms of surrender on the deck of the battleship *USS Missouri* on September 2, 1945. While restlessly awaiting repatriation Dickson, a journalist by profession, took the opportunity to write several letters to his loved ones, describing his thoughts and hopes as he looked for news from Australia. Dickson's fifteen letters to his wife, written during this interval, are the basis for this book. Through them, and the reminiscences they provoke, we can even catch glimpses of occasional acts of kindness by the Japanese, contrasted with the daily kindness the prisoners showed toward one another, often at considerable personal risk and sacrifice.

Dickson's letters are augmented by the recollections of his Pioneer friends, as well as writings and anecdotes, some published and some printed here for the first time, of fellow Australian, American and British ex-POWs who shared the Railway experience—and even a couple of Japanese who had contact with the p[risoners in Burma and Thailand.

In the concluding chapter, we will learn how some of Dickson's comrades feel, looking back on their experience from a lifetime's perspective. And we will reflect on how even after more than a half-century, many Japanese still have not learned the truth about their nation's wartime behavior.

The absence of bitterness and strength of will displayed in Dickson's remarkable letters draws us to examine more closely the life and spirit of one gallant Australian who survived, and overcame, so very much.

Thomas Cecil Dickson was born on October 6, 1902 in Geelong, Victoria, one of six children. His father, a pharmacist, was also Commodore of the Geelong Yacht Club, and the three boys, Stan, Cecil and John, became accomplished sailors under his guidance. Cecil was educated at Geelong Grammar School and Longerenong Agricultural College. As a young man he tried life as a boundary rider for a cattle ranch in Queensland, but found that his tastes had become too urbane for ranch life. However, his stint at Jackarooing was not a total waste of time; through friendship with a local soldier-settler, Dickson became attracted to the fellow's sister, Winifred [known to her family and friends as Freda] Dodgshun, whom he married in 1926.

Dickson's bride persuaded him to try life in her home town, Melbourne, where he found employment as a proofreader on the Melbourne *Argus.* Being the new man on staff, Dickson was assigned to the "lobster" shift, named for the color change observed in the eyes of those who toiled late at night in newspaper rooms. But he had the city to himself, so to speak, in the wee hours; and as a bicycle provided his transportation in those days, he took the liberty of riding it through the park to get home. Eventually, Dickson was able to put his land knowledge to use, rising to the position of Mining Editor on the *Argus.*

In 1940, when the 2nd Pioneer Battalion was being re-formed locally to meet the call of war, it became designated the 2/2 [for 2nd World War] Pioneers, and Dickson, along with his younger brother John, joined the Battalion on June 6 of that year. [see photo p. 4] The unit underwent rigorous training at Puckapunyal for what was expected to be desert warfare in the Middle East; but the survival techniques honed at 'Pucka' turned out to be invaluable during the ordeals of jungle life in Burma and Thailand. The Battalion was sent to Syria, and distinguished itself in combat against the Vichy French.

In January 1942, the combat-seasoned unit was rushed, aboard the *Orcades,* back to the Pacific to defend Australia. Instead, in a decision which remains controversial to this day [see chapter 2], the Battalion was put ashore at Java and placed under Dutch command. When the Dutch capitulated, the Pioneer Battalion was forced to surrender to the Japanese as well. Dickson and his comrades were taken prisoner, and as mentioned above, he joined thousands of other Australian, British, Dutch and American prisoners to build the Burma-Thailand Railway; and most prisoners remained in the region for nearly two years after its completion.

When Dickson finally got home in November 1945, he spent an idyllic vacation in Queenscliff with his wife, and then returned to the *Argus* He moved

*T. Cecil and John B. Dickson, Christmas 1940. This photo was taken
just before the Battalion departed for combat in the Middle East.*
(COURTESY OF JOHN B. DICKSON)

to the Melbourne *Age* briefly before starting his own publication, the *Australian Industrial and Mining Standard,* in the late 1940s. During 1946–48 he also served as press liaison officer to the Duke of Gloucester, when the Duke was appointed as His Majesty's Governor-General of Australia.

Subsequently, Dickson was persuaded to join the international financial investment firm, J.B. Were & Company, in its Melbourne office. But when a new manager fired a fellow Pioneer, Walter Summons, for whom Dickson had secured employment, Dickson became so incensed that he asked to be transferred to the firm's London office, where he remained for several years during the 1960s.

Freda Dickson's health began to fail, and the couple decided to return to Melbourne, where Freda died in 1968. Dickson traveled about for several years, visiting friends in England, the United States and other global spots of interest.

One object of frequent visitations for Dickson was Margaret Blair Eaton, whom he and Freda had met while posted in London with the Were firm. In 1976 he married Margaret, and brought her home to the Returned Services League War Veterans Village in Narrabeen, NSW, where Dickson's older brother, Stan, had already settled. The two brothers lived next door to one another in the Village for 12 years, until Cecil's death in August 1988, at the age of 85. His remains are interred in the family plot in Geelong.

After Cecil died, Margaret Dickson, sorting through her husband's papers, came upon a packet of letters he had written home to his first wife, just after being liberated from prison camp. At Christmas 1988, Margaret brought the letters along on a visit to Shelter Island, NY.

"Don't these sound just like Cec? I thought you'd like to see them", Margaret said as she handed me the packet. "I can hardly make out his handwriting in some places, though."

I offered to type them for her, and as I transcribed each line, I marvelled at the same humor—and absence of bitterness—that Cecil had displayed nearly 40 years later at the dinner table. "After all, more than 3800 consecutive meals of rice is a bit too much of a good thing!"

Barely two weeks after learning the nightmare was over, and still confined to the camp where he had endured such torment, this man could already look back and joke about rice! It struck me that my own mother seemed to display more residual anger about the Japanese, just because her favorite nephew, my cousin Bill Richardson, was scarred by his combat experiences on Guadalcanal, New Caledonia and Okinawa. He lived, but she never again knowingly bought

*Margaret and Cecil Diskson in front of the author's home,
Shelter Island, New York, May 1979.*

anything made in Japan, and neither did Bill, for that matter. So what kind of special breed were these Pioneers? The answer to my question has been offered, in many shadings, by Cecil's comrades. This is their story, and it is they who have made it come alive.

Many ex-POWs have kept their memories and mementos private for a lifetime; some have not even been shared with family members until now. Published here for the first time, for example, are the vivid recollections of Pioneer George Carroll, who was shipped to Japan to work as a laborer in factories and shipyards owned by private companies. Carroll's narrative is augmented by Pioneer Bill Mayne, who was torpedoed along with Carroll while travelling to Japan, and who worked with him in the same factory and shipyard locations.

Also published here for the first time are several photographs, taken in captivity, which were given to the author by Pioneer Cal Mitchell. To this day, secrecy has been maintained as to who actually took the photos, and how the camera[s] and film were hidden for over three years from the constant probings of Japanese bayonets, along with continual relocations. Until Mitchell shared these remarkable photos with the author, most of his fellow Pioneers had not seen them. When the snapshots were circulated at a Pioneer Association barbecue in Jell's Park, outside Melbourne, in October 1991, all believed the photos were taken just after liberation, while everyone was still in the camps and undernourished. As Pioneer Harry Bishop commented in a letter to the author the following month, "That is quite an achievement, as it means carrying a camera on many long marches, and there is a constant risk of bashing if it is found."

In addition, the Battalion Commanding Officer, Colonel Williams, took several photos with his own camera while in captivity; the best surviving print, in Chapter 2, shows the Australian officers' quarters in Java. Colonel Williams' description of how his film was preserved and returned to Australia also appears in Chapter 2.

As a result of the preparation of this book, both Mr. Mitchell and Colonel Williams have donated the captivity photographs shown here, to the Australian War Memorial in Canberra.

Just as these photographs allow the reader a gimpse of the desperate daily life in the prison camps of Java, Burma and Thailand, so Dickson's letters provide a series of windows through which we glimpse an Australian citizen-soldier looking homeward as he remembers the most brutal days experienced by any troops, anywhere, during the years of World War II.

1

A Sunday Lament

S unday, August 7, 1988, 2: 45 p.m. Cecil Dickson sets off with a jaunty air to join neighbors for a walk up the hill to the 3:00 p.m. service at the Chapel in the War Veterans Village in Narrabeen, NSW. Margaret Dickson recollects how natty her husband looked that afternoon in his Harris tweed jacket, and how high his spirits were.

Tom Gillespie, then Chairman of the Chapel Committee, describes greeting Dickson at the entrance to the Chapel, but watching in puzzlement as Dickson peers intently inside, then looks upward. "What does he see?" Gillespie wonders. An instant later Dickson, who stood 6'4", topples forward onto Gillespie, a "wee Scot" by some descriptions—and the two crash to the polished stone floor of the Chapel vestibule.

Margaret is summoned, along with Cecil's older brother, Stan, who lives next door. Together they sit, numbed, in the little room across from the Chapel, as the service goes on, draws to an end, and stunned worshippers begin quietly to leave the building. Two hours will pass before a physician appears to make the sad pronunciation, and to sign the necessary form. Then Margaret, supported by Stan, stumbles back down the hill, into the door of her home, and sinks into the little chair by the phone. With trembling fingers, she dials the overseas number to reach her daughter Susan, halfway around the globe on Shelter Island, New York.

* * * *

Sunday, August 7, 1988, 9:50 a.m.: The Reverend Peter D. MacLean is vesting in the sacristy at St. Mary's Episcopal Church for the 10 a.m. service. Peter has looked forward to this day for weeks, because the liturgy will be highlighted by my young visitor, James Lawrence Hamilton Carruthers, who has brought his bagpipes to play at the service.

9

Piper James L.H. Carruthers playing "The Flowers of the Forest" outside St. Mary's Episcopal Church, Shelter Island, New York, August 7, 1988.

Jamie is preparing to lead us into the front door of the church and up the aisle, playing "Going Home". But the air today is unbelievably heavy after a violent early morning thunderstorm, and out in the Parish Hall, he struggles, perspiring in his starched oxford shirt, woollen kilt and knee-high socks, to keep each pipe in its proper pitch.

As Peter starts to leave the sacristy, Susan Gross hurries into the side door of the Parish Hall, and moves toward him. He pauses as she pokes her head into the small room and says, "Ma called from Narrabeen at seven this morning. Cecil died today, on his way into the Chapel service." She turns away quickly and joins her husband, Ralph, to take their accustomed spot in the back pew.

Peter ponders a moment, then decides: this service will be a special sendoff for Cec—what a stroke of luck that Jamie is here! He whispers a few words to Jamie; he nods, and starts his measured steps. "Going home, going home, I am going home. . . ." Peter's vision blurs as he thinks of Cecil, natty in Harris tweeds, peering inside another sanctuary just a few hours earlier, and discovering he was already home.

As he climbs the chancel steps and turns toward the congregation, Peter's face contorts in a futile effort to control his tears, as he recalls how Cecil was one of the few men with whom a priest could share feelings about serving as a Marine Corps chaplain in Vietnam, about watching comrades die, and about how you minister to young men whose lives are being snatched away by strangers without reason. Suddenly sensing how his face must look right now, Peter says only: "Bagpipes always make me cry."

Later in the service, he descends the chancel steps to make what everyone expects will be the customary announcements of parish family business. Instead, with a husky voice and his eyes fixed on the carpet, Peter finds words to tell the sad news from Australia. Then he looks up and says, with all the authority that he, a Bishop's son, can claim: "Cecil Dickson taught us more about forgiveness than any clergyman—or any Bishop—has ever done."

Peter takes his seat and bows his head, listening as Jamie, standing on a hillock in the churchyard, pipes the classic Scottish lament, "The Flowers of the of the Forest".

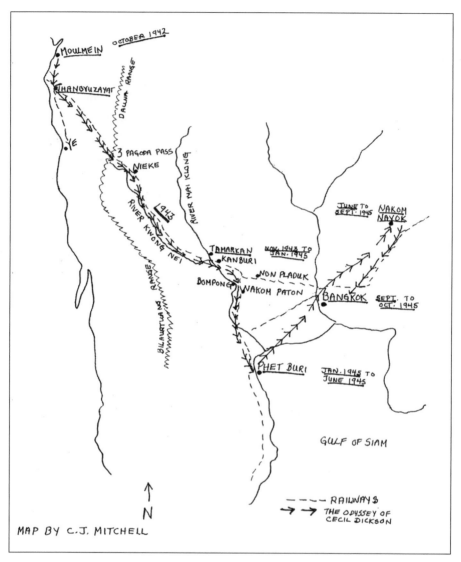

MAP BY C.J. MITCHELL

The odyssey of Cecil Dickson through Burma and Thailand,
October 1942 to October 1945.

2

It's Good Being Free

ugust 30, 1945: Barely two weeks after learning of the Japanese surrender, Staff Sergeant Cecil Dickson anxiously awaited word of how and when he would be sent home. He was in the enlisted men's camp near Nakom Nayok, Thailand; a second camp for non-commissioned officers was nearby, and a third camp, where POW officers had been gathered, was several miles down the road.

Some Americans were being flown out immediately, and had offered to take mail along. Dickson got hold of a small, scarce piece of paper, and in a dozen abbreviated sentences this seasoned journalist encapsulated the last three and a half years—telling his wife that he and his brother were OK, and hoping she would contact the *Argus* publisher to say that Dickson was alive, and available for eyewitness reporting.

2/2 Australian Pioneer Battalion
Nakom Nayok POW Camp
Thailand
August 30, 1945

Darling Old Binkie,

It's pretty good being free but the great day will be when I see the old Missus again. Hope you are as fit as I am. Rumour says we are flying to India. This globetrotting is all very well, but give me the shortest & quickest way home! John is here and in good fettle. I had charge of the 54 Pioneers in this camp, but am now looking after pay for the Australian wing. Been here 2 months (60 miles N.E. of Bangkok). Previous 6 months near Petburi (150 mi. S.W. of Bangkok). Till going there was 14 months at Tamarkan, near KAMBURI, near Thailand end of the famous railway line, construction of

13

which cost the lives of so many prisoners. After leaving Java in October '42
were 14 and a half months on the Burma section of the line. Year 1943 was a
bad one for everybody, but after coming to Tamarkan I picked up gradually &
was lucky not to return to the jungle. Remembrances family, friends, Mr. Knox
and staff. Longer letter next time perhaps.

Tons of love,

Pop

It had been a very tense month for all the prisoners: apprehension, exhilaration and caution had formed a tumble of emotions within each exhausted man's heart, and all with good reason. Since February, Dickson had been the highest-ranking Pioneer in his camp, because the Japanese moved officers and non-commissioned officers to different camps in early 1945. They planned to execute all POWs, beginning with officers, as soon as British General Lord Louis Mountbatten launched his expected invasion of Burma. By August 30, the wariness among prisoners still had not eased very much.

Excitement at the news of surrender, received on August 17 by Dickson and his camp-mates, and a day earlier in other locations, was tempered by the caution that although in many instances the Japanese and Koreans had quietly slipped away from the camps, they were still armed, and were likely to remain so until Emperor Hirohito's Foreign Minister formally signed the instrument of surrender, which had not yet happened. And it was an open question as to how long it might take for word of this formality to reach each armed Japanese, and what his individual reaction might be.

So tension in the camps crackled like static in the wireless sets which still had working batteries (or for which operators were able, with considerable relish, to commandeer fresh batteries from suddenly compliant Japanese). To compound the tension for the Australians, British and Dutch, just a week earlier, on August 23, the Office of Strategic Services (OSS) colonel in charge of operations in Thailand notified POW officers that all Americans were to be flown out of Thailand almost immediately, and American officers visited camps to tell their lucky compatriots the good news.

Resorting to humor to break the taut atmosphere (a tactic which served the prisoners so well for over 1,630 very dark days), someone formulated the following orders: "The Australians are to report to the nearest seaport; the Dutch are to go to the nearest railway station; the Americans are to report to the nearest airport, and the English are to be issued a new pair of shoes."[1] This witticism was to prove fairly accurate: most Americans had been home for a couple of months before many Australians, Dutch and English set foot on their beloved home shores.

So the best Dickson and his comrades could do on August 30 was to give a smile and a handclasp to their departing American friends, and if they were lucky enough, to hand over a scribbled note as well.

Dickson had no way of knowing, as he wrote his first letter home as a free man, that Freda did in fact receive all six cards he was allowed to send during his long captivity. And it would be another two weeks before he learned that close friends from his battalion were rescued at sea the previous September, returned to Australia, and reported in detail his whereabouts and living conditions.

"After leaving Java in October '42. . . ." These six words encompassed the few days of valiant battle, the heartbreak of forced surrender, the loss of hope for escape, and the horror of a ship voyage to Burma under what Dickson would later term "unspeakable conditions", without bothering to elaborate. As he wrote these words, Dickson no doubt assumed his wife had been notified that his battalion was forced to surrender on Java and that he was a Prisoner of War. But little did he know that Freda waited over a year before receiving official confirmation of his status, or that since November of last year, she had been all too aware of conditions in the camps, and increasingly worried for his safety.

The Dicksons' niece, Barbara Clements, recalled that: "When the newspapers began to print stories about the mistreatment of POWs, the situation at home grew even worse. It was a time of great strain for the family."[2]

Dickson's last letter as a free man had been written on board the troopship *Orcades* in early 1942, and until now he had no way of knowing whether any subsequent mail he was allowed to write in captivity ever did reach home.

The *Orcades* was the last ship in a hastily-assembled convoy rushing the Pioneers, now seasoned combat troops, from the Middle East toward home, to defend Australia against a feared Japanese invasion. To their everlasting regret, the Pioneers were loaded aboard wearing winter clothes, with only their backpacks and one blanket each—all baggage was put on another ship, which was sent on to Australia, with just a few members of the battalion on board. No one could foresee that the clothes on his back would be all he had for the next three and a half years. In his memoirs, the legendary ex-POW physician, Sir Edward "Weary" Dunlop recalled how he became separated, in a truly bureaucratic bungle, from nearly all his medical supplies and field hospital equipment, painstakingly assembled, when he, too, boarded the *Orcades*.[3]

As the *Orcades* sailed from Suez, about 60 Japanese troop transports were already in the South China Sea. Apparently as a token of support to the Dutch, whose homeland was already under Nazi occupation, and whose airfields in Java were vital—and also to divert those Japanese troopships away from Australia—the British High Command decided that the *Orcades* should land its troops on Java, to join the token Australian forces already attempting to hold the airports there. This was done over the vigorous protest of Australian Prime Minister John Curtin, among others. But as military historian D.M. Horner points out in his book, *High Command,* "The Americans recognized that Australia was a sovereign country; many British still tended to look upon Australia as a colony. British commanders often viewed Australian forces as an integral part of an imperial army (or navy or airforce) and they expected Australians to conform, without question, to British strategic direction."[4]

Horner records in detail the political wrangling surrounding the deployment of Australian troops in Java; for the bewildered Pioneers aboard the *Orcades,* this meant disembarking, being ordered to return to the ship, and disembarking the second time, at Batavia.

Half a century later, the controversy surrounding the Allied decision to leave Australian troops on Java still has not subsided, because that move caused nearly 3000 Australian military personnel to be captured by the Japanese. In February 1992, the dispute erupted anew when Queen Elizabeth visited Australia, and the recently-elected Prime Minister, Paul Keating, took the occasion to remind Britons that their government had "decided not to defend the Malaysian Peninsula, not to worry about Singapore, and not to give us our troops back [from Java] to keep ourselves from Japanese dominion."[5]

In retaliation, members of Parliament in London taunted Mr.Keating as presiding "over a country of ex-convicts." The continued use of this epithet keeps alive a smoldering resentment of the British for many Australians, who in turn regularly refer to the English as "Pommies", a corruption of the word for a well-known local fruit. Pomegranates were what the red-cheeked newcomers, bundled up in their woollens as they arrived from England on government grants, looked like to Australian children earlier in this century. So the neighborhood taunts began: "immygrant, jimmy-grant, pommy-grant!"[6]

Pioneer Captain Harry Bishop, in a 1992 letter to the author, reflected that when the Pioneers joined British Field Marshall Montgomery's forces to repel

General Erwin Rommel in the Middle Eastern desert, the British troops called the Australians "descendants of convicts" which, Bishop noted, "we did not appreciate". This type of name-calling was remembered by several other Pioneers as well, with special resentment from those who had volunteered to serve the Crown in wartime.

With 924 of their Battalion put ashore on Java, the Pioneers joined with the 2/3 Machinegun Battalion, under the command of Brigadier General A.S. Blackburn, and the resulting brigade, designated as Blackforce, was placed under Dutch command. The Pioneers fought fiercely against the Japanese, despite being issued outdated weapons and, on some occasions, using Biblical combat methods. Sergeant Harry Whelan, a member of the 2/3 Machinegun Battalion, remembered filling cloth bags with gravel from the ditches around their positions, and swinging the homemade missiles in hand-to-hand combat, in preference to using the Canadian Springfield rifles they had been issued, which lacked bayonets. "We actually did this—yes—a sort of David and Goliath maneuver", he recalled in a 1991 interview. In addition, as Cal Mitchell noted, the Springfield rifles had a .30 bore, so the Australians had to load their .303 rounds of ammunition by hand.

Almost as outdated as the weapons issued to the Pioneers was the intelligence they received about Dutch strength on Java. On one occasion, Dickson's friend Lieutenant Walter Summons, the unit's Intelligence Officer, asked Dutch Headquarters for information regarding Japanese deployment. The response: no update was available, because that morning's newspaper had not been delivered!

On March 2, the Dutch commander told Colonel Williams that, as far as he knew, there were no Japanese on the island. The next day, around noontime, a Dutch army intelligence report confirmed to Blackforce headquarters that there had been no Japanese landings on Java. Within minutes, five Japanese tanks approached the bridge which the Pioneers had been preparing to hold, at Llewiliang.

Some American members of the 131st Field Artillery, Texas National Guard, who were not allowed to engage in combat, watched the Pioneers' awesome fighting skills from a nearby hill. "I was proud to have been a POW with such brave soldiers", said Otto Schwarz, a survivor of the sinking of the *USS Houston,* after listening to the Texans tell about some of the Pioneer exploits. Another American ex-POW, Benjamin Dunn, a member of the California 26th Field Artillery Brigade, also sent to Java with the Texas unit, comments in his book, *The Bamboo Express,* ". . . The Dutch officials insisted they had the invasion under control.

They even permitted the Australian infantry to attack at night against overwhelming odds and without any help from the Dutch and Javanese infantry."[7]

This display of tenacity not only impressed the Japanese; it apparently made them believe they were dealing with two whole Australian divisions. Consequently, the Japanese invasion force headed for Australia was re-routed to Java (see Foreword).

It is estimated that the Pioneer unit killed at least 500 Japanese before bring forced to surrender. According to the Battalion History, on March 8 the Dutch decided to capitulate, and the Australians, being under Dutch command, had no choice but to surrender as well. On March 9, the Battalion was ordered to withdraw, and to destroy or disable all weapons and vehicles. Pioneer Lieutenant Walter Summons described the desperation of a "last mad rush to the south coast, hoping for ships . . ." which, of course, never materialized.[8]

Cecil Dickson wrote the chapter on Prisoners of War for the official *Story of the 2/2 Australian Pioneer Battalion,* and he graphically details how equipment was destroyed: "Much material found its way into fast-running mountain rivers, and . . . Pioneers saw to it that many dozens of motor-vehicles and Bren-carriers were wrecked by running them down steep ravines."[9] It was a wrenching decision for many members of the unit to discard their personal weapons.

However, 'A' Company of the Battalion did not receive the order to withdraw, and became cut off from the main force. Captain Ron Winning still recalled that time in precise detail, half a century later: "Our Commanding Officer, Lieut. Col. J.M. Williams, sent for me and gave me orders to move 'C' Company [Dickson's unit] out to a defensive position on the river, on our right flank. He expected we would be in action by nightfall. 'B' and 'D' Companies set an ambush on the main road, 'A' Company in reserve. I posted my guns and platoons, but for some reason the enemy attacked our left flank after losing heavily in the ambush. 'A' Company was sent out to the left and we never saw them again. They ran into the main Jap force and were decimated. We retreated and eventually ran out of land, and were captured."

The remnants of 'A' Company held out as guerrillas on Java for six months; until the only surviving officer, Lieutenant. R.W. Allen, was captured, along with Privates. V.L.J. McCrae and S.A. Baade, and brought to the jail at Batavia.

Perhaps the most poignant footnote to the Pioneers' combat experience in Java is this final communique, dated March 3, 1942, and preserved as received, typed on a portable typewriter, on yellow copy paper, in the archives of the Australian War Memorial at Canberra: "Capt. Guild and Lieuts. Stewart, Lang &

UNIT 2/2 Aust. Pioſ. Bn.

A.I.F. FORM C 2118A

WAR DIARY

(RENDER UNDER SECRET COVER)

For material required, see F.S.R. Vol. 1, Sec. 171

DATE	SUMMARY OF EVENTS	REFERENCES TO APPENDICES	C.O.s. REPORT AND COMMENTS ON MONTH
	Routine training details and information given in Casualty Returns are NOT required		(On Operations, Equipment, Movement, Health, Administration, etc.)

MONTH

YEAR

24 Feb.
Lt-Col.Williams at Force HQ. conference on evacuation plans. 2 raids, one raid on TJILITJAP dropped bombs and machine-gunned troops,4 casualties N.E. Hangar and posts hit. Other raid a lot of bombs dropped on D Coy area. After having been in COCHIN a further 3 days the Shillong and Niger Stroom leave in same convoy as before.

25 Feb.
Sophocles and Methura leave COCHIN without convoy.
A Coy. further preparing defences. D Coy practising A,B,& C plans for counter attack. HQ.Coy.co-operating with Brens.
2 Alarms.Big raid on TANJOENG PRIOK,BATAVIA,and KEMAJORN.Smoke of fires rising very high.

26 Feb.
Orders received by convoy ex COCHIN to break up and proceed on own course to FREMANTLE,AUSTRALIA.
JAVA Force.-- Patrols now getting excellent knowledge of bush.
A and HQ Coys. digging alternative positions. D Coy. again practising No report from B and C Coy. very heavy rain.Hot and sultry.No raids.New troops morale improving.

27 Feb.
Raids on all dromes,and very heavy raid on harbour. Casualties not known.
S.S."MU SUEH" sailed for COLOMBO with Major Joss aboard,being evacuated sick.

28 Feb.-2 Mar. *No information main body.*

3 Mar.
Capt. Guild and Lieutenants Stewart,Lang,and Allen reported missing by cable and othercasualties as per Part II Orders.This is the last advice from Bn.All communication with outside world cut off.Force now isolated.

9 Mar.
S.S. SOPHOCLES" arrives FREMANTLE.

AIF Mob Print Sec AIF 25M-141-6.

The position on the island unknown. The only Java after I left was unknown. The only Casualty list received from Bn being that of 3/4 March by Cable. Earlier casualties known not being notified. Bn strength on 28 Feb. was over 1000 men of whom were presumed missing after the 9th March in the absence of definite information. All German officers except Capt Guild were later reported by Batavia Radio to be prisoners of war.

Signature _____ 2/Lt Van Nooten

Last entries in official pages of the War Diary for 2/2 Australian Pioneer Battalion before the unit was captured on Java. Handwritten notations on right side of page were made by Major H.M. Joss, who was evacuated to Australia when he became ill.
(AUSTRALIAN WAR MEMORIAL, AWM 52 ITEM 8/6/2)

Allen reported missing by cable and all other casualties as per Part II orders. This is the last advice from Bn. All communication with outside world cut off. Force now isolated."[10] One can only guess as to the spirits of the Pioneer who sent that last, cryptic message.

For many Australians, contempt for the Dutch would linger throughout their years of captivity together, surfacing in many ways. As Harry Whelan phrased it: "We were put ashore on Java as a political gesture to the Dutch . . . to help (them) defend Java; and the next thing we knew, the Dutch had surrendered . . . I've read every account I could find on this, because three years and seven months of the best years of my life were wasted, and I've always wanted to know why."

But Brigadier Blackburn, for one, did not feel the Australian effort on Java was wasted. In a foreword to Walter Summons' book, compiled in 1946, the Brigadier wrote:

> To many of the men who took part in the campaign in Java and to many people in Australia, it seemed at the time that the landing of Australian troops in that island was a needless waste of men . . . I can say however, without hesitation, that the resistance put up by that small force of Australians against a crack Japanese Division was not wasted. At that critical time, March 1942, every day, perhaps every hour, during which the Japanese advance on Australia was delayed, meant a big gain to this country . . . it contributed in no small measure to the fact that Australia was saved from invasion.[11]

Harry Bishop, thinking back to that time, shared this thought in April of 1992:

> On Java we heard that one whole Jap convoy had no where to go. The rumour . . . was that [Australian General] Wavell set up . . . a propaganda campaign, with the cooperation of Americans, British and Dutch, to convince the Japs to land on Java. At this time, [the Japanese] could have landed anywhere on Western or northern Australia.
>
> I believe that [Gen.] Blamey's stubbornness allowed [American General Douglas] MacArthur to leave the Australians out of the Philippine campaign. This was a pity, as the Australian divisions

which returned from the Middle East inflicted the first defeat on the Japanese at Milne Bay, about the same time as the Coral Sea battle.

In retrospect, other Pioneer officers understood MacArthur's personal involvement with the Philippines, and were not surprised that he wanted to use his own troops for the invasion. Bishop continued:

> I was impressed with [Lieutenant General Sir Edmund] Herring's handling of Blamey. There were two sides to [Herring's] character, but he had a clear idea of what needed to be done, and the need to do it quickly. But on the other side he often left a poor impression. As an example, there was the Chiefs of Staff meeting in Washington, at which he went to sleep after being out late the night before.[12]

Author Benjamin Dunn wrote about how the American military contributed to the deception by allowing their vehicles to drive back and forth over the same roadways, in order to give the appearance of new equipment constantly arriving. But the scheme worked so well that it caused a handful of Allied officers to pay a very high price for this illusion, a few weeks later.

Recording those first few months of captivity for the Battalion History, Dickson wrote:

> It was difficult at this stage for members to realise that they were prisoners of war. Preoccupied with the task of taking over an island the size of Java, with its 42 million inhabitants, the Japanese allowed a maximum of freedom. Preconceived ideas of barbed-wire fences and armed guards had not yet eventuated, and the troops were free to visit shops and coffee-houses in the village, and even to hire a horse-drawn gharry to visit a neighbouring village, where other . . . Australians were quartered, and where a swimming pool provided facilities for many hours of enjoyment and sport. It was, from the point of view of the prisoners of war, an almost idyllic existence . . . Church parades were held regularly and were well attended' [in stark contrast to later days of captivity: see Chapter 15].
>
> During the stay at Leles the Japanese invited their prisoners to write letters home, with no limit as to length nor restrictions of subject. As these letters never reached home, it might be supposed

that they were sought by the Japanese merely with the object of gleaning as much information as possible, and that after close scrutiny by their intelligence service, they were destroyed. . . .

  Japanese troops in Leles area were apparently unsuspecting types who did not think to check up on whether wireless sets were being used by their prisoners, so the C.O. was able with his radio to receive B.B.C. and A.B.C. news daily. What he heard and relayed to the Battalion made it plain that Java had been so effectively isolated by enemy action that all thoughts of escape must be abandoned.[13]

Moreover, as Sergeant Crayton Gordon, a member of the Texas 131st Field Battalion remembers: "Those waters were full of sharks—man, no way did I want to jump in and swim!"

Dickson also notes, somewhat wistfully, a rare act of Japanese kindness he witnessed:

> There must also, by the way, have been a human streak among the Japanese whose duty it was to keep a casual eye on the Pioneers. One night one of them, wandering through the market-place occupied by the Battalion, stooped down to pull the blanket over one of the slumbering men who had come uncovered during his restless sleep. Time was to show that not all of his fellow-countrymen were capable of such an act of simple humanity.

He tells how one Pioneer hit upon a way to help his comrades dispel their sense of foreboding as they settled down to sleep:

> 'Slim' Maher, a well-known character of C company, enhanced his reputation for native humour . . . with an act that he repeated many times as the Battalion settled down to sleep. After 'lights-out', which was a misnomer as there were no lights to extinguish, he would recite in his penetrating voice, with appropriate emphasis, a broadcast advertisement for a popular brand of cough remedy that had become familiar to radio listeners at home. Drowsy men almost shivered as the voice of "Slim" quavered over "icy blasts" and advised his listeners what to take for the protection of their chests.[14]

In mid-May, the prisoners were moved to a new location on Java, called the

Bicycle Camp, and here their daily life took a decided turn for the worse. Dickson records what happened initially to jolt the prisoners:

> In charge of the camp was Lieut. Suzuki. He was not one of the
> vicious type of Japanese, but his sincerity was doubted, and if he
> ever did weep for the prisoners under his charge, the tears he shed
> were crocodile tears. It was while the camp was under his charge,
> and doubtless at his command, that the guards launched a campaign
> of vicious assaults on the prisoners of war—unprovoked bashings
> against which the victims had no redress. To Brig. Blackburn's
> protests against this harsh treatment, Suzuki would silkily reply that
> perhaps the prisoners were not saluting the guards properly (Japanese
> style) or standing properly to attention (Japanese style), and he would
> proceed to demonstrate the correct manner of carrying out these
> formalities. But the bashings continued.

Most POWs probably had no way of knowing that such treatment was a routine part of Japanese military training, and that Lieutenant Suzuki apparently decided, without explicitly announcing same, that the prisoners under this charge should be re-trained, "Japanese style." As Ruth Benedict points out in her study of Japanese culture, *The Chrysanthemum and the Sword: Patterns of Japanese Culture,* correct forms of respect to superiors were insisted upon rigorously within the military ranks, and recruits who failed to observe standards exactly came to expect a sudden blow to the face or body. Even a smile or casual gesture was considered disrespectful, and punishment was routinely swift and brutal—out of all proportion, by Western standards, to the perceived offense.[15] Benedict's study was written to be used as a handbook for American occupation troops in 1945, but for the hapless prisoners on Java in 1942, there were no handbooks issued, so the treatment they encountered was baffling. To their horror, it became a nerve-racking part of their daily lives for the next three years.

In as 1992 conversation, Crayton Gordon summed up the prisoners' initial contact with the Japanese this way: "There were three things about the Japanese way of life that made it so very, very hard on us: religion, discipline, and their standard of living. We didn't know much of anything about the Japanese culture when we were forced to surrender to them, but we sure learned pretty fast."[16]

Religion for the Japanese includes a code of conduct and honor, intertwined with cultural heritage, to create a deep sense of self. The belief that a *Kamikaze*, or "divine wind", spared their people from Genghis Khan in the Thirteenth Century, thus preserving their pure culture, reinforces the sends of oneness which is deeply embedded in the Japanese psyche.

This sense is arrived at through lifelong training which, if completed well, allows the will to be supreme over the "almost infinitely teachable body", as Benedict phrased it. Untimately, Benedict found, the purpose of such training is to free the Spirit to fulfill the Higher Law, which is duty to the Emperor. There is no such thing as standing up for what is right; the highest value for a Japanese is to fulfill whatever has been set forth as one's duty, at all costs, in order to maintain one's self-respect and, even more important, one's sense of honor.

Just as firmly intertwined in the Western cultural heritage is the Judeo-Christian tradition of human dignity, repentance and forgiveness. The concept of "forgiveness" appears several times in these pages; it is used not to convey pardon, but in the spiritual sense of abandoning the desire to "get even", as exemplified in the Biblical story of Joseph forgiving his brothers.[18]

But where East does not meet West is the attitude toward human life, and this is what Crayton Gordon meant when he said the Japanese religion made it "very, very hard on us." While the Christian tradition teaches that every life has dignity and value, and that redemption is possible, the Japanese culture holds that if one dishonors oneself, such as surrendering to the enemy, one's life has lost its value permanently, and one has stained the family name for many, many future generations. There is no redemption; the only honorable act left is to end one's life.

Discipline, and more especially self-discipline, is also part of lifetime training for Japanese in all walks of life. The tenets of the Zen religion were adopted in particular ways to the Japanese military code. By gaining control over his mind, a soldier is taught to believe that he can meet any situation, so that eventually there is no break between a man's will and his act. This single-mindedness and utter concentration in fulfilling one's task confounded the prisoners, who observed it time and time again, and it reminded "Weary" Dunlop of "Some of the defects of an insect society."[19] Yet former French Prime Minister Edith Cresson was roundly criticized in 1992 for describing the Japanese as "ants."[20]

As for the *standard of living* referred to by Crayton Gordon, this could perhaps be summarized as an assumption on the part of the Japanese that, for those contemptible Western soldiers who had allowed themselves to be taken prisoner, low living standards were to be expected.

During the month of May 1942, as the regimen being imposed upon them became more rigid and incomprehensible, the prisoners took every opportunity to calm their nerves with a touch of humor. Dickson recalls one such incident during the jittery days of May:

> The orderly-room corporal, Kitamura, was a fantastic little creature who wore high-heeled shoes. It was alleged that in Japan he was Suzuki's superior in a Government department, and it was even suggested that he had far more influence on camp policy than might have been expected from one of his rank. To demonstrate what a really good fellow he was, he once offered a prize of cigarettes for a literary competition among the prisoners. The choice of subjects included: "Your Home", "Your Life in Batavia", "A True Love Story", and last on the list, but by no means the least, "Mr. Kitamura"! Some of the entries written around the last named title were not submitted for judging.[21]

But toward the end of May, a monumental event occurred which was to shake each prisoner to his core: their highest-ranking officers were taken away for questioning, and were not seen again for a month. During that time, they were subjected to the most brutal and constant torture. Dickson describes some of the treatment inflicted upon the Pioneers' commanding officer, Colonel Williams, who is acknowledged in several accounts to have received the worst treatment by the Japanese of any POW:

> The C.O. in particular came in for a very rough handling, but even the threat to shoot him failed to extract from him any information that would have helped the enemy. After having refused to answer questions put to him by a Japanese Colonel, he was placed in a cell with 16 native prisoners. He had no mosquito net, and there was not enough room to lie down. With little variation, the food ration per day was a plate of rice with a fish head, eaten with the fingers. During the period of questioning, the C.O. was not permitted to shave, and he was allowed only an occasional wash. Persistent refusal to capitulate to the Japanese inquisitors was met by a variation of the "water treatment"—beer was forced into the C.O.'s lungs in an effort

to make him talk. On one occasion he was taken out before a firing squad. Instead of the volley he expected, he received the praise of the Japanese officer for his bravery, and was returned to his cell.

Author Leslie Hall adds even more excruciating details about the procedures to which Colonel Williams was subjected:

> Lieutenant Colonel Williams had been tied to a chair and his whole body bashed so badly, even his tormentors believed he was dying. When he did regain consciousness, dry rice was forced down his throat and a hose thrust into his mouth, allowing water to surge into his body. When the rice began to swell, his stomach was so swollen (it caused) intense agony. . . . For once [the Japanese] did not jump on and off his swelling abdomen, [and] nature came to his aid. . . . Many died from the rice and water punishment.[22]

Dickson's account continues: "Capt. (S.J.) Handasyde's refusal to answer Japanese questions earned a different type of torture. Small pieces of bamboo were placed between his fingers, which were twitched together while the bamboos were twisted."[23]

Pioneer Captains Ron Winning and A.H.J. Ross were given similar torment, and once again Leslie Hall supplies additional details:

> These officers . . . were strapped to chairs and bashed unmercifully with any weapon, be it wood or metal, the interrogating staff had to hand. Hour after hour the treatment went on and on and on. At times, a merciful fate intervened; they became oblivious to everything, unaware of darkness, light, days, hours or even meal times. The latter, few and far between.
>
> There was hardly any let up, even after cigarette lighter flames burned and blistered their swollen hands. The pain suffered then was maddening, but not enough to exact any information from the determined officers.[24]

Ron Winning remembered: "I was alert enough to tell the Japs that I was not at the ambush where they lost so heavily. I told them I was stationed at the airport, and finally they believed me."[25]

Dickson ends his account of this episode with typical understatement:

"When the C.O. and his officers were returned to the Bicycle Camp, the Japanese were none the wiser militarily, though no doubt they had been enlightened by the conduct of their prisoners."[26]

Many years later, author Benjamin Dunn, researching U.S. military files for his own book, may have found the major reason the Australian officers were subjected to such agony for so long: Japanese interrogators simply did not believe that there were only 500 American and less than 3000 Australian troops on Java, because Japanese businessmen and intelligence agents had said that 70,000 Americans and 40,000 Australians were on the way—and the interrogators therefore demanded to know where all these troops were, and when they were arriving. It was only as the month of June drew to a close, and their own sources brought different information, that the interrogators allowed the officers to return to their units.[27]

Ron Winning also recalled how the Japanese tormented POWs with their invasion plans—up to a point: "The Japs knew to a man how many Americans and Australians were on Java; their spies were on the wharf when we disembarked. However, they thought that reinforcements were on the way, which was quite incorrect. The battle which saved Australia from invasion was the Coral Sea Battle, when the Japs lost heavily to the US Naval Force. POW work forces were employed by the Japs loading their ships—the Jap soldiers took great delight in telling us what they were going to do in Australia. However, they didn't crow very much after the Coral Sea battle, and the ships that were loading supplies were finally used for their landing in New Guinea."[28]

In 1992, Colonel Williams confirmed the reasons for the treatment to which he was subjected, and his efforts to keep a record of it: "I took a number of photos . . . of Officers returning from one month's interrogation and torture when the Japanese were trying to find the location of the 6th, 7th and 9th [Australian] Divisions who were supposed to land in Java. Only a small number of negatives were suitable for enlargement. Three and a half years is a long time to keep undeveloped films . . ."[29]

The Battalion Commander had buried his film, hoping to preserve it as evidence in War Crimes trials. When he was shipped to Burma, his adjutant, Captain Edward Campbell, dug up the film and kept it with him all the way through a sea voyage to Japan (under deplorable conditions), and many months of constant relocation as a factory laborer there—all the while risking severe beating or death if the film were discovered. Campbell was able to personally hand-deliver the film to Colonel Williams at war's end, but as the Colonel mentioned, most of the negatives were badly deteriorated. In a letter to the author, he described how he got the films back to Australia on a priority basis, along with the list of Australian prisoners who were still alive:

> On 15 August 1945 Williams Force, composed mostly of 2/2 Pioneers, were in transit and had arrived at the Go-downs in Bangkok within days of the Japanese delivering peace in Thailand. No sooner had an official announcement been made when a small force of RAPWI (Recovery of Prisoners of War and Internees) officers arrived at our HQ to tell us they would supervise the return to Australia of all Prisoners of War. We then handed over a copy of our nominal roll.
>
> We also had a nominal roll of approximately 4000 names of Australian soldiers still alive at this date ready for dispatch to Australia, and I was selected by the senior officers in Bangkok to get this list to Australia by the quickest means. The only aircraft available was due to take off for Calcutta in one hour and I was available. I arrived at Calcutta that night. I also found another aircraft due for Columbo next morning, arriving there late afternoon. There was no cable office in Columbo, nor were any aircraft available. Eventually I caught a non-stop aircraft to Perth and landed at Melbourne on 11 September 1945 . . . I was tied up in Melbourne making sure every Pioneer was accounted for, especially in regards to medical history as a POW. I was one of the first ex-POWs to return to Melbourne, but I didn't see my wife or family in Sydney until I received my first three days leave on 25 December 1945.[30]

The news account of Colonel Williams arriving in Melbourne, published in the September 12, 1945 edition of the *Argus,* together with a photo showing him handing a briefcase containing the names of recovered Australian POWs— and his rolls of film—to a waiting officer, appears on page 29.

One of the few photos which survived appears on page 30. It shows the Australian officers' quarters in the Bicycle Camp. Colonel Williams said the officers planted a vegetable garden on the lawn, but the Japanese confiscated the harvest for their own use. "Once caught by the Japs we didn't try growing vegetables again", he commented.

It was in the Bicycle Camp that the POWs came to admire the Dutch women for their bravery. Staff Sergeant Tom O'Brien could recollect, even after half a century, vivid images of blond-haired women and children appearing each day

OFFICER BRINGS LIST OF 4,000 NAMES OF POW's IN SIAM

THERE was a dramatic moment at Essendon aerodrome last night, when Lieut-Colonel J. M. Williams, prisoner of war from Bangkok, Siam, stepped off a plane with a list of names of more than 4,000 Australian prisoners who were known to be alive in Siam at the end of August. He handed over the list to Major L. S. Walsh, of 2nd Echelon Records, who immediately rushed them to the city for transcription by a staff who were waiting to begin the long task of checking. They will remain on the job until it is completed.

Lieut-Colonel Williams, who comes from Sefton, NSW, was CO of the 2/2 Pioneer Battalion, a Victorian unit with a distinguished record in the Middle East. He suffered considerable ill-treatment and torture when captured by the Japanese.

The records which formed the list brought out by Lieut-Colonel Williams were kept by Australian prisoners themselves in Bangkok. The Japanese called in these lists, saying that they would preserve them, but once they got the lists they burnt them. Lieut-Colonel Williams, however, had kept a copy of the lists buried in the camp. He dug it up after the surrender and supplemented it with other names of men who came to the camp from outlying districts. The list gives the names of most of the 4,900 Australians who were in prison camps in Siam. Of these, 3,900 were described by Lieut-Colonel Williams as being recently fit. One thousand were receiving treatment in hospital. Most of these had dysentery, malaria, ulcers, or were suffering the effects of malnutrition.

HAS LIST OF CRIMINALS

Lieut-Colonel Williams said that he had a list of ... Japanese ...

veloped at once, and may give a pictorial record of some of the aspects of prison camp life. The pictures had to be taken surreptitiously.

NAMES OF POW's AT SINGAPORE

... Aus... at re... up of ...ss

LIEUT-COLONEL J. M. WILLIAMS (left), of Sydney, first POW to retur... from any Japanese camp, arriving in Me... and the second from Thailand ... bourne by plane from Perth last night. He is handing over to Major L. ... names of Army personnel reported to ha... Walsh lists of about 4,000 names of August. The names were collect... been alive in Thailand at the end of ... by pilots who flew supplies to the camps.

Excerpts from Melbourne Argus, *pages 1 and 3, September 12, 1945 edition, describing Colonel J.M. Williams as the first recovered POW to arrive in Australia, carrying a list of names and his film, hidden during captivity.* (COPIED FROM ORIGINALS AT RESEARCH CENTRE, AUSTRALIAN WAR MEMORIAL)

to sell sandwiches, cigarettes and candy to the prisoners. The Japanese would bash them with rifle butts, kick them and scatter their baskets of food. "But they didn't care—they were right back the next day", he said, shaking his head in wonder.

Lieutenant Cal Mitchell added his own indelible image: "After we were captured, we were marching along a road, and this young Dutch girl with long blond hair sent her little girl running toward us from the side of the road—she

*One of the few surviving photos taken secretly in captivity by Colonel Williams in
April 1942, at the Australian POW officers' quarters, Bicycle Camp, Java.
Plot in right foreground is where vegetables were grown by the prisoners, though later
confiscated by the Japanese. This film was buried, taken by sea to Japan and back,
and spent nearly three years in various hiding places, before being brought to
Australia for development by Colonel Williams.* (COURTESY OF J.M. WILLIAMS)

had long blond hair, too—to hand us sandwiches. The Jap guard bashed the little girl in the head with his rifle butt, and she fell down. The mother picked
her up and carried her off. I don't know what happened to her, but I'll never
forget that sight."[32]

And the contempt was still there in Tom O'Brien's voice as he muttered: "If
the Dutch men had been half as brave as their women, the Japs never would
have invaded Java." Several others around him nodded in agreement.[33]

As the weeks wore on in Java, the harsh realities of life under the Japanese
became more and more apparent. Because most of their equipment had been
left on board the transport ship, the Australians were issued no utensils with
which to cook food; and it took the resourcefulness of Harry Whelan, a pilot,
to visit the Dutch Air Force hangars and scrounge some tin cans for that pur-

pose. By June, rations had become increasingly poor, consisting only of rice and a small quantity of green vegetables in a stew, just barely flavored with pork. In growing numbers, the men fell ill with dengue fever, dysentery and severe eye infections, and tinea became rife throughout the camp.

Pioneers tried to keep up their spirits with work, regular exercises and games of volleyball, newly learned from the Americans. On June 17, they observed the anniversary of the unit's first battle in Syria, now adding to their remembrance with the missing men from 'A' Company. As Dickson noted, "The Pioneers recaptured for a brief quarter-hour something of the old 'Pucka'[Puckapunyal training camp] spirit—the spirit that had carried the unit successfully through its training days and earned for it a proud reputation on the field of battle."[34]

But the organized activities and diversions were abruptly ended in early July, when all POWs were forced to sign an oath of non-escape. Ironically for the Americans, Brigadier Blackburn, after initially holding out, authorized all men to sign the oath on the Fourth of July—American Independence Day.

On October 8, 1200 POWs were packed aboard the *Kinkon Maru,* embarking at the same wharf where they had tied up aboard the *Orcades,* just eight months earlier. They were taken to Changi Prison in Singapore, from which they departed a week later. This time, 1500 prisoners were squeezed aboard the *Maebisi Maru.* Before leaving, each POW was given a card to write home. Not only were these pieces of mail actually delivered to Australia, but the Japanese presented Colonel Williams with a bill for the postage! However, they broadcast some of the postcard messages over Singapore Radio; those few messages were picked up and relayed to the servicemen's families.

Under the command of Colonel Williams, the 1500 would become known as Williams Force, and would be taken to Moulmein, Burma, to begin constructing the railway from that end. Meanwhile, a second transport of approximately 1500 men, under Lieutenant Colonel "Weary" Dunlop, would be designated Dunlop Force, and would start work on the railway from the Thailand end.

Dickson merely refers to the voyage as being taken under "unspeakable conditions", but Harry Bishop describes vividly some of the hazards encountered by the men during that trip:

> The worst part was to climb down the hold every night at dusk, find the small space where one's gear had been placed, and then find space for everyone. In mid-afternoon on the fifth day we suddenly became

aware that there were three Liberator (bombers) above us in close formation at about 10,000 feet . . . the target was the other transport . . . they scored a hit amidships . . . the ship was sinking . . . there was no sign that lifeboats had been launched . . . the bombers turned and circled for their second run . . . I found a spot below the poop deck, and lay down. There was a noise like an express train, and then I felt a blow on the head . . . I had been hit by an electric iron which had been hanging behind the door. The whole ship had vibrated like a dog coming out of the water . . . A Japanese sailor fell backwards on the deck almost at my feet (dead) . . . several POWs were hit by shrapnel . . . the *USS Houston* survivors . . . told me that the (Japanese) Captain had a seaman lying on his back on the deck of the bridge, right alongside the wheel. His duty was to signal when he saw the bombs leave the plane. This gave the Captain a chance to shift his ship from the targeted line while the bombs fell. The Americans were very impressed by the Jap Captain's navigational skill![35]

Nevertheless, about 12 POW were killed during that raid. They were buried at the St. Patrick's Mission in Moulmein.

At Moulmein, the group was divided into two units: Williams Force still included most of the Pioneers, although Ron Winning was detached to act as adjutant of the second unit, named Black Force after Lieutenant Colonel C. Black of the 2/3rd Motor Transport Company. Survivors of the *H.M.A.S. Perth* were attached to Williams Force. By the time the war ended, 2/2 Pioneers were recovered in seven different locations: Thailand, Java, Singapore, Indo-China (Vietnam), Sumatra, Borneo and Japan.

Of the 867 members of the Battalion who became prisoners of the Japanese, slightly more than half were in Williams Force in Burma. 118 'A' Company personnel were missing in action; most later left Java and worked on the Thailand end of the railway. Fourteen Pioneers under Captain Harry became part of No. 5 Branch, and worked on the Burma section of the line. 68 remained in Java. Dickson was Quartermaster of 'C' Company, in Williams Force.

Until the railway was completed at the end of 1943, Williams Force was under the command of Lieutenant Colonel Nagatomo [later executed at the Tokyo War Crimes Trials, at which Colonel Williams was a major witness]. Several accounts have appeared in various publications of Colonel Nagatomo's initial address to the troops of Williams Force, but it took Dickson to note that the Japanese commander chose to deliver his remarks in French, from which they were translated into English by a Dutchman. Dickson's summary follows:

> The gist of his remarks was that the men before him were but a rabble—the skeleton of a broken army. By the infinite grace of His Imperial Majesty the Emperor, their lives had been spared. They were now expected in effect to enter with unbounded enthusiasm into the task of assisting Japan in her high-minded endeavour of bringing civilisation and happiness to the world, most especially to South-East Asia. He was good enough to warn any potential slackers that idleness would be looked upon with grave disfavour. A muffled sound from the men on parade greeted his masterly oration. If Nagatomo's ears were keen and his powers of interpretation good, he would have recognised in it a rather prolonged and ill-suppressed demonstration of mirth. Nevertheless, despite an outward show of nonchalance, deep down in the hearts of prisoners there were growing misgivings as to the future.[36]

The misgivings of the prisoners were not lessened by Nagatomo's assurance that even though Japan had not ratified the Geneva Conventions with reference to treatment of Prisoners of War (signed by most other nations July 27, 1929), his government intended to act as if it had done so. Ironically, a memorandum delivered by the Japanese government to the United States Department of State via the Spanish Embassy in Washington, D.C. on February 24, 1942, also gave assurances that the treaty stipulations signed at Geneva would be applied to "civil, as well as military prisoners who find themselves under Japanese jurisdiction."[37] With each passing day of their captivity, the POWs were reminded anew of how empty these assurances would be.

3

Too Much of a Good Thing

ugust 30, 1945: Having been lucky enough to obtain two pieces of paper in one day, Dickson began a second letter to his wife, but he quickly ran out of space, and it would be another six days before he resumed writing it.

Dickson deliberately re-phrased several points from the note he rushed to send off earlier that day, just in case this one reached Melbourne first:

From: VX 19618
S/Sgt. T.C. Dickson
2/2 Aust. Pioneer Bn.
Nakom Nai POW Camp
Thailand
August 30, 1945

My old Darling,

Of all the exciting events of the last week or two, this is by no means the least—to be able once again to communicate with you in a more or less normal manner. Next to seeing you again—which looks like being a reality very soon, the thing I look forward to is hearing from you and knowing you are fit. Of the latter I feel quite confident, but to hear direct from you, that you are well, will be a great joy. In all the long time we have been apart I have always felt that we have been close in spirit. What a magnificent day it will be when we are really together again. I know you will be anxious to know how I am. You will be glad to hear that you are not getting a physical wreck back on your hands. I am really quite fit, and have been for more than a year. My bad period was late 1943 and early 1944, as it was with many others. Very bad food and jungle conditions generally were responsible for that. After coming to

Thailand early in '44 was fortunate enough not to return to the jungle, and have gradually picked up ever since. Apart from the fact that I can do with some glasses, I am practically as good as pre-POW days, and will be fully so on a good course of normal food. After all, more than 3800 consecutive meals of rice is a bit too much of a good thing! John also, who is in this camp, is in good form, although at present suffering from a broken collarbone—not serious. In mid'43 he had a bad time but made a really good recovery. Now that should be enough about the family health!

This is not a bad place—paddy fields with mountains close at hand. Until two months ago we had been for six months near PETBURI, 100 miles or so south-west of Bangkok. (This place is about 60 miles north-east of Bangkok.) Today's report is that we are to be flown to India, to recuperate at Bangalore, a hill station inland from Madras. Time will prove whether that is correct or not. As soon as the war ended officers were sent to take command, they having been separated from the other ranks at the beginning of this year.

[Here is where Dickson ran out of paper.]

How easily a string of well-chosen words can minimize endless days of horror! "My bad period was late 1943 and early 1944, as it was with many others", Dickson wrote matter-of-factly. But all available accounts and diaries recorded daily conditions during this time which were so unbelievable that the reader sometimes needs to scan sentences a second time, before absorbing them fully.

As Leslie Hall pointed out, Dickson's unit, Williams Force, had the toughest job on the railway. No doubt the Japanese couldn't believe their luck at capturing a whole battalion of rugged Australians, and an engineering battalion at that! So it is not surprising that Williams Force became the core of 'No. 1 Mobile Force ', and mobile it was; on the move constantly, under worsening weather, supply and jungle conditions. The heavy monsoon rains became incessant, as did the screams of the guards. "Speedo! Speedo!" They would shout in broken English, all the time pelting the POWs with rocks, as the prisoners tried to complete their impossible quotas of work with primitive or worn tools.

Although the British had considered building a railway in this location some years earlier, the idea was abandoned after a field survey clearly showed that supplying construction crews—and keeping them healthy in jungles infested with malaria-carrying mosquitos—would be impossible. What an irony that so many POWs from the British Empire would die a few years later, proving this point to the determined servants of the Japanese Empire!

Crew of prisoners working by firelight at night, driving piles for Railway trestle, 1943. On one occasion, a crew released the pile suddenly, hoping to strike the Japanese engineer standing below. The plot failed by inches.
(MURRAY GRIFFIN: *BRIDGE WORK, THAILAND RAILWAY,* PEN AND BRUSH AND BROWN INK OVER PENCIL, HEIGHTENED WITH WHITE, 51.4 X 35.6 CM. AUSTRALIAN WAR MEMORIAL, AWM 25107)

Of course, the British saw the railway as a possible convenience; whereas its construction was undertaken by the Japanese as a desperate necessity, after American submarines and British bombers so successfully disrupted Japan's cargo shipping routes through the China Sea.

Sergeant Kevin Nolan recalled how the POWs managed to slow—and sabotage—construction as much as possible, in spite of the rantings, rock peltings and beatings of their captors:

> At different times I worked on all phases of the railway line.
> The first task allotted to us was clearing the route of the proposed
> embankment. This entails some very hard work clearing thick stands
> of bamboo. The hollowed out bamboo provided some very welcome
> water containers, and also served as vats for fermenting rice, fruit
> and vegetable peelings, etc. Cal Mitchell was one distiller, and I well
> remember him regaling myself and 'Twin' Lew Whitfeld with a dram
> on a couple of occasions at the 35 Kilo camp [Whitfeld was later
> kicked to death by a guard—see chapter 9].
>
> Trees large and small were felled, and the arrival of elephants
> which removed the large trunks was most welcome.
>
> The next variation was to be required to dig and transport on
> 'tungahs' (two oat sacks suspended on bamboo rods) an amount of
> earth which could be comfortably shifted in half a day; however, it
> took all but two gangs a full day. The two in question would not
> listen to reason, being keen to get back to camp and play volleyball.
> We were still pretty fit then. Nippon became suspicious and
> progressively increased the requirements until it did take all day
> to accomplish.
>
> Then came a stint in a bridge building gang, [beginning by]
> felling poles and lashing them into a scaffold 20 feet high. Sometimes
> I was on the end of one of 60 or so ropes pulled to the accompaniment
> of a chant. A better job was being one of four up the scaffold,
> controlling ropes that kept the pile directly under the 'monkey',
> a heavy weight that slid up and down a steel pointed shaft six
> centimeters thick and three metres long.
>
> On one occasion we plotted what would now be labelled
> 'attempted murder'. As the monkey rose, the shaft left the guide hole
> in the top of the pile fractionally, whereupon on this occasion, we
> jerked the pile aside so that on the down stroke the shaft speared
> into the ground, narrowly missing its target, the Jap engineer officer

who was measuring the effectiveness of each thump. We managed
to convince him that it had been a most regrettable accident. Had
it been fatal, I wonder what the consequences would have been?

The technique employed in the construction was so inept that
we hoped we would never be required to traverse these structures
[but some were, and their careful sabotage made the journey nerve-
racking indeed].

Later we went back to the final stage of the embankment. The
meeting of the two converging ends [of the Railway, one end begun in
Thailand, and the other in Burma] was set for the deadline of March
28, 1943. That night, as in many others, we worked under oil flares.
However, despite much screaming and ranting by the Japanese, the
meeting was not achieved until the early hours of the morning. No
doubt the fact that in some cases the labourers were having tungahs
filled from pits on one side, carrying them over to the other side,
tipping them and reloading with the same dirt and returning it to
whence it originally came—had some bearing on this delay. In the
gloom, there appeared to be much activity, but there wasn't much
progress.

Next came the laying of wooden sleepers, followed by positioning
of the heavy iron rails. By this time our physical condition was
beginning to deteriorate and we found these tasks somewhat
exhausting. The sleepers had to be bored, mostly by hand, and then
the rails spiked onto them. I then discovered that I could hit a dog
spike with about as much consistency as I hit a golf ball. Nippon
was not amused.

A bit of comic relief came into life then when I, with seven others,
was formed into a rail straightening gang. We would set out in the
morning and with huge crowbars straighten the snake-like line of
rails and sleepers which had wauped so badly in the heat of the day.
By the time we had covered a mile or so the sun was at it again and
our straightened section was twisted again. The Jap sergeant in charge
of us was a reasonable and intelligent man, and realising the utter
futility of the operation, he used to get us well out of sight and repair
into the bush, where he would conduct miniature sports meetings.
Then towards evening we would straighten out the track on the way
back to camp. Unfortunately that job didn't last very long. The
section was ballasted, with the result that our labours with the bars
really ground us down.[1]

Leslie Hall adds a poignant note about the elephants mentioned by Nolan:

> The Nipponese, accepting the advice of the Australians, decided to corduroy (the mud-filled roadway) . . . trees had to be felled and carried . . . it was at this point the massive and wonderful elephants came to the aid of the POW. Even though they, too, were ill-fed, they seemed to sense the need of the prisoners . . . and without even a mahout [keeper], wrapped their trunks around heavy logs, to the balance point, and carried them to the lay-down area.[2]

But the assistance of the elephants was short-lived; according to Colonel Williams, the Japanese decided that a few Australians could do more work than an elephant.

And POW author Ernest Gordon's blue eyes still sparkled as he recollected how the prisoners sabotaged each step as much as they could, whenever a guard's back was turned: "Shearing a bolt, splitting wood—even planting termite's nests in structures, whenever one was found along the way." [3]

No wonder the ex-POWs were so incensed when Pierre Boulle's portrayal became immortalized in a popular movie, depicting the prisoners as being inspired by their leadership to show the Japanese what a good job they could do! POW artist Ronald Searle summarized the feelings of many: "As for *The Bridge on the River Kwai,* it crossed the river only in the imagination of its author; his idea of British behaviour under the Japanese was equally bizarre." [4]

It is difficult for most Westerners to imagine accomplishing anything in a climate where annual rainfall is the highest in the world, averaging 400 inches per year; and where roadways, campsites and everything else becomes mired in knee-deep mud during the long monsoon season. Yet the POWs were forced to work every day, and often long into the night, during the awful year of 1943, until the converging parts were finally joined at the 153-kilo peg, near Nieke, Thailand on October 17, 1943.

For this occasion, the Japanese command staged a ridiculous propaganda film, to be shown back home—and the 'stars' weren't even in the show! The emaciated prisoners were kept out of sight, while water was thrown on the bodies of well-fed Japanese 'workers', to simulate sweat. Spikes were painted gold for the joining ceremony; dignitaries stood by proudly as a brass band played in honor of the hard-toiling Japanese nationals who had singlehandedly created this important supply link for the Imperial Army.

Perhaps one reason the prisoners were not shown is that Article 31 of the 1929 Geneva Conventions reads: "Work which a prisoner is called upon to perform shall have no direct connection with the operations of the War."

Yet just a day before the film was made, Colonel Williams secretly recorded in his diary: "The sick boys, who worked 18 hours, were not allowed to eat the meal taken out to them . . . the night shift returned to camp at 1330 hours after completing 31 hours straight. The day workers are still out and no one has any idea when they will be back. No instructions to send a meal, or meals, out to them. We can just wait . . . Capt. Handasyde was badly beaten today . . . the guard didn't like the look on his face . . . two more . . . succumbed to the ravages of the diseases which plagued them, and their bodies were laid to rest in the one peaceful area of this encampment . . . (just before dawn) the railway from Singapore to Moulmein, Burma became a fact. But at what a price! The lives of many thousands of prisoners of war and Burmese civilians!"[5].

The most consistent figures put the death toll—just for the construction of the railway—at 12,568 POW, and between 50,000 and 80,000 civilian laborers.[6]. The toll would keep mounting steadily, reaching over 15,000 by August 1945, and beyond.

So the creation of the Japanese propaganda film was all the more grating for the POWs to watch, capping as it did their previous weeks at the worst campsites yet endured. Since January of that year, the Japanese had been recording the weight, height and chest measurement of each prisoner, every month. One of the most chilling entries in Colonel Williams' diary is this one: "Based on recent experiences at hospital camps, once the combined weight of prisoners decreases, so do rations, accordingly." 7.

This policy, incidentally, was applied, on orders from Tokyo, to military and civilian prisoners in other locations, including women and children, who had the misfortune of being interned by the Japanese.[8].

Conditions and rations worsened steadily through the year, as work became harder and the hours longer. Weakening bodies invited disease, and there were plenty of insects to transport it. By early August, Colonel Williams noted desperately: "Three days into August and our living conditions are worsening by the minute. The non-stop rain has made a mockery of the huts' roof structure, and the centre walkway is almost knee deep in mud. Water is pouring from top and sides. However, the men are so wearied and done in, they just flop down on their bedspaces and seek solace in sleep . . . Informed we have to reduce our rice intake from 350 grammes per man per day to 250. If it was starvation previously, what now! Kitchen fires hard to keep alight with green wet wood . . . no matter . . . the Japanese demand hot water be provided for their daily baths . . . is it any wonder so many men are fading away."[9]

As usual, Colonel. Williams protested conditions vigorously, and finally got permission to slaughter a yak cow. He notes bitterly: "The Nipponese confiscated the greater portion of the beast and gave the prisoners the ribs (can't eat bones), one shoulder, and half of one leg . . . impossible to feed hundreds of men on such a meagre issue, but at least the sick will appreciate what broth can be made from it . . ."

On September 28, Williams Force had arrived at 130 Kilo camp, which by all accounts, even that of a Japanese officer, was the worst yet seen: two roofless huts, barely able to accomodate 600 men, became home to 900; no kitchen, therefore no food could be prepared. It rained all night, and not one POW slept. For two days, the Japanese took all the POW tools to build a hut and kitchen for themselves, making it impossible for the prisoners to cut wood. With no fires, there could be no cooking, even in the open.

Takashi Nagase, then an interpreter for the dreaded *kempe tai* [military police], saw the 130 Kilo camp, and nearly half a century later, he still remembered it in detail:

> A funeral procession of prisoners was coming up. Comrades were carrying a body on a stretcher which was covered with a faded Union Jack, followed by a Japanese soldier with a gun. At the rear of the procession, four or five vultures followed with their heads moving to and fro . . . I was shocked at the sight of the camp when I walked through the bamboo fence. There were nothing but shabby looking huts without roofs. The floors of the huts were covered with bamboo which was split in two. The floor bamboos were laid with the curved side up. On the rugged floor sick prisoners were shivering in soaking blankets. Rain oozed out from worn-out blankets every time the POWs, who were stricken with malaria, rolled over on their side. . . .[10]

Incidentally, Nagase was posing as an inspector on this occasion, in order to get information from the prisoners, primarily by searching their belongings—which probably explains some of the sudden 'raids' of POW possessions about which Colonel Williams complained so often throughout their captivity.

Cecil Dickson may well have been one of the malaria victims the Japanese officer saw that day in September 1943: he contracted the disease in May of that year, and had approximately 20 relapses to July 1944. He would suffer periodic bouts of malaria for the rest of his life. In his soldier's pay book [see page137] Dickson also lists conjunctivitis, failing vision, infected sores, and beri-beri, the last-mentioned from November 1943 through January 1944.

Dickson's greatest anxiety about health, however, may have been when his younger brother John contracted cholera in mid-1943 [the 'bad time' Dickson cryptically refers to in his letter]. In later years he would often mention with wonderment how John, isolated in the cholera hut with half a hundred others, was one of just five men to walk out alive.

Although John made a 'really good recovery', according to his brother, the younger Dickson's condition remained considerably weakened throughout the rest of their internment, and he was hospitalized immediately upon his return to Melbourne.

Barbara Clements remembered that: "John and Cecil both had iron wills, and were full of stubborn determination. Nothing would break their spirit." It had to be a large dose of determination which allowed John Dickson to walk out of that cholera hut, when no other medicine was made available to the POWs.

Colonel Williams would ask for volunteers to man the isolation hut, and some always stepped forward, despite the obvious risk. As a result, it was not uncommon for some to give their own lives, tending to their mates. Leslie Hall summed up the situation this way: "In the almost intolerable conditions existing in POW camps in Burma and Thailand, the word *mate* held greater significance than in any other sphere of life. Selfishness was rare. Few ever gave it a thought; 90% never knew the meaning of the expression."[11].

In a bizarre twist, the only way the cholera patients could immediately reciprocate the risks their fellow POW took in caring for them, was to provide a sanctuary for precious items such as diaries, cameras and drawings. Ronald Searle tells how whenever possible, he hid his sketches of camp life under the pillow of a cholera patient, because the Japanese were terrified of the disease, and the cholera hut was the one spot in camp guaranteed not to be searched.[12].

Despite their drastic food shortages, the men of Williams Force at one point gave up their rations after Colonel Williams visited the 'hospital' at 55 Kilo camp and saw that the kitchen there had been without rice for two days. The Pioneers commanding officer had made it a point to check the hospital camp, being aware of remarks made by Japanese officers, such as: "Your sick shall starve until they die or go back to work . . . no work, no food."[13].

Was it possible the Japanese were making a mockery of Christian scripture, quoting the words of St. Paul to his followers: "If any would not work, neither should he eat"?[14]. More likely, the Japanese were observing their own regulations, which held that sick soldiers were useless, and should be abandoned or shot for failing to carry out their duties. Anthropologist Ruth Benedict, in her study of Japanese culture, cites instances in New Guinea and the Philippines where hospitalized Japanese soldiers were killed, and their medical officers committed suicide. She also quotes an American colonel, Harold Glattley, who told the *Washington Post* in a 1945 interview that during three years as a POW on Formosa, he saw no doctors for Japanese soldiers.[15].

It must have been impressive, though baffling, for the Japanese to watch POWs feeding their sick first, and tending to them constantly. Perhaps no single act more vividly contrasted the spiritual and cultural heritages of captor and captive, and no one dared to test that gap more boldly than "Weary" Dunlop. Here, in his own words, is his account of a truly remarkable incident:

> I recall that the Japanese commandant in Chunkai Camp, court-martialled me summarily for operating on a Japanese soldier who failed to carry out his camp duties. He took a dramatic 'swish' at my neck with his gleaming Samurai sword, which however stopped quivering at my neck, then said, 'No, here is my sword, please honour me by killing yourself.'
>
> I returned an eloquent account of all the reasons why Australians did not commit 'hari-kiri'. His fierce brown eyes were locked on mine and he summed up, 'You mean that you are such a great coward you will not kill yourself?' To which I replied, 'You were right about one thing; I won't kill myself.'
>
> So I finished up in the 'box house' with my patient, Akimoto, that poltroon.[16]

A desperate situation was made nearly impossible to bear for the starving POWs as the local camp guards and their cooks insisted on confiscating, or at least taking a cut of, the rations which were being sent in for the prisoners. Just a week after the Railway was completed, Colonel Williams' diary reads: "As ration carriers have to pass the Nip kitchen to get to ours, the fat Nipponese cook snatches what he wants from our containers. Hence, low rations for the

The photo on the left shows brothers Cal (left) and Alan Mitchell, midway through a 136-mile training hike at Shepparton, Victoria, in July 1940. Right: *The Mitchell brothers, Alan (left) and Cal (seated) with Basil Ransome (standing) shortly after release, Bangkok, September 1945. Many ex-POWs sent similar photos home in advance of their arrival, hoping to assure families of their "good health."* (COURTESY OF C.J. MITCHELL)

prisoners . . . they took at least 100 men's potato entitlements from the last delivery." By Armistice Day, November 11, the CO's diary contains one of its starkest entries: "We are completely out of foodstuffs. No meals can be served today." Two days later: "A herd of seven yaks all went to the Japs—not one cut for the prisoners." On this occasion, his protest yielded 40 pounds of meat; but by then, they were down to one meal per day. And on November 17, he records that the prisoners had to carry in rations for the Japanese, but none were supplied at all to the POWs.[17]

Reflecting four decades later on that desperate and debilitating year of forced labor in 1943, speaking with a sadness which must have been especially acute for a physician, "Weary" Dunlop said in an interview: "The trouble was that if you were sinewy, indestructible, if you were a good workman, you got sent back and back and back on these terrible tasks with utterly inadequate food. You could see these magnificently strong men with great hearts who slowly went to pieces, and died."[18]

It should come as no surprise, then, to learn that when John Dickson finally arrived in Melbourne, family members were shocked at his condition. The
oldest of the three brothers, Stan, was there with daughter Jeanette, who recalls:
"No one could believe how thin Uncle John was. He weighed just over three
stones [about 50 pounds]. Every rib was broken from malnutrition." And
despite Cecil's cheery assurances that he was "practically as good as pre-POW
days," when he docked in Melbourne after nearly two additional months of
good food, Barbara Clements, remembers that "Uncle Cec still looked like a
scarecrow."

Of course, to the POWs who had been starved for so long, just the opportunity to eat three meals a day made them feel so robust, by comparison, that it
didn't occur to them they might look otherwise. Cal Mitchell, his brother Alan
and their friend Basil Ransome couldn't wait to have a photographer take their
picture in Bangkok, and they gleefully sent it home "so our families could stop
worrying", Cal remembered. "That photo caused much distress and weeping
about how thin we were, and how old we looked", he added ruefully.

So while he tried to minimize his own health problems and those of his
brother in this second letter home, Dickson knew that he has good reason to
worry about his wife's condition. During their marriage, she had suffered several miscarriages, which left the couple childless—a great and lasting disappointment. Freda's doctor had detected a weak heart, and advised against further
attempts at parenthood. And while Dickson was interned, his wife suffered a
bout of rheumatic fever. It seemed to her niece Barbara that "Aunt Freda was
ill the whole time Uncle Cec was away. To us, as children, it was a period of terrible sadness. My father (Freda's brother Hornby) and my uncle Cam (Freda's
brother-in-law) died during that time; Aunt Freda was so ill; Uncle Cec was a
POW. . . ."[19]

Years later, Dickson would confide that when he first came down the gang-
plank from the *Circassia* on November 3, 1945, he moved along the walkway,
chatting through the chain-link fence with a very pleasant lady for about ten
minutes—before realizing he was talking to his wife.

4

The Most Exciting Day

S eptember 1, 1945: It has been fifteen long days since the camp bugler sounded reveille English-style, signalling the end of imprisonment—but not of confinement, For Dickson and his fellow POWs who remained at Nakom Nayok, patience was being strained not only by the priority departure of the Americans, but also by the continuing need to stay put and await word of their own travel arrangements. Today, at last, the strain had been broken by the arrival of supplies by air, and medical officers by truck—a sure sign that the countryside was becoming more secure.

Dickson was one of the lucky few to get a piece of airmail stationery from among the newly-arrived supplies. He dared to hope that he would be home in time for his wedding anniversary.

Nakom Nayok Camp
Thailand
September 1, 1945

Dearest Old Binks,

Things are moving fast here now re our departure, which gives me a slight hope of being with you by October 2 {their anniversary}. Don't pin too much hope on it but there is just a chance. I have written to you already. This note, however, might beat the other home. An American friend, who left here a few days ago, was to send you a cable, also one to Stan re John's safety, so I hope these reached their destinations. Just to let the office know that I am still on the map I sent off, per another departed American, an account of how we received the news—which might & might not turn up. There is a very limited number of letters going on this air-mail. I was fortunate enough to get one, and would be glad if you would write immediately to the addresses on the back (or wire for preference) informing the people concerned that their husbands (respectively Capts. Edwards, Winning & Lovett, Flying Officer

*Matheson, Sgt. Dixon & Pvt. Redcliffe) and sons (Capt. Howitt & Cpl. Battye)
are well. On second thoughts, hang the expense and make it all telegrams!
Tremendous excitement to-day. First an American plane dropped two Americans, a
Thai, and then personal gear into the camp, then a British plane circled round
parachuting down books, recent papers, cigarettes and a host of other stuff. There
are two schools of thought about the journey home. One is that we fly to India via
Rangoon; the other that we catch a ship at Bangkok for Australia direct. A party
of stretcher sick has just left the camp for Bangkok to be flown to India. Cheerio
old darling. Seeing you soon—and won't it be magnificent!*

Tons of love, Pop

[Names and addresses of telegram recipients followed, neatly printed
in block letters in a double column.]

'SECURITY: THINK BEFORE YOU WRITE' is printed across the envelope's flap. What an irony! How he would have liked to actually write letters
home these past 44 months; but all he got to do was cross out inappropriate
pre-printed lines on postcards supplied by the Imperial Japanese Army, about
once every six months. When he had been sick, he would cross out the phrase:
'I have not had any illness.' And then he could cram a dozen well-chosen words
into two and a half lines of space at the bottom of the card, and wonder whether
it would ever leave the camp.

Despite the fact that he was only allowed to date one card (in May 1944),
Dickson cleverly found ways to signal when some were being written. The second card, for example, gives a traditional New Year's greeting, and refers to
Freda's upcoming birthday, February 2. Perhaps the most dramatic reference is
his use of the word 'message' instead of 'letter' in his final card, telling his wife
that some of the radio messages being sent by the Relatives Association, are
being received over clandestine wireless sets.

As Dickson would describe the situation some years later, in compiling the
'Prisoners of War' chapter for his Battalion's history:

December 1943 was notable for one great event. It was the arrival of
the first mail that the prisoners received from home. Much of it was
written in July 1942, so it was almost 18 months in reaching its
destination. It had been written before messages from relatives were
restricted to 25 words, and the pages of news from home were a
wonderful tonic to the weary men. They were in real need of a tonic

then. Food supplies were at their worst and the deathroll was mounting daily. The letters revived thoughts and hopes of home, which now seemed so far distant and remote. The men knew that to those dearest to them in Australia anxiety would be their daily companion, for the men in captivity were behind a dark curtain and it would be natural for those who could not see behind it to fear the worst for their men. The sympathetic thoughts therefore flowed to, as well as from, Australia.

All that the prisoners could do to help allay the fears of their families at home was to take advantage of the opportunity, about once every six months, to send them a card. Most of these cards were already printed, and of course the words were supplied by the Japanese, requiring only the signature of the sender. They gave no hint of the real conditions that existed in the camps. They praised the captors for their treatment of the prisoners, who were alleged to be extremely grateful for the benefits being bestowed on them by their kindly and generous hosts. In return for these nauseating epistles the prisoners received 25-word postcards from home. These were written once a month, but they were released by the Japanese at very irregular intervals. It was not uncommon for 12 months to pass without an issue of inward mail, and some men received no word at all from home during the whole of their captivity. When mail was handed out by the Japanese, however, it had a tremendously uplifting effect on the morale of its receivers.[1]

None of his wife's long letters were delivered, but occasionally Dickson got a 25-word note. Fellow Pioneer Walter Summons compiled a record of the dates he remembers writing a postcard, and the date his family received it in Melbourne:

Written October 12, 1942, received September 13, 1943
Written January 22, 1943, received October 6, 1943
Written May 31, 1943, received November 30, 1943
Written February 1, 1944, received January 6, 1945

*Following pages: The six postcards sent home by Cecil Dickson, 1942–45.
The first card was written from Java, before the Japanese disrtibuted
printed forms. Some arrived in Melbourne a year after being written.*
(PHOTOGRAPHED FROM THE ORIGINALS COURTESY OF MRS. T.C. DICKSON)

VX19618, STAFF-SGT. T. C. DICKSON.

DARLING BINKIE,

VERY FIT. IN GOOD
SPIRITS. HOPE YOU SAME. LONGING
HEAR FROM YOU. TWO THORNS WELL.
LOVE OLD DARLING, ALSO MOTHER,
FAMILIES,

POP.

IMPERIAL JAPANESE ARMY.

I am interned at The War Prisoners Camp at
Moulmein in Burma.

My health is (good, ~~usual, poor~~)

~~I have not had any illness.~~

~~I (am) (have been) in hospital.~~

~~I am (not) working (for pay at _____ per day).~~

~~My salary is _____ per month.~~

I am with friends. MAY 1943 BRING HAPPINESS

OLD GIRL. MANY HAPPY RETURNS OF FEB. 2.

LOVE TO MOTHER AND ALL THE FAMILIES

From POP

IMPERIAL JAPANESE ARMY

I am interned at The War Prisoners Camp at
Moulmein in Burma.

My health is (good, ~~usual, poor~~)

~~I have not had any illness.~~

I (am) ~~(have been)~~ in hospital.

I am (not) working ~~(for pay at _____ per day).~~

~~My salary is _____ per month.~~

I am with friends (JOHN, McCARTHY, NOLAN)

RECOVERING FROM TEMPORARY SICKNESS,

OTHERWISE FIT. HOPE YOU WELL. LOVE OLD DEAR.

From POP.

IMPERIAL JAPANESE ARMY.

Our present place, quarters, and work is unchanged since last card sent to you. The rains have finished, it is now beautiful weather. I am working healthily ~~(sick)~~. We receive newspapers printed in English which reveal world events.

We have joyfully received a present of some milk, tea, margarine, sugar and cigarettes from the Japanese Authorities.

We are very anxious to hear from home, but some prisoners have received letters or cables.

Everyone is hopeful of a speedy end to the war and with faith in the future we look forward to a happy reunion soon.

With best wishes for a cheerful Christmas.

YOUR FIRST LETTERS RECEIVED. SPECIAL RE-MEMBRANCES ELLA & NEEDHAMS, LOVE, OLD GIRL

From *T.C. Dickson*

IMPERIAL JAPANESE ARMY

Date *19-5-44*

Your mails ~~(and ———)~~ are received with thanks.
My health is (good, ~~usual, poor~~).
~~I am ill in hospital.~~
~~I am working for pay (I am paid monthly salary).~~
I am not working.
My best regards to *ALL. NOT ENOUGH SPACE TO GET*

SENTIMENTAL! JOHN WELL, KEN BLOOMING, LOVE OLD GIRL

Yours ever,

Pop

IMPERIAL JAPANESE ARMY.

I am still in a P. O. W. Camp near Moulmein, Burma. There are 20,000 Prisoners, being Australian, Dutch, English, and American. There are several camps of 2/3000 prisoners who work at settled labour daily.

We are quartered in very plain huts. The climate is good. Our life is now easier with regard to food, medicine and clothes. The Japanese Commander sincerely endeavours to treat prisoners kindly.

Officers' salary is based on salary of Japanese Officers of the same rank and every prisoner who performs labour or duty is given daily wages from 25 cents (minimum) to 45 cents, according to rank and work.

Canteens are established where we can buy some extra foods and smokes. By courtesy of the Japanese Commander we conduct concerts in the camps, and a limited number go to a picture show about once per month.

FEELING FIT – JOHN ALSO – AND OF COURSE THINK-ING OF THE OLD LADY A LOT. WILL BE THRILLED TO RECEIVE MAIL

Pop.

Ernest Gordon, a captain in the Argyll and Sutherland Highlanders, was one of the POWs who received no mail at all during his entire captivity, a fact he attributes primarily to Japanese indifference to record-keeping and somewhat bureaucratic lassitude on the part of the International Red Cross. A member of a secret service group in Singapore, Gordon escaped with a handful of others on a sailboat, and almost got to Ceylon before being spotted and captured by a Japanese tanker. The Japanese simply never bothered to add these few stragglers to the list of POWs they had supplied to the Red Cross, so Gordon was listed as "missing in action and presumed killed." His family had no inkling that he was alive until April, 1945 when, by some miracle, one of his pre-printed post-cards was delivered to their home in Scotland.

A further twist to Gordon's story is that just one person *did* know of his whereabouts: a USSteel executive with whom Gordon had become friends in Singapore. Once a month, the American sent Gordon a cablegram through the Red Cross, asking how he was doing. (Despite this regular contact, no one at the Red Cross thought to pass this information along to Gordon's family). None of these cables reached him until one day, while Gordon was working on the Railway, a Japanese vehicle drove up to the worksite. Out stepped an officer, demanding that Gordon be identified.

"I thought, this is it; they've discovered my diary or something, and I'm going to be killed", Gordon recalled. "Instead, the Japanese hands me this cable, with a flourish, and they all thought I must be someone very important." His family did not learn he was free until they received an official cable in September 1945, and he was not able to communicate with them until he reached Rangoon that same month.[2]

Freda Dickson could only guess whether her husband was still alive by the time she held each soiled, long-delayed piece of stiff manila paper, with just a few words in his handwriting. After all, she hadn't even heard that he was a prisoner until a year after the fact.

Her anxiety had increased tenfold, or so it seemed, over the past nine months—ever since some POWs being shipped to Japan had been torpedoed, then rescued by the same United States submarines, in September 1944. Nine Pioneers were among those rescued and brought back to Stewart House, near Brisbane, on October 18, 1944. The stories they told intelligence officers about conditions in the Burma-Thailand POW camps were so appalling that for several weeks, the dramatic rescue of these men at sea was kept secret, while the governments of Britain, the United States and Australia anguished over whether to reveal such atrocities to the public.

Finally, on November 17, 1944, Acting Prime Minister Forde addressed the House of Representatives in Canberra, as simultaneous announcements were being made in Washington and London. After he described the daily horrors the POWs were enduring, the public was outraged—but the families of those POWs were chilled beyond belief.

Leo Cornelius, one of the nine rescued Pioneers, described the tremendous burden placed on the handful of recovered POWs by anxious families:

"One of the greatest difficulties of my life was the meeting in Melbourne of relatives in Pioneer and [HMAS] *Perth* survivors, especially when the soldier concerned was deceased or ill when you last saw him . . . we were under specific orders not to release bad news, under any circumstances."

As word spread of their return, the repatriated POWs were besieged with calls and visits from anxious families of those still held prisoner. The inquiries turned into what Cornelius describes as "An avalanche, which caused some of us to go into seclusion."

He describes the poignance of his personal experience, heightened by concern for the well-being of an elderly aunt with whom he was living:

"It was not unusual for her to wake about 7 a.m. to tell me there were several people waiting to talk to me. When I protested she occasionally broke into tears and said, 'Some of them have been here for hours—in fact, since daylight.'"3

Perhaps the only comfort for Freda Dickson at that time was to realize that Cecil had *not* been selected for transport to Japan. The one dated postcard she received became especially significant, because it was written in May 1944, after POWs had been selected for that journey. This was the only time the Japanese allowed a date to be placed on outgoing correspondence; the concession was a direct result of International Red Cross protests earlier that year.

As her niece Barbara verified, reading and hearing first-hand accounts of such monumental hardships, especially from some of the men in Cecil's unit, made it very, very difficult for Freda Dickson and other POW relatives to sustain hope for their loved ones' safe return. But they tried to comfort each other with weekly meetings, where they shared information and offered mutual support. And they kept up their system of sending monthly postcards and messages, in the hope that some would be received.

No doubt Prime Minister Forde caught the sentiments of such families in his concluding sentences of that November 1944 address:

> The Government regrets that these disclosures have to be made, but it is convinced it is necessary that the Japanese government should know that we are in possession of the facts and will hold them responsible. All the rescued men speak of the high courage shown by their comrades. Everywhere and in all circumstances, the Australians have maintained matchless morale. They have shown themselves undaunted in the face of death. The many who have survived privation and disease in the jungle have developed spiritual and physical powers to triumph over adversity and their captors. Let us look forward to the day of their release.

Now that release had come, and Dickson's efforts at spreading the news about friends who survived—would succeed. Apparently Freda, being a good journalist's wife, contacted Mr. Knox at the *Argus* as soon as she received this letter, and the list of names appears in a story under Dickson's byline on September 13, 1945. Just over a week later, on September 22, his news account of the camp's activity on September 1 was printed in the paper. A reproduction of the article, obtained from the archives of the *Herald and Weekly Sun,* preceded by an editor's note explaining who has filed the story, is printed below:

POW's MOST EXCITING DAY
Liberation in Siam Camp

From WO T. CECIL DICKSON, mining editor of THE ARGUS before enlisting in 1940, who was recently liberated from a Siam POW camp.

The most exciting day at Nakom Nai POW camp, Siam, since August 17, when 2,500 British, Australian, Dutch and American prisoners were told that the war was over, was September 1.

Shortly after breakfast that morning a US transport plane dropped packages into the camp from a height of 300 feet.

An hour later a British machine, circling at a low altitude, dropped package after package into a small square. Before the end of the day the men had been issued with toilet and shaving soap, razor blades, cigarettes, and other almost forgotten luxuries.

Meanwhile a third plane, having failed to find the camp, had

POW's MOST EXCITING DAY

Liberation In Siam Camp

From **WO T. CECIL DICKSON,** mining editor of **THE ARGUS** before enlisting in 1940, who was recently liberated from a Siam POW camp.

The most exciting day at Nakou Nai POW camp, Siam, since August 17, when 2,500 British, Australian, Dutch, and American prisoners were told that the war was over, was September 1.

Shortly after breakfast that morning a US transport plane dropped packages into the camp from a height of 300 feet.

An hour later a British machine, circling at a low altitude, dropped package after package into a small square. Before the end of the day the men had been issued with toilet and shaving soap, razor blades, cigarettes, and other almost forgotten luxuries.

Meanwhile a third plane, having failed to find the camp, had dropped four British medical officers with great quantities of medical supplies into a paddyfield some miles away. They reached the camp by motor-truck later in the day.

One of the four, a 23-year-old English major, on landing, screwed a black-taped monocle into his eye and asked a group of Siamese "where the deuce the prisoners of war were to be found."

34 AIF UNITS REPRESENTED

Five hundred and fifty Australians from 34 separate units, under Captain J. J. Edwards, MC, 2/3 Machinegun Batt, of Adelaide, were among the personnel at Nakou Nai. The 2/4th Machinegun Batt was represented by 63 men, the 2/2nd Pioneer Batt by 54, and the 2/40th Inf Batt by 53.

The period between the end of the war and actual liberation was in some respects a trying one for the men. But their high spirits and morale averted what could have become an intolerable situation.

Although nominally free, they were still behind a high bamboo fence, forbidden to leave camp and taste the joys outside. Patience was the only course, especially as the district teemed with armed Japanese.

NOT VINDICTIVE RACE

Whatever the failings of the British race, vindictiveness is not one. Hardly a POW at Nakou Nai, or anywhere else for that matter, had but good cause in the preceding 3½ years to take violent vengeance when the day came against Japanese and Koreans.

But the day did come, and hardly a hair on a short-cropped Japanese head was hurt. Relief at their release banished the spirit of revenge from men's hearts.

Only one incident occurred at Nakou Nai camp. One of the newly appointed British camp police found himself face to face with the most hated Korean in tne camp, by whom he had been bashed only a week before. The Korean, who was drunk, made friendly advances to the camp policeman, who felled him in one blow.

News article sent by Dickson to the Melbourne Argus just after liberation, in late August 1945. It appeared in the September 22 1945 edition.
(COURTESY OF THE HERALD AND WEEKLY TIMES, MELBOURNE)

dropped four British medical officers with great quantities of medical supplies into a paddyfield some miles away. They reached the camp by motor-truck later in the day.

One of the four, a 23-year-old English major, on landing, screwed a black-taped monocle into his eye and asked a group of Siamese 'where the deuce the prisoners of war were to be found.'

34 A I F UNITS REPRESENTED

Five hundred and fifty Australians from 34 separate units, under Captain J.J. Edwards, MC 2/3 Machinegun Batt, of Adelaide, were among the personnel at Nakom Nai. The 2/4th Machinegun Batt was represented by 63 men, the 2/2nd Pioneer Batt by 54, and the 2/40th Inf Batt by 53.

The period between the end of the war and actual liberation was in some respects a trying one for the men. But their high spirits and morale averted what could have become an intolerable situation.

Although nominally free, they were still behind a high bamboo fence, forbidden to leave camp and taste the joys outside. Patience was the only course, especially as the district teemed with armed Japanese.

NOT VINDICTIVE RACE

Whatever the failings of the British race, vindictiveness is not one. Hardly a POW at Nakom Nai, or anywhere else for that matter, had but good cause in the preceding $3^{1}/_{2}$ years to take violent vengeance when the day came against Japanese and Koreans.

But the day did come, and hardly a hair on a short-cropped Japanese head was hurt. Relief at their release banished the spirit of revenge from men's hearts.

Only one incident occurred at Nakom Nai camp. One of the newly appointed British camp police found himself face to face with the most hated Korean in the camp, by whom he had been bashed only a week before. The Korean, who was drunk, made friendly advances to the camp policeman, who felled him in one blow.

The benign attitude of newly-freed POW toward Japanese camp personnel was a source of continuing puzzlement and debate even to some of their commanding officers, especially in view of how close all POWs came to being executed.

Cal Mitchell remembered: "Our hidden wireless sets picked up the information that on August 22, the Japs planned to start executing all POWs, beginning with the officers. We beat the deadline by just six days! And of course, the non-commissioned officers were just as well organized as the officers.[4]

Harry Whelan loved to tell the story about how a Japanese interpreter, seeking to ingratiate himself with "Weary" Dunlop, read him the order that if Japan surrendered, all POWs were to be executed first: "Taking his turn to have a little fun, at last, at the Jap's expense, 'Weary' pointed out that since under the code of *Bushido* a Japanese had dishonored himself if he surrendered, and would be required to commit hari-kiri, 'Weary' and his fellow officers would have liked to witness the ceremony . . ."[5]

Sir Edward, commenting on the incident, pointed out that "All prisoners were to be eliminated, so that my presence at the hari-kiri ceremony was impractical."[6]

However, the Allies had for some months previously been parachuting commandos into the jungle near as many POW camps as could be located, with the purpose of training Thai villagers to assist in storming the camps at the first sound of gunfire. Interpreter Takashi Nagase recalled seeing those commandos arriving, and searching for them—mostly in vain, apparently: "On full moon nights, Allied spies dropped by blue parachute in groups of five. We spent many nights searching for them throughout the jungle and grassy fields."[7]

The POWs also learned through radio broadcasts that, since their campsites were presumed by British intelligence to be a location for Japanese troops, the RAF was planning to bomb them—on August 17! As Ernest Gordon observed: "Had the war continued for two more weeks, we would have copped it one way or another, at the hand of friend or foe."

Echoing Dickson's report in the *Argus* story, Gordon wrote: "Though we now held the power, it never occurred to us to raise a hand against them . . . The liberators wanted to shoot the Japanese on the spot. Only the intervention of the victims prevented them. Captors were spared by their captives."[8]

But Mitchell was one officer who would not have been inclined to such leniency, had he been with his troops on the day of liberation. He emphasized: "As regards the attention given to the Japanese after the capitulation I must say we were all rather surprised by the actions, or rather lack of action, by our troops. I brought this up with them at the time and they were greatly surprised. It could be summed up by the remark 'What! And be as big a lot of bastards as them?' "[9]

Christian values wear many labels.

5

Undreamed of Luxury

September 5, 1945: Dickson finally located more paper to continue the letter he had interrupted on August 30. Pages 317 and 318 of an accounting ledger, lined horizontaly in blue with a vertical red margin column, served his purpose.

In the last couple of days, he had retrieved several letters from his wife, which had been brought to his camp from a more distant Japanese headquarters. Undistributed mail was found at almost every location, and handed out as quickly as possible to the eager POWs.

Trying to read his wife's letters in sequence, Dickson began to catch up on family news, and not all of it was pleasant. He learned for the first time that his brother-in-law, Cam, had died several months earlier. Many POWs experienced similar shocks upon opening those first letters from home.

There is no salutation on this letter, because Dickson was picking up where he left off six days previously:

Having gone so far, special small sheets of paper were issued for the letter on August 30, so I'm finishing the one I began on that day. None of our officers came to this camp, but I had letters from Capts. Winning and Bishop, who had gone to other camps. Both were well.

Yesterday was full of excitement. Three planes dropped a large quantity of food, etc. One's tastes have become so simple through having so little for so long that all of this stuff that is being poured in on us now is like undreamed of luxury. Everyone is putting on weight (including yours truly) as a result of the enormous improvement in food, vitamin tablets, etc.

A couple of days ago I had the pleasure of walking out of the camp and experiencing the feeling of freedom. Two of the officers and a sergeant were also of the party. Hailing a Jap truck outside the camp, we went into town, about

8 miles away. Quite a fair place, although 20 miles from the railway.
Friendly people, plenty of Japs and Koreans—and even armed Jap guards at
the main corners—I think to keep order among their own people (troops). We
ate lunch in the market surrounded by 20 or 30 Thais—one speaking good
English interpreting for the rest.

Re mail from you. Five of the long letters did not reach me and I received
most of the 25 worders up to May 1944. As you say, it is hard to imagine
50 Canterbury Road without Cam. I was very grieved to hear the news about
the poor old chap. There will be an enormous amount for you to tell me about
the doings when I reach home.

Latest report is that we are flying to Singapore, although officially our
postal address, which I append below, is India. Unless you hear otherwise,
write there, but I hope we will be with you before there is time for an exchange
of letters. In the meantime look after yourself old darling. Remembrances to
family and friends.

Your loving

Pop

Many POWs found mixed blessings when they finally received batches of mail from home. One of the most poignant accounts of searching in vain for familiar handwriting, was told by Leslie Hall in his manuscript of family history, "The Queen of Hearts." Hall kept pestering the postal staff to look, and look again, for a letter in his mother's handwriting. Exasperated, the postal clerk said: "Here's the pile; look for yourself." In rapid succession, Hall found several pieces of mail addressed to him from various relatives, but still none from his mother. Finally, he opened one from his sister, only to discover that his mother had died a year and a half ago. How often he had pictured his reunion with her—he would lift his petite mother and swing her in circles, as he had done so many times. Now, all he could look forward to was a visit to her grave. Heartbroken, he wandered into the orderly room; and when a friend approached, Hall could only point to the sheet of paper in his hand.[1]

For quite a few returning POWs, the anticipation of arrival was mingled with apprehension about who might not be there to greet them at home. One POW returning on Dickson's troopship, the *Circassia,* got such bad news when he phoned home from Fremantle, the ship's first stop, that the poor soldier just quietly slipped overboard during the night, on the way to Melbourne (see Chapter 16).

Arrival in Australia would also bring an unwelcome task to those, like Hall, who felt an obligation to seek out relatives of POWs who had died in the camps and try to offer words of comfort, as if details of a final rest in peace might help to assuage the searing news which many families had just received.

While he waited for passage home, nothing pleased Dickson and his friends more than encountering Japanese and Koreans trying to blend into the landscape, and forcing them to salute. To all military forces, of course, saluting is a required act of respect, to be displayed first by the one junior in rank. Since the Japanese considered all POWs to be of lesser importance than even the lowliest Japanese private, nothing apparently brought swifter retribution—or just a handy excuse to administer a beating—than the failure to salute promptly. Even among their own ranks, breaches of respect brought incredibly brutal responses.

The insistence on "respect" was all the more galling to POWs, especially officers, not only because of the frequently brutal and temperamental behavior of their captors, but also because the prisoners were often under the command of junior-ranking Japanese. At one location during 1943, the camp commandant was a three-star private!

As Harry Whelan explained: "You had to be careful; if you did one thing to displease them, then they had it in for you. For example, if you wore a hat, you were supposed to salute; if not, you bowed from the waist. I saw a man kicked to death because he was too sick to stand up and salute."

This exaggerated protocol was even demanded of civilians. One Dutch woman, interned in Sumatra with her two young children, was apparently "marked", as Whelan would say, in the early days of her captivity. Perhaps she failed to bow correctly, "Japanese style", during daily *tenko* (roll call). Every single day for the next three years, she was beaten, no matter how exemplary her behavoir might have been—and her children were made to watch.

In his diaries, Colonel Williams frequently referred to a "saluting blitz", in which POWs were beaten repeatedly for allegedly failing to salute rapidly enough—usually when they were midway through a task. At one point, he noted, guards took to sneaking up behind working parties of POWs and using the element of surprise as an excuse to administer a fearful bashing.[2] One camp commandant even complained to the Pioneer CO that "The Australian troops must conform as do the Americans and British, and salute the Great Nipponese. The Australian attitude is to treat Nipponese like cows and pigs. This must cease; saluting must improve."[3]

Dickson found a brilliant way to beat the Japanese at their own game, and he managed to do it by combining the three priorities which, when breached, caused the greatest discomfort in Japanese culture: observing protocol; avoiding embarrassment; and never appearing to be taken by surprise. In one camp, he timed his morning rounds to coincide with the moment when a particular Japanese officer was standing outdoors in his silk bathrobe, concentrating on his image in a propped-up mirror as he lathered shaving soap on to his face. At that precise moment, Dickson would round the corner and salute smartly, forcing the Japanese to drop his razor (usually in the dirt) and return the salute, while dripping shaving cream all over his silk robe. This was one of Dickson's favorite stories, and just about every one of his friends told it with renewed glee, nearly half a century later.

Because of their constant insistence on proper saluting, nothing apparently made the Japanese feel the reality of surrender more than the sudden requirement that *they,* and not the Caucasians, must now salute first. Former interpreter Takashi Nagase confirms this: "Shortly after the surrender, I was forced to salute an Allied group of soldiers in a busy street in Bangkok . . . I had to salute the Caucasians, who had been our prisoners until recently, in the local people's presence. I had never felt such a heavy saluting arm . . . then a real feeling of surrender struck me."[4]

Apparently the post-liberation transition was more orderly at Nakom Nayok than at certain other locations. Hardly anyone in the Allied military forces, be they liberators or POWs, shared the confidence of the Supreme Allied Commander, General Douglas MacArthur, that the Japanese would lay down their arms once instructed to do so by their Emperor. It was a fortune of history, at least in this respect, that the American commander was so well-schooled in Japanese culture. MacArthur insisted that the Emperor's representative, Foreign Minister Mamoru Shigemitsu, sign the formal surrender in public, and some very tense days passed before Hirohito finally agreed to have Shigemitsu board the battleship *Missouri* in Tokyo Bay for the ceremony.

As was his custom, MacArthur made sure of full media coverage (just ask any Pacific war correspondent how many times the General strode ashore in Leyte Gulf, the Philippines, in October 1944 to declare 'I have returned' for the cameras). He knew that once the Emperor's representative was seen carrying out the ceremony of surrender in full view, it would be incumbent on his subjects to do likewise. More important to Allied troops, and especially to POWs in such remote locations, once Japanese troops from general to lowliest guard heard their Emperor's voice on the radio instructing them to lay down their arms, *they did so,* much to the astonishment and great relief of all.

By contrast, where word of the Emperor's actions had not reached his troops in Burma, the situation was dangerously different. Nagase tells of his experience accompanying British and Australian officers of the Allied War Graves Commission to Burma on September 24, some five weeks after the surrender was official. In one of those little ironies of history, this incident took place near Thanbyuzayat, Burma, where the POWs were forced to begin construction of the Railway:

> The moment the train pulled in at the open platform the clicks of unlocking safeties of rifles were heard from every direction. Japanese soldiers . . . got up with guns at the ready. Their piercing eyes were focused on the Allied party. The surrounding circle was becoming smaller and smaller . . . the Allied party did not have enough time to get their arms, which lay in the next [rail car]. They did nothing but stand still . . .
>
> I shouted to the NCO: 'Didn't you get some news about us?' He gave us a blank look . . . [finally] the commanding officer showed up . . . I approached [him] and said in a low voice, 'Lieutenant Colonel, would you please salute the Captain of the Allies?' The Lieutenant Colonel looked offended.
>
> [Australian] Captain White had gotten off the rail car and taken up stance for taking the salute from the Japanese officer, who had turned up in full uniform . . . the Lieutenant Colonel . . . raised his right arm wearily and slowly to salute the Australian without approaching him, which might have been a sign of his resistance . . .
>
> Captain White received the Lieutenant Colonel's salute . . . [and] returned the salute by swinging his right arm from his side straight up above the shoulder in the typical Australian way. Then he made a big sound with both heels of his boots.[5]

Even in Thailand, not all Japanese camp personnel sat quietly waiting for someone in the Allied command to show up and collect their weapons. Possibly the most jittery days of August were endured by the POWs at Tamuan, a campsite in northern Thailand, near the mountains. Harry Whelan was there, as was Leslie Hall.

Whelan describes the scene:

For some weeks prior to August 16, we would awaken to find the camp surrounded by Jap soldiers with machine guns, etc. They had made us fill in all slit trenches in the camp, and it was pretty obvious that they intended harm to us . . . our lives were undoubtedly saved by the atomic bomb.

When the war ended the Japanese were still in force in the vicinity, and still occupied the guard house with a machine gun prominently displayed on a tripod. We were very wary for probably the first two weeks after news of surrender.

All officers, other than a few doctors, had been separated from us some months previously and Tamuan camp was, from a POW point of view, commanded by a British Regimental Sergeant Major named Edkins, who had been in the British army for over 20 years. He had plenty of common sense and did a good job—much better, in my opinion, than some of the officers had done.

Probably two weeks after the war's end a British paratrooper, Captain Ross, plus a corporal (I think his name was Phillips) drove into the camp. They had parachuted into the area, walked to a road and held up and commandeered a Japanese truck. I subsequently heard that he had gone to the Japanese guard house, demanded to see the senior Japanese officer and an interpreter (all prison camps had a Jap who could speak English). I understand that Captain Ross told Colonel Ishi, the Japanese commandant, that he, Captain Ross, was now in command, and that if Ishi did not do as he as told he would shoot him. I was in some minor position of authority in the camp, and had access to Corporal Phillips. I queried the wisdom of a two man army talking to the Jap commandant in this manner. The corporal replied that Captain Ross was a mad bastard, but a brave one! Anyway, Captain Ross got away with it and from then on, things improved. Colonel Ishi was, I understand, executed as a war criminal . . .

I remember that flags appeared from somewhere. We soon had the Stars and Stripes and the Union Jack flying over the camp. Later on, we flew an Australian flag . . .

Unfortunately, there were still a lot of very sick men in the camp, and I seem to remember there were deaths nearly every day . . .[6]

Leslie Hall wrote of the continuing deaths at Tamuan: "The sad part was [that] for some, the unbelievable happening was just too late. The sounding of "The Last Post" was a solemn reminder all diseases and illnesses had not automatically ended the moment peace had been declared. Many had been too ill to even *learn they were free again* [before succumbing]."[7]

The raising of long-hidden flags was surely one of the greatest sights for sore POW eyes in mid-August 1945. Dickson remembered that one of his camp-mates had sewn a Union Jack inside his shirt, and its tattered, sweat-stained remnant was proudly hoisted at Nakom Nayok, while everyone sang "God Save The King". Even the Americans joined in, and one Texas farm lad came to Dickson with tears streaming down his face, put his arm around Dickson's shoulder, and sobbed: "*I sang* 'God Save The King'! I cried horse's turds when I did it, but *I sang it!*"

No flag was in the railroad car with Cal Mitchell in the marshaling yards at Bangkok: "It was near midnight and we were a trainload of Australians and Dutch. When the announcement was made by a senior officer, the Dutch stood and sang their national anthem, and then we rose and sang 'God Save The King'. If there was a dry eye among us, it would have been an exception."

The initial absence of their nation's flag caused much consternation among the Americans at Nakom Nayok, and Benjamin Dunn tells how they labored to create one:

> The Dutch soldiers had worn green straw hats with bright red linings so we collected some of those and salvaged the linings. I still had a single piece of white tenting large enough for a flag, and I had a piece of keel which was just the right shade of blue for the field. We carefully marked off the stars in the field and then colored around them with the blue keel, leaving the stars white. I still had a needle and some white thread I had unraveled from the canvas I had borrowed in Singapore; I helped to sew the red and white stripes together.
>
> We worked on the Flag for two days and finally completed it. A soldier and a sailor were appointed to stand at attention as the Flag was raised on the large bamboo pole that was erected in front of the American hut . . . I was chosen as the soldier . . . I remember the emotion that gripped me on that occasion. To see that Flag slowly raised to eminence over this camp of the enemy, at whose hands we had suffered for so long, was an experience the memory of which will remain with me forever.
>
> Our Flag was heavier than most because of the material in it, but a good breeze had sprung up and when the wind struck it and it rippled, it was absolutely breathtaking. It was the first American

Flag we had seen flying for three and a half years, and when one was
on the ground looking up at it, he couldn't see a flaw in it—and for
what it meant to us, there wasn't a flaw in it or what it stood for.

When we got word that we were going to leave the camp, our First
Sergeant took possession of the Flag. I haven't forgotten and won't
ever forget that he took the Flag. I thought any of us who made the
Flag should have had it . . . I hope he has it to this day and that he
is as proud of it as we were.[8]

A homemade Australian flag, conceived by Pioneer Harold Ramsay in Japan,
may have been the signal which brought relief supplies to the POWs there (see
chapter 8).

Flags were among the precious items hidden in the hollow legs of those
POW who had endured amputations to avoid death from spreading leg ulcers,
because no medication was made available to them. Kevin Nolan remembered
British and Australian flags emerging from these novel hiding places, as well
as his first post-liberation assignment:

Immediately Colonel Albert Coates, the northern equivalent of
'Weary' Dunlop, took command of the camp (Nakom Paton) and
posted a piquet on the only gateway into the compound. This
consisted of a sergeant (me) and six men.

Can you imagine how my knees knocked when, immaculately
dressed in a loin cloth and bare feet, and armed with a bamboo stick,
I had to explain to the two top Jap officers that they could leave the
camp for the evening, but they must leave their pistols and swords
in the guard house until their return! I am very proud of the fact
that this order was accomplished mainly by sign language. I was
completely astounded by the meekness of these formerly arrogant
brutes who complied without argument.

These (same) two were two of about eight referred to in Cec's
letter of September 29, '45, when I was detailed to escort them to
a detention camp in Bangkok. Now dressed in jungle greens, and
complete with boots and a hat, and armed with rifles, we sat them
up on boxes on the back of a tray truck, whilst my two off siders and
I perched on the cabin roof very alert and watchful, maybe hoping
they would do something foolish. They didn't; in fact they were so
meek and mild, bowing and scraping, it was almost sickening. I
handed them over to a Captain of a Ghurka regiment and left, feeling

that they were in good hands—and that they had got the message
that no nonsense would be tolerated![9]

Perhaps one of the most daring post-liberation forays was made by Pioneer
Captain Ron Winning:

> When the war ended, I was in Nakom Nayok officer's camp. About
> ten days after the end I was sent for by the senior Allied officer
> and myself, a British Captain and a Dutch Captain were ordered
> to proceed north with two trucks and two English-speaking Jap
> sergeants to find 1500 POW somewhere in northern Thailand.
> We eventually found them, and took command.
>
> Then an English officer, of Z Special Force parachuted in, and a
> few days later he gave me orders to take 40 unarmed men to the
> aerodrome at Takli and take over all the arms of the Jap aerodrome
> guard regiment. This I did, and ordered the Jap commander to hand
> over his sword. I still have it.[10]

Cal Mitchell remembered that the British had set up an underground headquarters in Bangkok, which was operating for quite a while before the war
ended. When a young British Major arrived at one POW camp, he was surprised to find that the Japanese there were still armed. So he had his signaller
send a message to the headquarters in Bangkok, saying that the Major was
about to disarm all Japanese in his area. According to Mitchell, due to a lingering uncertainty on the part of Allied commanders as to whether the Japanese
would abide by the Emperor's announced wishes, the headquarters sent a message right back to the Major: "Under no account disarm Japanese in your area."
The Major replied: "Have already disarmed all Japanese in my area," to which
headquarters responded: "Good show."

Good show indeed, all the way around, as POWs took their first bold steps
of freedom.

6

A Would-Be Correspondent

September 9, 1945: As a journalist, Dickson knew he was sitting on the biggest news story of the year, and he would have liked nothing better than to resume his profession right then, and cover the story as an eyewitness. The discovery, recovery and treatment of POWs had become daily page one news worldwide, and Dickson yearned to put his talents to use as a correspondent, but red tape would prevent such a transfer from taking place. He would have to be content with the slim satisfaction of learning, a couple of months later that two of his articles did find their way into the pages of the *Argus*.

Dickson wrote this letter without paragraph indentations in order to save paper:

Nakom Nayok
Thailand
September 9, 1945

Dear old Binks,

The mail position from this end has undergone a great improvement. We are now permitted to send four letters a week. If you don't receive the whole four from me you'll know that I've reserved an occasional one for 365 Elizabeth Street {home of his brother, Stan}. Incidentally, I'm making an effort to have myself transferred to Bangkok on the news side. These things are not easy when one is still a member of the army, so nothing may come of it. But it's worth trying. In the meantime keep it under your hat. All of this does not sound much like going home! The position in that regard is at present obscure, and one can only hope that developments will be faster than would appear likely at present. Oct. 2 {their anniversary} seems a rather forlorn chance! But however long it is I feel sure we both have the patience to see it out, old dear. The great excitement yesterday was a visit from Lady Louis Mountbatten. No other woman with her. She went down 'big' with the troops, and is certainly a charming personality. Pretty obviously she has been under a big strain but I should say she was a very capable woman. She was the first white one we had seen for more than three years! I saw Ken Kingston at Batavia, and last year at Tamarkan {Thailand}, where I spent 13 months. He left from there to go to Japan and I hope is safe. Ken Barrett also left on a Japan party, but as far as I can hear he was not on the ship that was sunk with a heavy deathroll among the prisoners. I was at Thanbuzayat, Burma, when the camp was bombed twice in June 1943. About 30 prisoners were killed in the two raids. On Nov. 29 last year, when the anti-aircraft positions close to the Tamarkan camp were bombed by 21 Liberators, the corner of the camp copped it and we lost 16 men. The A.A. {anti aircraft guns} and bridge, also close to the camp, were raided several times in the following couple of months, but we were prepared with slit trenches, etc. and had only one more man killed. Most of these camps were slap up against military objectives. At Nonpladuk, 35 miles from Tamarkan, a railway junction, about 100 prisoners were killed in one raid. Another 40 were lost on a train that was attacked by aircraft. Taking these events into consideration, (with others not mentioned) and the enormous deathroll on the construction of the line itself, one is extremely fortunate to be kicking along still. However, enough of these unpleasant things. The food continues good & one is still laying on flesh. An RAF Dakota dropped more food to-day. It looks as if yours truly will be busy in the next day or two, as pay is expected to arrive from Bangkok. It's a great luxury, by the way, to smoke Players cigarettes, dropped from the air, after some of the muck, wrapped in any sort of paper you could get hold of, that we have had to put up with.

Love till next letter day my old darling,

Your ever loving Pop

Dickson's frustration was compounded by the ability of a fledgling journalist, Rohan Rivett, who had been placed in an Australian Army officer's unit throughout his internment, to pull strings, get home first, and "scoop" Dickson with a series of lengthy articles in the very newspaper at which Dickson was a staff editor!

Understandably, the editors at the *Argus* were only too happy to print Rivett's accounts. The series, which appeared in the paper in mid-September 1945, became the basis for his best-selling book, *Behind Bamboo,* which Rivett managed to complete in November 1945, making it the first of many books published on this subject. At the time of its publication in May, 1946, the *Argus* asked none other than returned Mining Editor T. Cecil Dickson to review Rivett's book. Here are some excerpts of his review, which appeared in the May 18, 1946 edition of the *Argus:*

> The tendency of some young writers to over-emphasize the first
> person is understandable. In this case the author's rather obvious
> efforts to portray himself as the war correspondent would have been
> more convincing had he shown greater concern for the accuracy of
> detail demanded by what, after all, is a job of reporting.
>
> Some of the errors which occur in this book are venial offences
> against a cardinal principle of journalism. Others, such as a grossly
> inaccurate statement of the time and place of a fellow prisoner's death,
> which occurred more than 1,000 miles away and a year later than is
> stated, are unjustifiable. Working against time to catch the book
> market while it is still 'hot' is no exoneration.

Although he later became well known as a campaigning newspaper editor, Rivett was a controversial figure in the POW camps. He had been employed as a trainee at the Malaya Broadcasting Corporation for about three months when the Japanese overran Southeast Asia, and Rivett, along with many other British subjects, was captured in Sumatra. He was interned with survivors of the *HMAS Perth* and *USS Houston,* and eventually reached Java.

Rivett's father, a well-connected figure in Australian government and social circles, feared his son would be killed by the Japanese, who tended to view journalists, and especially correspondents, as spies. So the elder Rivett arranged for Rohan to be assigned to an Australian Army officers unit, giving him all privileges of officers' rank, including the Officers Mess. This irritated many commissioned officers; as one reflected some years later: "In our unit there were many young men from backgrounds of privilege or influence, but they chose to enlist in the ranks, like everyone else, and never tried to use family connections to gain special favors."

More irritating than Rivett's sudden arrival in their midst was his tendency to offer his somewhat liberal points of view in lectures to fellow officers. One one occasion, a Pioneer officer recalls, "Rivett concluded a speech with these stirring words: 'It won't be the British who liberate us; it won't be the Americans either. The great Red Army will liberate us!' That went down like a wet sock with the troops, of course."

Far more welcome among the POWs was Lady Louis Mountbatten, wife of the British General. This extraordinary woman insisted on visiting a number of POW camp locations immediately following the Japanese surrender, which was by all accounts quite a daring feat. She was tall and good-looking; needless to say, her appearances were a great morale-booster to the weary POW. Pioneer Lieutenant Gordon Hamilton in a letter to his family just a day before Dickson penned his note, wrote:

> Lady Mountbatten paid us a visit yesterday together with her staff
> of two Colonels A.T.S. and numerous Army officers up to a Major
> General R.A.M.C., on a camp inspection. She was the most pleasant
> and natural person possible. Shook hands all round and chatted
> breezily for about half an hour. They say she is indefatigable, and
> already had visited some of our Jungle Camps inland. When
> communications were difficult, she wanted to be dropped by
> parachute, in lieu of any other means of coming. She arrived yesterday
> sitting in the very uncomfortable front seat of a battle-buggy, while
> her numerous retinue rode in comfortable limousines. It was a thrill
> meeting her, though.[1].

Lady Mountbatten visited Tamuan camp as the British POWs were being flown to India. Harry Whelan remembered the day: "By this time we all had a shirt, a pair of long trousers and a pair of khaki sandshoes, so we were able to look fairly tidy for her ladyship. [She] visited the so-called hospital, which was just an ordinary hut with no medical facilities whatever. I believe she was appalled at the way the Japs had behaved toward POW." 2.

On the eighth anniversary of the terrible Allied air raid at Tamarkan camp, Dickson wrote an article for publication, describing in dramatic detail the events he refers to in his letter. The published version has not been located, but his original draft was recently discovered by Mrs. Dickson, and it appears below in its entirety. The reader may note that the first person singular pronoun does not appear once, and only in the last paragraph does Dickson reveal that he was an eyewitness to the events:

OUR BOMBERS CAME

The 29th of November is a date which British prisoners of the
Japanese at Tamarkan, Siam in 1944 have cause to remember. Eight
years ago to-day Allied aircraft launched a long series of attacks aimed
at a railway bridge and Japanese anti-aircraft post just outside the

camp boundary. It was the beginning of the end of a long captivity. But it added a new hazard, bombs dropped by friends, to an already hazardous existence rife with death, disease and malnutrition.

A week or so before the attacks began, Allied aircraft dropped pamphlets in the vicinity of Tamarkan camp. They were addressed 'To all British Prisoners of War.' They surveyed the successful progress of Allied operations in Europe and the Pacific, and concluded: 'Take heart; we are coming. (Signed) South-East Asia Command.' After November 29, when the ground shook with 1,000 pound bombs exploding and machine gun bursts at the attacking aircraft, one wit at Tamarkan suggested that 'Take heart; we are coming' should now be amended to 'Take cover; we are here'!

Allied prisoners in Siam, survivors of the force that had worked on the Burma-Siam Railway, were at the time concentrated mainly in five large camps situated along a 35-mile stretch at the Siam end of the new railway. These camps were Tamarkan, Chungkai, Kanburi, Tamuan and Nonpladuk. And not far from Nonpladuk, which was at the junction of the new railway with the old Bangkok-Singapore main line, was Nakompaton, a hospital camp housing some 7,000 sick P.O.W.'s.

A year had passed since the new line was completed by forced P.O.W. and coolie labour. Through heavy jungle country, it linked, for the first time in history, the railway systems of Burma and Siam. For 12 months the railway had been used by the Japanese to transport reinforcements and supplies to their army in Burma. Its construction, which cost the lives of 15,000 Allied prisoners, had taken more than a year. Late in October, 1943, trains were traversing its whole length, and by the end of February, 1944, most of the survivors had been moved to Siam.

Like Chungkai, three miles away, Tamarkan held 4500 Allied prisoners. Mainly British and Australians, as well as Dutch and a few Americans, they were under the charge of Lt.-Colonel [C.G.W.] Anderson, the Australian C.O. who won the Victoria Cross in the Malayan campaign. Life at Tamarkan was bearable after those hideous months in the jungle. There was not much work, and there was enough food to live on.

For a year, Allied aircraft had passed regularly overhead on their way to bomb objectives in and around Bangkok and the coastal areas. It was a source of infinite satisfaction to the inmates that, although the Japanese anti-aircraft guns invariably opened fire on the passing bombers, not once did they score a hit.

During September 1944, an ugly rumour circulated among the
prisoners at Tamarkan. It was said that there had been a raid by Allied
planes at Nonpladuk, 35 miles distant, and that 100 Allied P.O.W.'s
had been killed by bombs that fell in their camp.

So persistent did the rumour become that senior P.O.W. officers at
Tamarkan announced on parade one evening that it lacked official
confirmation and should therefore be disregarded. The rumour
unhappily proved to be true. Allied aircraft had carried out a highly
successful night raid on the Nonpladuk railway junction, yards and
workshop. The last stick of bombs had fallen in the P.O.W. camp.
There were no slit trenches in the camp, and in addition to the 100
killed a further 100 prisoners had been wounded.

At Tamarkan, the fear grew that the experience might be repeated
there.

Evening parade was held just before sundown, when for the second
time each day the prisoners were counted and checked by the Japanese
guards. On the evening of November 29, 1944, the fall-in bugle
sounded as usual and the 4500 prisoners formed up in their various
sections on the parade ground.

Apart from patients in the camp hospital, a few prisoners were
exempt from the parade—men sick in their huts and members of a
late work party which had just returned to camp.

Officers and NCOs were checking their sections, when the sound
of approaching aircraft was heard. Eyes turned to the northwest.
There, in formation, at an altitude of about 6000 feet, were 21
Liberators. They were headed straight for the camp. First reaction
among the assembled men was of admiration; through the ranks ran
that thrill of excitement that the spectacle of friendly aircraft never
failed to provoke.

The Liberators continued their straight course toward the camp.
Suddenly excitement gave place to misgiving. This time, it was
obvious, the bombers meant business. The peace of evening was
shattered as they raked the ground below with their machine-guns
and cannon. In the anti-aircraft post, the Japs were caught napping,
but not for long. They sprang to action and quickly returned the fire.

Forty bombs rained down, and the earth shook again with the
concussion of their explosions as they buried themselves in the soft
earth. The Japanese had opened fire just in time to destroy the
bombers' aim. Intended for the anti-aircraft post, only three of the

bombs went near their objective. Most of them fell between the post and the camp fence. Four fell in the camp.

With shells still bursting around them and flak raining down on the camp, the bombers passed overhead. Their silver bodies glinted in the rays of the setting sun as they banked in a wide arc, formation unbroken, to return in the direction whence they had come. At that stage of the war their base must have been at least 1000 miles distant.

Before the sun had finally dipped below the horizon, the inmates of Tamarkan had begun to count the cost of that brief visit. Had the raid occurred ten minutes earlier two or three hundred men must have been killed; every hut was partly wrecked.

Daylight had gone when all men in the camp except hospital cases were called on parade again. A count showed that 16 men were missing.

Next morning a pathetic procession moved out through the camp gate. It was bound for the cemetery, a mile away. On improvised stretchers were the bodies of fourteen men that had been recovered.

Two of the stretchers were draped with large flags. One was the Union Jack; the other a red lion on a yellow background—the Scottish standard. For more than two and a half years these emblems had been carried around in the kits of their owners. Despite many kit inspections, the Japanese had never seen fit to confiscate them.

Fourteen men were buried in Tamarkan that day. But the raid had reduced the camp strength by sixteen.

And so the air raid siren had frequent use during the next few months. For, in the words of the troops, it was 'on again' every few days as Allied aircraft hammered at the large steel and concrete bridge that carried the supply line across the river on its way to Burma.

During one raid a prisoner was killed by a machine-gun bullet from a low-flying plane, and another man lost his arm. The canteen and one of the large living huts were burnt down after being set alight by stray incendiary bullets.

On the other side of the picture, severe damage was inflicted on the bridge, and eventually four of the five anti-aircraft guns were put out of action with the loss of 150 Japanese lives.

Lt.-Colonel Anderson protested several times to the Japanese that such close proximity to a military objective was no fit place to hold defenceless prisoners of war. The Japanese were unconvinced. Lieut. Naguchi, the camp adjutant, better known as Bluebeard, had what he considered the unanswerable reply. 'You are soldiers', he said; 'therefore you should be prepared to die at any time.'

To give Bluebeard his due, during air raids he was the only person in the area above ground. His buck teeth revealed by a wide grin, he would walk about, oblivious of flying flak and bomb splinters and stray machine-gun bullets, obviously enjoying the whole proceedings.

By the end of February, 1945, even the Japanese found the position untenable, and they ordered abandonment of the camp. The flags were pulled down; and the inmates were dispersed among other camps in Siam. Only the cemetery remained—a reminder that Tamarkan P.O.W. camp once stood there.

What about the two missing bodies that were not found after the raid of the 29th November? Not until after the war were the facts about them revealed. Two British prisoners had taken advantage of the confusion and escaped to a nearby village where American paratroops had been placed. There they remained secure until Japan signed the instrument of surrender.

If only we had known that such a haven was so close at hand! It was as well, perhaps, that we did not. With all the good will in the world, the paratroopers might have found some difficulty in accommodating 4500 escaped prisoners.

Cal Mitchell remembered one Allied aircraft which was a welcome, though somewhat mysterious sight, flying daily over the camps. It was a Mosquito reconnaissance plane, and it flew very high, out of the reach of Japanese anti-aircraft guns. "It was so high, all we could see were the vapor trails. The Japs called it the 'come-look-see, go-back-speako' plane. When we got to Bangkok, we found out that the pilot was Australian, from Scone, NSW. His brother was a POW in the camps."[3]

The airman had especially requested that assignment, as his way of sending signals of hope to his brother, far below.

7

Finally, Some Money!

September 9, 1945: Again, Dickson uses no paragraph structure in order to save space on his one precious sheet of air mail stationery:

Nakom Nayok
Thailand
September 9, 1945 (sent by air)

My old Darling,

This is an unexpected note out of the blue, and I was lucky enough again to land one, although there were not enough to go round. I don't know how the ordinary letters are travelling. I should think by air—but if not then this one should reach you ahead of some I have written earlier. Still no sign of a move, but we hope for an unexpected order any day. As pay sergeant I had a busy morning. With tikals {Thai currency} valued at 7d. each, we disbursed more than 85,000 tikals among the Australians at the rate of 170 tikals per man to those who wanted it. I took my share. Although there's not a great deal to spend it on except food, which is plentiful anyhow, it might come in useful, and represents only p.5 out of the paybook if it is deducted, which is uncertain. I might take another look round the town—perhaps to-morrow. Have not been out of the camp since I was in there eight days ago. More excitement to-day. Another plane arrived about mid-day and disgorged bundles of clothing and foodstuffs (including Guest's Famous Biscuits!) marmalade, 1XL {one extra large} jam, etc. This time it was not one of the mere twin-engined Dakotas, but a large four-engined bomber (R.A.F.) which disgorged the packages (some with parachutes & some without) through the bomb doors. Having done so it swooped down to the camp to less than 100 ft. before returning in the direction of

Rangoon. I have no doubt these displays have a nasty taste in the mouths of our yellow friends, many thousands of whom are down the road a couple of miles away. We are right in the depths of the monsoon now. For the last couple of months the rain has been in very heavy thunderstorms, quickly over. But it poured heavily the whole of last night, and looks like doing so to-night. Fortunately the atap roof above me does not leak. Incidentally, I have not slept in anything but a bamboo and atap hut for 3 years, so look forward to a civilised home again. These atap buildings are pretty airy affairs, usually with low eaves and no walls, with bamboo sleeping platforms, but in this warm to hot climate that is no hardship. With the departure of most of the British and the Maylay volunteers I lost quite a few friends. The Dutch are not popular but I had some good friends among them also.

Tons of love,

Pop

Serving as paymaster for the whole Australian wing still in Nakom Nayok camp, Dickson was at last able to distribute some pocket money to his countrymen—a little over five pounds, or roughly $15.00, was the allotment. His letter touches on what was to become a raging controversy between ex-POWs at the Australian government during the next several years: how much back pay was due to POWs, and whether they were entitled to a meal allowance for all the meals they *didn't* have while in captivity(see concluding chapter.) For example, some 500 surviving Americans who toiled with Dickson and his friends on the Burma Railway received, by a 1948 Act of Congress, just $1.00 per day for "missed meals" while in captivity—the same amount issued to all other Americans who survived as prisoners of the Japanese in the Pacific.

The issuance of pay was a double-edged thing. On the one hand, the military authorities couldn't arrange to ship POWs home very quickly, so the stranded soldiers were entitled to some "walking-around money" while they waited. On the other hand, officials were apparently reluctant to put too much at one time in the hands of ex-POWs. This policy denied the newly -freed soldiers some of the simple first tastes of freedom, and was much resented. As Cal Mitchell remarked, "They treated us like children, really; never wanting to give us much at a time. Some time elapsed before any pay was issued, and then only one pound per week [under $3.00]. Perhaps it was thought that the substantial sums in our pay books would be splurged on wine, women and song. It was most frustrating having so little money. A bottle of whiskey (so called) was one pound. However, it was discovered that banks in Bangkok would accept cheques and many of us availed ourselves of this benefit. The money was shared out and settlements were effected upon our return home."[1]

In this letter, Dickson gets around to describing the grass huts in which he had been living for the past three and a half years (see the two photos, taken in captivity, which show the interiors of these structures, pp.80-81). With characteristic aplomb, he claims that, given the climate, this hut structure was "no hardship." Nevertheless, a fairly clean hut, with intact roof, must have been a vivid contrast to the dilapidated ones he had often encountered along the way.

Although Dickson acknowledged he was looking forward to a "civilised home" again, some ex-POWs took a while to get used to beds and mattresses. Harry Whelan remembered being given a kapok mattress to sleep on in Bangkok, but he and his companions all wound up on the cement floor, preferring the hard surface to which they had become so accustomed!

In his closing sentence, Dickson emphasizes the unpopularity of Dutch POWs. As mentioned earlier, POWs of other nationalities, who had been put under Dutch command on Java, bitterly resented the swift decision by the Dutch to surrender there, giving other military units no choice but to follow along. Benjamin Dunn reflected the anger of many:

> On March 8, 1942, a Major said in effect "The Dutch High Command has agreed upon terms for capitulation to the Japanese. You are all to lay down your arms and surrender." He continued with tears in his eyes, "It is not the choice of the Americans—but the Dutch."
>
> This came as a real jolt . . . none of us had even seen a Jap . . . we were being forced to surrender by the Dutch and Javanese because they didn't want to defend the island. That Dutchman, who gave us that talk back at Camp Singosari, had lied when he said, 'We will fight shoulder to shoulder with our American, British and Australian allies and inflict severe losses on the enemy!'
>
> The decision to surrender made by the Dutch probably did save the lives of many Australians and Americans, but it was held against them [the Dutch] for the duration of the war.[2]

In later years, discussing his quartermaster duties as a POW, Dickson would remark to his family that, despite his efforts to be scrupulously fair in doling out equal amounts of a pitifully small yak carcass to each unit, for example, the

The photo above was taken secretly by an Australian prisoner at Kanchanaburi, Thailand, in early 1945, before it became exclusively an officers' camp. Prisoners are standing outside the rear entrance to long huts, constructed of bamboo and foliage.
(COURTESY OF C.J. MITCHELL, AWM P1502/08)

The photo below was also taken by an Australian prisoner, inside a hut at Tamarkan, Thailand, in early 1944. All POWs are clearly aware tha the picture is being taken. The camera and film will then probably be buried in the ground at a spot known only to the owner. A prisoner risks severe beating or death if either the camera or film is discovered by the Japanese. (COURTESY OF C.J. MITCHELL, AWM P1502/03)

Australian prisoner gets his comrades to look toward the camera for another secret photo, Kanchanaburi, Thailand, 1944. Note the POWs' possessions hanging from the rafters and along the aisle. (COURTESY OF C.J. MITCHELL, AWM P1502/06)

Dutch nevertheless would frequently complain about their portion—"As if they somehow felt entitled to more than anyone else", he would add, in bewilderment.

Invariably, this attitude would provoke some POWs to grumble: "It was you who got us into this mess in the first place . . ." And the Dutch did not exactly boost their popularity when Colonel Williams, on one occasion, discovered that the Netherlanders had eaten not only their own share of rations, but had consumed the provisions for the Australians as well.[3]

Leslie Hall noted that oddly enough, although many of the Dutch captives had lived in Southeast Asia for several years, most were repelled by the version of rice served in the camps, so they tried to get more meat instead. He believes that Australian eating habits were a key to their higher rate of survival: "The Australians ate everything available and sought more. The American troops despised rice and consumed less than their issue. The Dutch, although avid rice eaters normally, ate less than anyone."[4]

As for the British, many soldiers had grown up in the cities of England, so their diets had not been as well-balanced as those of Australians or Americans.

Worse still, they were quite unaccustomed to rice; some even found it hard to swallow. Possibly these factors were key reasons why the British death rate was higher than that of any other POW nationality in the camps, according to figures from the Australian War Memorial and the Allied War Graves Registry.

Probably the most serious incident involving a Dutch POW occurred at Tamarkan camp, when a Dutch interpreter was found to have turned in three Americans who smuggled several copies of a propaganda newspaper, *Bangkok Chronicles,* into the camp. As a result, the Americans were tortured and beaten for several days by the *kempe tai.* One of the Americans caught up with the Dutchman after liberation, and beat the daylights out of him. The American stopped short of killing the interpreter when told that the Dutchman was scheduled to be tried back in Holland, as a Nazi collaborator.[5]

Of course, the Dutch were well aware of the resentment, and sometimes outright contempt, aimed in their direction by fellow POWs. Benjamin Dunn wrote of a touching deathbed confession by one young Dutch flying officer, as both lay in a hospital hut: "Knowing he was dying and being still rational, [he] talked to me of the shame he had of his fellow countrymen for their failure to resist longer and harder in the defense of Java. He said he thought Americans had a lot more courage than the Dutch and that we helped each other more in times of trial."[6]

Dunn also credits a Dutch physician, Dr. Han Hekking, with keeping the death rate remarkably low among American POWs. Dr. Hekking, who had been born and reared in the Dutch East Indies, was assigned as camp physician to survivors of the *USS Houston* and the Texas 131st Field Artillery, who constituted most of the Americans toiling on the Railway. (Dunn and 17 fellow members of the 26th US Field Artillery were assigned to the Texas unit in Java.)

At least one Australian found a plus in the Dutch outspokenness about entitlements. J.G. 'Tom' Morris recorded in his diary an incident when the Japanese Commander of all POWs in Thailand, Lieutenant Colonel Y. Nagatomo, visited the miserable 55 Kilo hospital in November 1943. "The Senior Dutch officer, [speaking] fearlessly and in good English, took the occasion to berate Nagatomo for failing to distribute Red Cross parcels and mail, and demanded to have them. It was a great boost to our morale."[7]

Within a month, that brave Dutchman was dead from starvation, disease, and parcels sent but not distributed. He was laid to rest at Thanbyuzayat cemetery, along with 437 of his countrymen.

8

All This Mail!

Nakom Nayok
Thailand
September 12, 1945

P.S. did I tell you that thanks to the RAF I now bathe with the old favorite
Lux soap?

Dear old Binks,

You'll be getting almost sick of receiving letters from me! I spent yesterday in
Nakom Nayok with John and another. On returning to camp about 8: 30 there
awaited me three cards from you—July 23, November 19 and December 31
(all 1944). Prompt mail service, what! One of the Jap methods of being
unpleasant seemed to be to procrastinate over the censorship and handing out of
incoming mail. Had quite a good day in the town. Did nothing much more
than wander about, poke into about every second shop (of which there would be
quite 200, although the place is only a glorified village), and dawdle over a
couple of meals. Chicken is the usual motif, served in open cafes in the roofed-in
market. The usual buying of 'souvenirs' goes on but I have seen nothing as yet
that I should care to take home. One of the features of Nakom Nayok (which
we pronounce Nakom Nai) is the fast-flowing river which divides it roughly
in half. One crosses it in small boats propelled by one oar, at 10 cents a crossing.
Keeping it up against the swift current is a work of art. John, as usual, was
frequently surrounded by large numbers of kids, who are legion, and who
up to the age of about five wear only their birthday suits. They all have the
expression 'OK—, No. 1' with which they give the thumbs up. With my new
shorts and shirt I wore the old webbing belt, which I have managed to preserve!
Before setting out I had to let it out a hole in each side, and it was still a little
tight. The East doesn't seem to cater for No. 10 feet, so I had to wear clogs,

which are simply a wooden sole with a single strap across the toes. The last pair of socks I possessed was the one I bought at the Leviathan. You might remember the favourable comment they produced on the beach at Pt. Lonsdale from Mesdames Pratt and Purcell. They have, however, been defunct for more than two years now. I was very pleased to hear that {Leo} Cornelius was safe home. He, {Vic} Clifford and {Jack} Hocking I knew. They are the only three of whose return we have heard. They were certainly very fortunate. I was not considered for the Japan parties, being at the time classified as sick and over 40. We expect a move to Bangkok in two or three days—thence, let's hope, it won't be too long before we continue to Singapore and so home. And, let there be no moaning at the bar when I step ashore! That, perhaps, does not convey what I want to say, which is—a quiet reunion somewhere with the old Missus without any beating of drums or fanfare of trumpets. I'd like to arrive unexpectedly and walk in through the door. But whatever the circumstances, it will be the best day ever, and I won't really mind how it occurs. Cheerio, old darling.

    Pop

The most recent communication Dickson had received so far from his wife was penned on New Year's Eve, 1944, as she faced the beginning of a fourth year without a glimpse of her beloved husband. Several accounts by ex-POWs indicate a remarkably efficient delivery system by the Japanese High Command, considering the remote location of most POW camps. The cruelty was on the part of local camp commandants, who simply refused to distribute incoming mail, and who were apparently quite lax in sending out the pitifully few postcards POWs were allowed to write, judging by the arrival times of those cards in Melbourne (see Chapter 4).

Newly-liberated POWs in other locations found large sacks of undistributed mail; often they seemed to know just where to look. As Dickson remarked, this was just "one of the Jap methods of being unpleasant."

Along with undistributed letters, POWs and their liberators frequently found unopened Red Cross boxes, the contents of which were often rancid or rotted beyond use. Failing to distribute these parcels, which usually contained lifesaving medicines as well as food and clothing, went beyond "unpleasant" and crossed over to criminal behavior (see Chapter 9). Perhaps because prisoners had only recently been moved there, no Red Cross parcels were stored at Nakom Nayok; clothing was in especially short supply, and the first new clothes arrived by air-drops.[1]

*An Australian prisoner dares to carry his camera outdoors, while POWs of
all nationalities line up at a canteen, Kanchanaburi, Thailand, 1944.
'Coffee' was usually burnt rice and hot water. Note the remnants of uniforms and
makeshift utensils: no new clothing or supplies had been issued in over three years*
(COURTESY OF C.J. MITCHELL, AWM P1502/06)

Efforts by the prisoners to preserve, patch and mend their clothing for three
and a half years were a true test of ingenuity. As mentioned in chapter 2, most
of the Pioneers' gear was on a second ship, which steamed for Australia while
the *Orcades* deposited the Battalion on Java. So when captured, members of the
unit had only the clothes on their backs, and whatever spare articles they might
have in their backpacks. Luckily for the Pioneers, they were not inclined to trust
the assurances of the Japanese, who told all POWs that everything would be
provided in new locations, and they need not trouble themselves to carry such
things as utensils or first aid kits. Unhappily, many British soldiers did take
those assurances at face value; as a result, the Australians felt obliged to share
suddenly-precious utensils, so that fellow POWs might at least have a container to hold food rations. And the contents of small, personal first aid kits became
prized like gemstones, until they gradually disappeared.

Probably the most foresighted of newly-captured POWs was Harry Bishop, a member of Dickson's C Company. After the surrender in Java, Bishop spotted a Chinese businessman who sold cloth. "I thought maybe it might be useful to have some military cloth with us, so I bought a bolt from him, signed for it, and told him I would pay for it later, *which I did*", he emphasized proudly. "I carried it with me from Java to Burma, and it certainly came in handy. Quite a few men were able to patch up their garments with pieces of that cloth."[2]

Although Dickson mentions in this letter that he wore clogs to town, once his boots rotted in the jungle, he was barefoot during most of his captivity. Years later, Margaret Dickson marvelled at her recollection of how intact Cecil's feet were. "There wasn't a mark on them, in spite of all the years of tramping over rocks and thorns and what-have-you. Even Cec wondered at his luck of never scratching or cutting his feet while building that infamous railway!"[3]

Dickson also told about how a tailor in one camp advised him to cut his trousers into shorts, which he did, salvaging the extra cloth to serve as two pillows. One by one, the 'pillows' were used to patch his shirt, in an effort to keep the scorching sun off his back.

Predictably, the subject of clothing became a sore point between the Pioneer Commanding Officer and Japanese authorities; equally predictably, the Japanese withheld needed items, even when available.

As early as February 1943, Colonel Williams already painted a desperate picture regarding clothing for his men. A diary entry reads:

> A general warning, 'If any man received any clothing and still had
> some in his possession, he would be punished'. How they expected
> men to work in any kind of weighty cloth in the tropical heat, is
> beyond anyone's imagination. But, the Nipponese did!
>
> In day time, and especially out on the line job, the temperature
> feels anywhere in the vicinity of 120 degrees Farenheit, as men haul
> the ropes to pull up the piledriver or swing a pick and/or shovel.
>
> As the line of men moved along and they were seen to be wearing
> any kind of rag at all, no shirt or shorts were issued.
>
> If what they were wearing was torn or worn out they were told to
> mend the article concerned. The fact no needles, cotton or material
> of any type was on issue, mattered not. As far as the (well named)
> Economy Officer cared, if they were wearing something, that was it.

They were clothed, even if it was merely a 'G' string that only protected one's modesty, it was sufficient.

The fact it was completely beyond the point of repair due to climatic conditions still did not matter . . . A lad, wearing a pair of shorts that could only be accepted as a grass skirt, was refused a replacement. Not one man in the whole camp had received any clothing replacement for over twelve months. The shorts, or part thereof, they wore had been issued to them in the Far East, being their last issue of clothing (one pair of shorts each); no shirts since the Middle East. Every pair of shorts now worn had long since lost identity as such. What they wore was merely rotted material.[4]

By mid-September of that horrible year, writing from the filthiest camp conditions yet encountered, Colonel Williams fairly exploded with words in his diary:

Time and again Force commanders have made appeals to the Jap. authorities for an issue of suitable footwear to all POW. On rare occasions clogs and rubberised slipper type of footwear have been made available, but never in a quantity. In any case what was issued were not suitable for the work being done and were so fragile they soon wore out.

Major Meagher was aware boots were stored at the Base camp and were to remain there until the rainy season was over. So much for the vaunted kindness of the Nipponese![5]

It probably would have been no consolation to POWs if they had known that 'G' strings were the common attire for Japanese peasant farm laborers; an observation made by women prisoners on Sumatra, as they noted that Japanese soldiers who guarded them reverted to their customary garb of civilian life. Women prisoners were even ordered to sew such loincloths for use by their captors; but they sweetened the task by sewing pins inside the hems, and embroidering an occasional thistle on the corner, as an exquisite subliminal message.[6]

The enforced daily toiling of POWs in the jungles of Burma and Thailand probably marked the first time that people of northern European descent had been used as coolie labor in such a tropical climate, and the lack of proper clothing cost many dearly. For the rest of his life, Dickson would be plagued by cancerous skin lesions, which were periodically removed.

The Japanese were probably aware that fair-skinned Caucasians were at greater risk of developing such problems, and Dickson's light complexion, together with his age and health at the moment of selection, spared him from a hazardous voyage to Japan, and a new experience of forced labor. The selection of POWs to work in the factories, mines and shipyards of Japan was another clear violation of Article 31 of the 1929 Geneva Conventions, since the locations to which prisoners were sent exclusively involved the manufacture of products for use in the war.

A total of 115 Pioneers were picked to be shipped to Japan, in a move which journalist and former United States submarine officer Clay Blair, Jr. recognized as particularly cruel—plucking POWs at random from the midst of their friends, and throwing them among strangers to perform yet another type of hard labor in the factories and shipyards of their captor's homeland.[7]

On June 24, 1944, a ship carrying fifteen Pioneers was torpedoed and sunk; nine members of the unit drowned. The remaining six continued their journey to Japan on another vessel; they were all recovered there at war's end.

An even larger contingent of Pioneers, 73 in all, left Saigon on September 4, 1944. Eight days later that ship was also sunk by United States submarines, near Formosa, and 55 Pioneers drowned. The luckiest survivors included those mentioned by Dickson in his letter: Leo Cornelius, Vic Clifford and Jack Hocking. They were among nine Pioneers who were finally pulled aboard the very submarines which had attacked their convoy.

As mentioned in Chapter 4, great secrecy surrounded the rescue of these men. When they passed through Guadalcanal on their way to Australia, security was so tight that no one stationed there had any idea of the ordeals the POWs had just endured. Edith Monks Stark was a 28-yearold American Red Cross worker, helping to operate a service canteen on Guadalcanal at that time. She remembered:

> A truck passed us, carrying a group of Australians. They were skin
> and bones—such scarecrows—and they looked so sad. I was told they
> were prisoners of war who had been rescued. I asked why they looked
> so sad, if they were on their way home. I was told it was 'because
> nobody expects them.' When we pressed for more information, we
> were told their families didn't even know they were alive, and some
> of the wives might have remarried. So they were going home to a very
> uncertain future. I never saw the group again, after they passed by in
> the truck.[8]

For 48 years, Edith Stark's puzzlement about the sad-looking Australians remained, until a chance conversation in Shelter Island, New York in May 1992 brought forth the truth.

By an odd coincidence, another nine Pioneers were rescued from the same torpedoed ship, the *Rakuyu Maru*—but by a Japanese vessel. Typically, the Pioneers had found each other, and most managed to cling together, floating on real or makeshift rafts, until they were allowed to climb aboard a Japanese cruiser.

Probably the luckiest Pioneers selected for what they termed "Japan Parties" were the 27 who remained in Saigon, after the Japanese decided not to attempt another shipment of POW labor to Japan.

Several detailed accounts have been written about the incredible experiences of those Japan-bound POWs, and quite a few have been sought out and interviewed over the years. However, no one ever tracked down Pioneer George Carroll, who along with Bill Mayne, Harold Ramsey and six other Pioneers, were among those hauled aboard the Japanese cruiser mentioned above, to continue their fateful journey.

Here, for the first time, is Carroll's story, as told in a lengthy interview in Melbourne, in October 1991. Carroll's narrative is augmented by the recollections of Bill Mayne, who shared the same experience, both at sea and in Japan, for 10 months in 1944–45:

The ship was sunk at 2 a.m. We jumped overboard, then got back on the ship during the day, till evening when it sank. The torpedo missed the hull. Only one person was killed on the ship. He was a Jap!

We scrounged supplies. The Jap escort vessels came back. The lifeboats were adrift. I was one of the last ones off the ship. There was a small dinghy with two Japs in it. It sank. I and one Jap got back on it. We thought the escort vessel would pick up POWs. By nightfall we got 14 lifeboats rounded up. There were about 20 to a boat. I was with Rowley Richards and Vic Duncan. We tied the boats together. A typhoon came up, and we cut loose. Three boats stayed together, but when we woke up we were all by ourselves. We heard machine gun fire; we thought a Jap sub had surfaced.

We saw ships in the distance; they passed. We thought they were mirages. On the fourth day, we saw three ships. They were Jap cruisers. They picked us up. As each POW climbed aboard, we got a hit in the head or back with a baton or rifle butt, or whatever they had handy. I fell back into the lifeboat from the force of the blow, and had to climb up and get another whack. They put the POWs in front of a double-barreled gun. The captain spoke English. The Japs had no rations, hardly. They gave us broken biscuits soaked in brandy.

We went to a port, Sangai, in Hainan Province, China. We were put on an oil tanker. There was an air raid that night. The bombers missed us—bad shots!

We were on a US whaling vessel which had been captured by the Japs and re-named the *Kibibi Maru.* There were 150 POW on board. Everyone was packed below deck for three or four days. They were steel hatches. We were being constantly fired upon by Allied ships. On the fourth day we were allowed up for fresh air. We met the commander—he hadn't been home for eight years! He was in charge of troops going to Japan. He improved our conditions.

There were 20 ships in our convoy. When the shooting began, our ship turned to avoid a torpedo, and a boatload of Japanese women and children got the torpedo. Finally, we saw Japan. It was a thrill! We had just half a cup of water and a rice cake per day. As we came into Tokyo Bay, the ship behind us got torpedoed.

By the time we got into Moji, I could hardly stand up. I was half blind, and covered with oil. The Japs gave each of us a small box of rice and a turnip—that was it!

Bill Mayne adds:

We boarded a train at Moji and travelled northwards we thought, although the blinds were drawn and we were told not to look out. We managed to peek now and then. We arrived at Yokohama station where we detrained amidst a crowd of curious Japanese workers who just stopped and stared at the bedraggled men who got off the train. Some of us were naked; some had on only a pair of shorts. Eventually the guards produced some blankets for us; apart from our nakedness, the day was very cold. [The winter of 1944–45 in Japan was the coldest in 42 years.]

Fifty of us were sent to Kawasaki, a camp in a compound with a bamboo fence containing a long hut, Jap sergeant and guard quarters, communal bath, kitchen, store shed and small parade ground. Everything was constructed of bamboo. The camp comprised mainly American and Dutch POWs.

George Carroll continues:

Kawasaki was not too bad. We walked to Yokohama to work, at
4 a.m. We worked till dark, making submarine fans and wheels for
trains. We got two meals a day. If you worked well, you'd get one
cigarette a day. This—*Pommy*—tried to get us to follow this work
incentive. *We—didn't—want—to—do—that!* The British were in
charge of our workforce. There were civilian Jap guards in our camp,
and military ones at the factory. The Aussies had to follow what the
Pommys said.

Mayne remembered an especially hard rule:

A rule of the camp regarding sickness: you had to report to the doctor
the night before to be excused from work, and still have to front the
Jap sergeant for his OK. On this particular morning, I awoke with a
fever and high temperature; but because I had not reported sick the
night before, I marched off to work. On arrival at the industrial works
I asked the guard could I lie down on one of the benches in the
canteen where we had our midday meal (I had a temperature of 103).
He said OK; I had just lain down when the Boss guard (we
nicknamed him Rubberneck) started laying into me with a five foot
hectonal (an inch-thick stick he always carried); after that he bashed
me around the head and told me to follow him. He took me to the
section where I worked (I was in a section where we made condenser
tanks for submarines; my job was to take the buckles out of quarter-
inch and half-inch 20 ft. by 15 ft. steel plates, with an 8 or 16-pound
sledge hammer). Rubberneck spoke to my Jap foreman and the next
thing I was told was to swing this 16 pound hammer all day, non-
stop. I was afraid to stop, because after we finished work for the day
we were taken upstairs to a disused canteen, and if you had been
noticed talking to the Japs or not working, your number was called
out. Then they practiced jujitsu on you. Some terrible beatings were
received there.

A lot of the boys had trouble holding their water after being fed a
diet of rice and very watery soup three times a day, every day; so by
the time we were ready to start our walk to work (approximately three
miles), many had bursting bladders. After walking in the snow with
only sandshoes for footwear, blokes would begin relieving themselves

as we walked along, leaving a telltale trail in the snow. The Japs did not like this; if you were caught you got a bashing. To overcome this, those with severe problems carried a tin or bottle in their overcoat pocket and emptied it at work.[9]

It is interesting to note that British, Australian and Dutch women held captive on Sumatra were repelled at the constant sight of Japanese soldiers relieving themselves at will, anywhere they happened to be, in front of whoever might be around at the moment.[10]

Carroll's narrative continues:

Toward the end of 1944, the air raids began. Tons of ammo were blown up. We heard bombs being dropped. We saw Tokyo burnt to the ground. There were 800–900 planes one night. They dropped canisters of fireballs. Everything wooden between Yokohama, Kawasaki and Tokyo was burned. We lost a few POWs in those raids.

The Japs took us to a market yard. We didn't know what would become of us. We went to a factory at Kawasaki. We slept and worked there. It was 24 hours a day of work. We thought surely the bombs would come, and they did. We went to another factory, at Yokohama, after the first one was bombed out. We made submarine plates there.

In Yokohama there was snow. We had no boots. We were given shirts and pants made of material like hessian bags, dyed green, to wear. The more dirt and grease we got on us, the more it kept us warm. We wore caps with our names and a number on the back. We would sweep the snow off the equipment, but it was snowing so hard, it came right back. The hessian cloth was thin, like paper. Things got bad; there were more guards.

A Jap general gave each of us a Red Cross parcel, with a pair of boots and some clothes in it, because Prince Konoi was coming to inspect our factory. They took back the clothes after the Prince finished his inspection.

On Christmas, we got half a day off. We had a Red Cross box, shared by six people. I saw the interpreter shaking the Red Cross boxes, and taking what he wanted, before we got them.

Mayne remembered more about George Carroll and Red Cross boxes:

Christmas 1944 we received one Red Cross food parcel between three men. That was the only food parcel we got in Japan apart from the two we got illegally; this came about through an air raid. One night we had just finished our evening meal when the sirens started. We were ordered to get into our bed and we just laid there and listened to the krump of the bombs falling; they were getting closer. All of a sudden we were told to grab everything we could and get out quick. When we got out the sky was bright with the glow from the fires, which were engulfing us as far as we could see. We had only gone about 100 yards when a stick of incendiary bombs fell on our camp; all went up in flames as we watched. After walking for miles dodging the fires, we rested in an oil refinery for the night. In the morning we marched through the burnt out streets of Yokohama and surrounds. Eventually we got back to our work factory where we settled down in another disused canteen. While we were looking at what belongings we still had, George Carroll produced two Red Cross food parcels, which he shared among a few mates, myself and Harold Ramsey included. It appears that while everybody was in a hurry to leave camp, George went to this shed where the parcels were kept and helped himself. He carried them all night at the risk of severe beating or death.

During air raids we were ordered down into the shelters, such as they were, very little ventilation and only room to stand. Nobody could sit, and to pass the time we would start a discussion on our main topic: food. If our mothers and wives could have listened in, they would have heard how their meals were appreciated and missed. We had Dutch wanting to know how Aussies cooked; Yanks asking how the Dutch prepared food; and so on. We all had a special recipe we were going to try when we got home. Hunger was always with us.

Carroll tells how things began to change for the better, as 1945 began:

On New Year's Day, 1945, they came around again and transferred the healthiest of us to Niigata, a rural town farther north. It took us three or four days to get there. The POWs were allowed to listen to radio news and to read the [local] papers. We were astonished till we figured out why—there was no news of the war in their papers. The people didn't even know there was a war on!

It was a pleasure to walk to work, between the seaport, the airport and the factory. There were much easier conditions. We dug a hole under the fence and got food. It was worth the little bashing if we got caught.

Once again, Carroll has omitted his role in a truly remarkable episode, and Mayne gives the details:

[Niigata] was an industrial city straddling a river. Had the Japs not surrendered, we learned later, Niigata would have been next on the list for an atom bomb. [It] was a more relaxed camp, with electric light that the occupants made good use of, by making frypans and many other electrical gadgets. Just about every second night we would have a blackout—somebody was testing another invention!

During our stay there, [Pioneer] Harold Ramsay had a birthday. He wanted something special for his meal on that day. One day just before his birthday, while walking back to camp along the main road, we passed this vegetable garden. Harold suggested that we raid it that night. Our camp was surrounded by a high wooden paling fence, and every night each man had to do one hour fire picquet; a guard came around and asked your number. When your turn was up, you woke up the next person.

We asked a mate, [fellow Pioneer] Jim White, to stand picquet in place of the bloke who should be doing the shift. We wanted him to stand guard and wait for us to come back. What we did was dig under the fence after the guard had done his round; then after we had crawled under the fence Jim filled in the hole and waited for our return. Outside the camp was a large railway siding where shunting was going on all night. We had to keep away from the fence because a battery of anti-aircraft guns were emplaced there. Having got past these obstacles, we had to go about 1000 yards to a highway; we crossed that and came into the field where the vegetables were. Trying to find what vegetables we wanted was quite some job in the dark; every so often we had to drop flat whenever a car or truck passed. Eventually we got enough to satisfy us and we headed back to camp where we gave our signal, hoping the guard had not noticed the disturbed soil—or perhaps was not standing right there, having a quiet smoke. Luckily, Jim returned our signal, so we started digging and finally got under the fence and back to our bunks. Harold got his special birthday meal!

While we were at work one day, word went around that the Commandant's chickens had been knocked off. Guards had been ordered to search all POWs to find the chickens. As it happened, a Canadian used to trap rats overnight and cook them up in the morning. This particular morning he was doing just that, when the guard came in and saw the can bubbling away over the brassiere. He accused the Canadian of stealing the Commandant's chooks. The Canadian said they were rats, but the Jap, not believing him, set about eating what he thought was chicken. No more was said about the chickens, and the Commandant never did find out who pinched them.

Carroll reveals, among other things, another way the POWs supplemented their diet, at the expense of some university students who were helping the war effort:

There were 60,000 Japs employed in the factory. It was *very* big, and manufactured submarines. There were university students by the hundreds who also came to work here.

We were feeding the furnaces at a coke, coal and iron foundry. They gave you a basket of scrap iron—some of it was from Australia! You had to fill the basket, run up and stack it in the feeder. We sat down and began working much more slowly—we didn't want to help their war effort! We said we couldn't stand the pace—this worked! The Japs laughed at our Australian foolishness.

Ramsay and I got a job pushing two Japs around taking stock orders. This lasted one week; then we got the Japs to push, by bribing them with stolen food, and so the Australians sat in the cart.

The students came in groups of 50. They left their lunch boxes in a certain spot. The POWs stole their dinners. We ate 20 and threw the rest in the sea. Our baskets of rice were all dirty from the factory soot. When you went home at the end of the day, you weren't searched. We had enough tobacco and cigarettes copped from the students for 20 or 30 people! Jobs were allotted every day, but two Japs picked me and one mate, Ramsay, for the same jobs each day.

Soon the Yanks started dropping 10-ton sea mines. One landed in our camp, and went 15 feet down into the ground. One plane crewman who was shot down, gave info about how to defuse the bomb. He defused it, and the Japs made him part of our workforce.

We stood at the dock one night, and watched two ships go out and
hit mines and sink. All crew were lost. We didn't work for four days
while the bodies were cleared from the harbor.

We could see Nagasaki across the way, when we walked to work.
One day as we were going to the factory, the air raid alarm sounded,
and we took cover. When the all-clear sounded and we came out, we
looked across and all you could see were just two chimneys standing.
I'll never forget that sight. It was the result of high explosive
firebombs, *before* the atom bomb was dropped there.

Mayne adds that, during the final week of the war, "Leaflets [were dropped]
on our camp showing what damage a big bomb did, and underneath that a
drawing of a small bomb and the amount of damage that did; so we knew
something big had happened."

Carroll's story resumes:

The bombing was stepped up. We had to help dismantle the factory
to be shipped further north. The bigger bombs missed us—we were
lucky. One day we looked and saw three planes from the *USS
Lexington* strafing our camp.

The raids began in the daytime. We made an Australian flag—I'll
have to give Ramsay credit for that one—to fly in the camp, hoping
the planes would see us. We saw an aircraft carrier [after the
announcement that the war was over]. All the Japs left the camp.
Planes from the carrier dropped a parachute. We raised our flag. Then
they came again and dropped everything they could from the ship!
Guess they saw our flag! Then five planes a day dropped 10 tons of
supplies to POWs—clothes, boots—they dropped one load five miles
away. When we got there, the Japs had scavenged all of it. There was
a population of 50 million Japs, and 200 POWs. We had to put up a
fence again to protect ourselves from the scavengers. We made the Jap
guards and police come back to protect us. For 10 days, we began
getting haircuts and boot shines from the Japs. It was just like
heaven!

A British official parachuted into our camp. He had a two-way
radio. We did not know another British POW camp was 15 miles
away. They never got a thing. They were captured in the Aleutians
and were in desperate shape. We found them and shared our stuff.

Mayne adds a poignant note about sharing:

[When the Americans dropped food supplies] There were always some chocolates or cigarettes broken. All food was now controlled by our quartermaster, and we had already taken charge of all the rice the Japs had been holding, So by now we had plenty to eat. Any broken biscuits, chocolate or cigarettes we could help ourselves to; not many blokes were bothering about them because we had all the food we could eat. A British friend and I decided we would give some to an aged Jap who had been our foreman. This Tommy and I had been on a gang pushing small rail trucks around this vast area of railway tracks, picking up all the different pieces of moldings from around the various furnaces. Our Jap foreman did not harass us; he just let us get on with our job, and just before our lunch break he would allow us to go and collect grass which we would boil up and eat with our rice. Other times he would give us a pipeful of hair tobacco each, to smoke.

Armed with broken biscuits, chocolate and cigarettes, we went to the factory and found out where this old Jap lived. We gave him our gift, and he could not thank us enough; like us, he had not seen these things for some time. He invited us to have a meal with his family. We accepted, and when we left, both of us gave him a note with our name, unit, number, etc. to give the occupation forces, in which we outlined the humane way he treated us. After we arrived home, we received word from the American forces that he had been granted a double ration of rice, for the kindness shown toward us.

Right after the Japs told us the war was over, they said they would have to stay and guard us from the civilian population. We were told to stay in the camp, but we had other ideas. My British mate and I went for a walk into town, and had a shave and haircut. The barber did the job with a cutthroat razor, and a few thoughts went through my mind as he was shaving my throat; but all went well, and he did not charge us for his services. In wandering around town, we came across a brewery, so we walked in there, picked up a case of beer and walked out. This was the first alcohol we had had for three and a half years, apart from a small glass of saki the Commandant had given us very soon after the cessation of hostilities, during a display of dancing by geisha girls.

*Recovered Australian prisoners at Yokohama Railway station, Japan,
late August 1945, displaying a handmade Australian flag. Pioneers in
the photo are Pte. George Carroll (far left); Pte. Jim White (fourth from left);
Pte. Harold Ramsey (centre); and Pte. Bill Mayne (second from right).
Unfortunately, in the confusion the flag was left behind in a U.S. Army truck.*
(AUSTRALIAN WAR MEMORIAL, AWM 19202)

It seems as if the Pioneers in Japan had a more pleasant, and less frustrating, post-liberation experience than their fellow members of the unit in Thailand, and a quicker start to their trip home. Carroll describes the stages of that exhilarating, final path to Australia:

> At the end of August 1945 we travelled for one and a half days to Tokyo on a clean train, with Jap servants and white towels. When we got there we saw millions of civilians and Yanks. They escorted us to the airport. In the confusion, we left our handmade flag behind us in the US truck. I've always regretted that.
>
> All our gear was burnt in the air raids. They gave us soap and a towel to shower, then we had a medical inspection and clean clothes.

We went home either on a hospital ship or by plane. I flew out in a B-29. When we left Tokyo, the pilot took us over the A-bomb site at Hiroshima. We landed in Okinawa, and were there a month. The Japs were still fighting. We took off from Okinawa in a C-54, and crash landed in a snowstorm in Luzon. We landed in a field. For two weeks, while they fixed the plane, we were treated like royalty. Then from Luzon, we flew to Manila. We had to circle the airport, so they took us hedge-hopping through Corregidor.

When we landed in the military airfield in Manila and saw all those planes, we laughed remembering that in the factory [in Japan], we had five minutes of propaganda every day. They gave us figures of how many US planes had been shot down the day before. We knew the figures were so exaggerated, because if they were true, we knew there wouldn't be a plane left in the world!

Mayne remembered one thing about the Manila airport: "When we landed there, a band started playing 'Waltzing Matilda'—what a lovely sound! We realised at last we were going home!"

Carroll continues his homeward-bound narrative:

Prisoners of all nationalities were in Manila, at a holding camp where you got the OK to be shipped home. We were under American command, and we were treated real good. There were just six men to a tent, and a real mattress to sleep on. Someone made your bed and washed your clothes. The Americans waited on us hand and foot, and prepared whatever we wanted for breakfast. They gave us the privilege of making the Jap prisoners work, picking up litter while kneeling. If they didn't do it properly, we'd tip it over and make them do it again.

A doctor visited the sick all the time. We saw movies, and they issued us three sets of clothes. One rainy day, we were handed over to a British officer, because we were to be transported home on a British ship. He stood us at attention in the rain. An American officer came upon the scene, chewed out that Pommy real good, and sent us back in our tents and told us to rest.

A typhoon held up the boat which was to ship us home. We went out in pontoon boats to a British aircraft carrier, the *Formidable*. The waves were 10 feet high, and we lost some men trying to get aboard. I couldn't figure out why they didn't wait a while to have us board, but the captain of the carrier said he had to rendezvous with his fleet, and he was in a hurry.

We sailed into Sydney in November '45. I took a train to Albury, where I had worked and lived in a boarding house. I had no family, and the old lady who ran the boarding house had been notified that I had been taken prisoner and presumed dead, so she got rid of all my clothes and belongings.

I got two months leave, then came to Watsonia. I got 12 months leave, then got out of the Army. One of the first things I did when I got home was to get a set of false teeth. I had broken mine on Java just before we were taken prisoner—so I had no teeth at all for over three years!

Looking back, I can't emphasize too strongly my gratitude to the Americans, and their decision to use the atom bomb. I'm convinced it saved our lives, and the U.S. saved Australia from the Japanese.

Just about every ex-POW interviewed during the preparation of this book, has expressed that same sentiment, using almost the exact words spoken by George Carroll.

9

Moving Out

S eptember 14, 1945: Almost a month to the day after hearing he was free, Dickson had finally started the first leg of his trip home; at last he was writing from Bangkok. Unfortunately for the ex-POWs at Nakom Nayok, their camp was located right in the middle of Japanese defensive positions in northern Thailand, and was described as a particularly difficult place to reach from points south.

For the first time, he refers to a specific major act of brutality about which he had heard, committed on a Pioneer.

Bankok {sic}
Thailand
September 14, 1945

Darling old Binks,

Note new address! Day before yesterday we had a sudden order to be ready for the move next day. As everyone was becoming very 'browned off' at things, to use the Tommies' expression, the news was extra welcome. Travelled the 80 miles from Nakom Nayok yesterday by motor-truck with Jap drivers. Very unkind, perhaps, but I had a certain amount of pleasure in ordering the offsider of the truck of which I was in charge out of the front seat, which I occupied with another staff sgt. who was in the party, while his nibs climbed up in the back with the troops. Also a certain amount of pleasure in receiving the salutes of Jap. soldiers and officers en route. What a change! They do realise, I think, that they have lost the war, and have knuckled down pretty well to the changed conditions. The trouncing they have had in Burma, as well as closer to their homeland, no doubt has helped to make them see the light. Their attitudes toward us had eased considerably in the latter stages of our period as their guests, but some of them, even up to the last, were pretty truculent. The story has reached me in a letter from one of our officers of the bayoneting to death on August 14, last day of the war, of a Pioneer, after he had been kept tied to a tree for 23 days and fed on rice and water for 18 of them. If that story is true, which I believe it is, the Japs responsible will pay dearly for it. The journey down to Bankok took me back to many a run down the Geelong road in Lea. It is flat country, with paddy-fields as far as the eye could see on either side of the road. One different note was a narrow canal running alongside the road of a fair distance, up & down which an occasional barge, propelled by sail or oar, passed. We are in quite good quarters here. I believe it is the Chinese School of Commerce, recently occupied as Japanese Kinpie (military police) H.Q. Post-war mail has begun to arrive. Only A's to C's have been sorted so far. Look out if there isn't one from you in the D's! Last night we (John, 2 others & myself) went in to the city per the local taxi service, the vehicle being rubber-tyred tricycles, with a hooded seat for two at the rear. The place was rather dark as the electricity supply is not yet fully restored, it having been put somewhat out of joint by our bombs. Power stations, railway workshops, docks etc. here were hit hard, and the bombers used to pass straight over us at Tamarkan on moonlight nights to do it. There was little else to do than find an eating establishment, and wash the meal down with a bottle of beer each at the enormous price of 17 tikals (10/) {shillings} a bottle. But it was the first for a long time, and it was good. Some of our convoy from Nakom Nayok yesterday were cut off & sent to another camp, at the University. Sixty of them left by air for Singapore this morning. So perhaps I might be next!

Lots of love,

Pop

The incident mentioned here was detailed by a fellow Pioneer Gordon Hamilton, in a September 8, 1945 letter to his family. Hamilton also alludes to a second incident, involving a sick Pioneer:

We have just heard after the death of Pvt. Durkin of our Battalion. He had a bout of malaria and wandered off from a working party in north Siam, and was caught 2 days later. He was chained to a tree for 21 days, tortured and beaten, cigarettes butted on his face etc., and on the 14 Aug. last (2 days before surrender signed) was taken out and bayonetted to death after digging his own grave. One case of *many* such!

Poor old Lew Whitfeld died as a result of kicks in the stomach by one of our guards.

Not only was this extreme brutality inflicted on someone from their own unit, but as in so many other cases, the torture was inflicted for an act which had a perfectly reasonable explanation. And thus was drawn the line between major and minor war crimes: Private Durkin was not trying to escape; he was not concealing a wireless radio or a camera. All of these infractions were recognized risks. But this POW was delirious with fever, and wandered away from the camp because he was disoriented by illness.

Another incident which, if possible, traumatized the Pioneers even more, was the one involving Lewis Whitfeld. This particular episode was so devastating because it occurred right in their midst. Cal Mitchell told how it happened:

At the 131 Kilo camp, Lew was a walking skeleton and was also virtually blind. The blindness was caused by dietary deficiency [read: malnutrition caused by starvation]. He had big brown eyes, and he could hardly see out of them. I can still remember those beautiful big eyes. He had just come out of hospital and was sitting near us—we were playing cards on one of the bunks—when this Korean known as 'The Maggot' appeared. Of course Lew couldn't see him, and was beaten and kicked (for failing to stand and salute the guard). He died three days later.

Together with others I forwarded a statutory declaration to the War Crimes Tribunal. Just recently, in a book I read where, in 1947 in Singapore, 'The Maggot' was hanged for this crime. I had not until then known what had transpired at his trial.[1]

There is evidence to suggest that some Japanese military personnel sent to staff the POW camps considered themselves deeply humiliated and insulted by the assignment. It has been stated that they were, all too often, those who for some reason had been found inadequate to offer more active service to the emperor. British writer Lavinia Warner, for example, interviewing a group of women who had survived Japanese internment, learned that their camp commandant had often expressed his feeling that to be put in charge of prisoners was humilating enough, but to be placed in charge of *female* prisoners was doubly so.[2]

However, former *Kempe tai* interpreter Takashi Nagase pointed out in a 1992 letter to the author that many camp commandants were reserve officers, called back to serve in that capacity, and it was his observation that most seemed content with their assignment. But he acknowledged that some camp officers, especially younger ones, may have been disappointed at not having more glorious military opportunities—and thus a greater chance for promotion in rank—and concedes that they may have tended to take out their frustrations on the prisoners.[3]

Cal Mitchell noted that: "Mention of the poor types of Japs and Koreans in charge of POWs was quite true. However, I am sorry to say that this could be said of most other nations. It is a natural thought [for a commanding officer] when asked to supply personnel for other units, to get rid of the most useless or unpleasant people."[4]

The most consistently vicious camp personnel were, by all accounts, Korean guards. Nagase, who had frequent contact with staff personnel at many POW camps in Java, Burma and Thailand, states that Koreans: "All volunteered to be Japanese soldiers, but I am so sorry that against their expectation, their treatment by the Japanese [was] not good, and the training was so severe that they were much disappointed. But they tried very hard to become true Japanese soldiers."[5] However, information supplied to Benjamin Dunn by fellow American prisoners reveals that toward the end of the war, several Koreans relaxed a bit and began conversing with POW officers. Some Koreans admitted that they were serving as camp guards as their own prison sentence, having been convicted of some crime back home. This revelation appears to give the term "criminal behavior" a truly double meaning. As Dunn put it, "Woe be to the poor prisoners who happened to be in a camp guarded by Koreans who were being punished or disciplined."[6]

No doubt POWs took little solace in occasionally seeing the Japanese use swift brutality on one of their own staff. In a retrospective radio broadcast, one Australian ex-POW recalled standing in the camp guardhouse and watching, in horror, as a Japanese officer knocked a sergeant to the ground for a "back-talking" remark. The officer began kicking the sergeant, who never uttered a sound as he was slowly kicked to death.[7]

The slightest appearance of insubordination brought such swift punishment, that it kept everyone's nerves on edge. Colonel Williams noted in his diary:

"The guards are particularly vicious today, and one lad had his head split open when struck with a heavy piece of wood. When the Force Commander [Williams] protested vigorously he was told the cause of attack was due to a smile at the guard by the man concerned. Prisoners are not allowed the privilege of smiling."[8]

Of course, POWs had no way of knowing that in the Japanese culture, children are taught from an early age that expressions of familiarity, even smiling, are regarded as acts of insolence, and must be avoided.[9]

According to the Rescript for Soldiers and Sailors, written by Emperor Meiji in 1882, one's "sincerity" made one's acts acceptable, as long as the act was carried out to fulfill duty to the emperor. By the time a Japanese soldier finished his training, he had repeatedly been subjected to the situation he feared most: surprise and humiliation, because "hazing" at the hands of upperclassmen was frequent. For the rest of his life, the recruit would look for a way to settle the score with an individual tormentor—but at the same time, he often couldn't wait to pass on similar humiliations to anyone who might come under his control. He was likely to graduate with a heightened insistence on respect; in his own training, a sudden blow was often used to teach "insight", and a failure to show respect frequently led to disastrous reprisals.[10]

Even the continuing brutality of relentlessly driving POWs to work on the Railway far into the night, with no sleep, appears to have a precedent in Japanese military training. A British colonel who was allowed to observe Japanese training methods in 1934–35, once questioned the captain in charge of some recruits why he was driving the soldiers to a new task, after three days and two nights without sleep. Why not let them rest up and be fresh for the next day, he asked. "They already know how to sleep", the captain replied. "They need training in how to stay awake."[11]

The Japanese recruits in that training exercise may have been learning a form of discipline for a few days, but their exercise was not stretched for months on end while they were being starved and beaten daily. Colonel Williams observed that for the POWs under his command, "On the Burma Railway we had no time to ourselves. We were building a railway for the Japanese and never at any time did we have any more than six hours sleep. On one period the men worked 72 hours without a break."[12]

Some of the most baffling aspect of Japanese behavior, as far as the prisoners were concerned, may have occurred in the weeks following surrender. Quite a few ex-POWs told stories similar to the one Cal Mitchell related, which occurred in Bangkok, when a Japanese officer approached an Australian officer, extended his hand, and said: "Now we are friends." Mitchell still seemed astonished at the recollection, even after a lifetime. "Imagine! All the brutality and starvation was just to be put out of mind—he wanted the fellow to shake hands, just like that!" He snapped his fingers.[13]

One United States-educated Japanese woman has summed up her countrymen's outlook in a way which may offer some clue to the seemingly nonchalant attitude the ex-POW found so hard to fathom. Michiko Asano, who has served as Vice-President for Education in the College Women's Association of Japan, recently wrote to a Wellesley College classmate: "We Japanese . . . try to hide the things past which are not comfortable to talk about. For decades we have been doing this."[14] Mrs. Asano has seen this pattern of behavior beginning to change, but she recognized that for over half a century, it has prevented young Japanese from learning much about their country's role in World War II.

For Railway survivors, the memories were too searing to dismiss with a handshake.

10

In Touch With Things Again

Dear old Binks,

Another day nearer home! Last evening one Sgt. Dixon and I paid a visit to Bankok's Chinatown, and had lots of fun. We dropped in at Chinese wedding feasts, private mah-jongg clubs—in fact anywhere giving forth sounds of life. The old (and not so old) Chinks dispensed hospitality in the shape of iced lemonade, cigarettes, and China tea, and we didn't remain long enough anywhere to outstay the welcome. I haven't yet located New Bankok, which I believe is quite modern and not unlike Haifa in Palestine. Perhaps to-morrow I might get there. One of the troubles in finding one's way about is that unless you take French leave you don't leave here until about dark. It is then raining & continues to do so for a couple of hours, so it's pretty dark with no street lighting in operation. Another handicap is financial. Owing to shortage of power the trains are not running at night, and the run into the city by jarru {the tricycle taxi he described in previous letter} costs at least 5 tikals. Meals begin at about twice that price. Cigarettes cost at least 20 cents each—that is the smokable ones. The Odeon theatre puts on pictures for the troops free every second night. The films are flown over from Rangoon. There is an excellent and substantive theatre in the grounds here to seat 500–600. It is being rewired for sound. To-night a concert is being held there. As I write I can hear the band rehearsing—the best music I have heard for years. I now have thank goodness a new pair of boots. A perfect fit. Put them on for the first time when I went out last night, and suffered none of the ill effects usual with new footwear. My last pair konked out two and a half years ago. We are gradually coming back into

touch with things again. There was a parade for General Shin (I think that
was the name), commander of the 14th British army, which did such good
work in Burma. He was driven out of that country by the Nips in '42, and
has been doing battle with them ever since. Knowing them as he does, and
knowing their treatment of prisoners, he is not letting them down too lightly in
Malaya and Singapore, where his army is in occupation. Owing to the fat
condition of the Jap major-general who had charge of prison camps in Malaya
and the somewhat lighter condition of some of his former guests, he {Gen. Shin}
told us, he has the aforesaid major-general on a 'controlled diet'. That
gentleman is also doing a strenuous course of exercise in his bare feet very close
to the point of a bayonet—just to let him know what the 'exercise' he has given
his former prisoners was like. Gen. Shin remarked that he thought the Nip's
physical condition would be greatly improved at the end of a week's treatment!
We also had an Australian lieutenant along this morning who left home since
the war ended. He told us about conditions in Australia generally and
answered a lot of questions. Love to you old dear and remembrances to family
and friends.

   Pop

Next to the rare religious services they were allowed (see Chapter 15), the
equally rare musical performances and outdoor concerts kept feelings of hope
and humanity alive for the POWs during their endless months of degradation
and death.

If one picture is worth a thousand words, the photograph on page 109, taken
secretly in captivity and, like the others displayed in these pages, buried, dug
up and re-buried at constant risk of death for so many years—says more than
any verbal description could possibly accomplish, about what the opportunity
to hear music meant to these men who were starved in so many different ways.

For example, one Australian (wearing hat), seated in the right foreground
next to the man standing closest to the camera, is so sick he cannot hold his
head up—but he is there. Further down the line, another POW, seated, leans
on a friend's back for support. According to donor Cal Mitchell, the picture was
taken at Kanchanaburi (also called Kanburi) camp in early 1945, when conditions had improved somewhat; but the men are still pitifully thin. Note that
many are looking toward the camera, apparently aware that their photograph
is being taken, and probably wondering if it will ever be seen by anyone. No

This photo taken by an Australian prisoner at Kanchanaburi, Thailand, in early 1944, shows mostly Australian and some Dutch POWs assembling for a rare outdoor concert. No matter how sick, every man attended. Note the POW seated in the foreground, wearing a hat, too weak to raise his head. Several POWs look toward the camera; photogapher was especially bold to attempt a snapshot at such a large gathering. The low railing was also used as a communion rail for the equally rare religious services.
(COURTESY OF C.J. MITCHELL, AWM P1502/02).

doubt few dreamed that it might one day be on display at the Australian War Memorial in Canberra.

In the POW exhibit at the War Memorial, several musical instruments are displayed. They were crafted, hammered and pieced together from various materials, as Mitchell attests: "At Kanburi, some fellows were really quite ingenious. They made violins, using cat and other animal gut; carved flutes from bamboo, wrote musical scores from memory, and created an orchestra of sorts. When the commandant was in a good mood, the orchestra was allowed to give a concert now and then. Of course everyone came."

Colonel Williams proudly describes one concert, on November 20, 1943, in the worst of the days on the Railway, as "A professional, refreshing show that proved, beyond doubt, no matter the suffering, there is always a group who can minimise miserable moments and build up morale."[1]

If the entries in the Battalion commander's diary can be taken as a gauge, the November 1943 concert may have been the first since February 1943, which in turn was the first since November 1942. So "every now and then" seems to have meant every six months or so.

Another POW, Australian Driver Thomas Fagan, also describes a rare 1943 concert, given by and for sick prisoners: "Last night was a great lift for all of us; the Nips allowed the boys to put on a concert. Hard to believe how sick men can change so rapidly. A bit of a sing-song, some laughter, a joke or two and one's anguish is, for a few minutes, gone. We enjoyed the show even though those who rendered items did so only with a great deal of willpower. They, too, suffered from various ailments and a few propped themselves up on bamboo crutches. What a fantastic lot!"[2]

Leslie Hall mentioned that a frequent request at concerts was to hear a rendition of the "Colonel Bogey March", commonly used in British training drills, and therefore one of the more accurate touches in the film, *The Bridge Over the River Kwai*. But most of the time, he noted sadly, the only music POWs heard with any frequency was "Taps" or "The Last Post".

Prisoners were often punished if they whistled or sang on the Railway, but frequently at night, some found a way to cheer up everyone within earshot, by whistling tunes softly, or by daring to sing. Hall remembers one musician called "The Tiger Rag King", who was apparently allowed to wander from hut to hut at the 55 Kilo hospital camp, playing his mini concertina. Far beyond the light recreation usually associated with wandering minstrels, his music meant so much because it was literally the only medicine available to those who lay and listened in the dark.

By contrast, the Japanese sometimes indulged in light recreation by picking POWs at random, and subjecting them to various forms of torment to fill idle moments, such as lunch breaks along the Railway. Artist Ronald Searle captured such a moment for all time in his drawing, titled "Lunchtime Games", which is now part of the Imperial War Museum collection in London, and which is reproduced in his text, *To the Kwai—and Back.*[3]

On this particular day the selectee was an Australian, judging by his hat. All his friends could do was to gather nearby and glare or scowl at the tormentors, which they are certainly doing. Seated in a ridiculously out-of-place upholstered lounge chair (probably appropriated from a nearby prosperous Thai household) is the Japanese camp overseer, with a red star on his pith helmet. His boot is propped against the prisoner's thigh, and he holds a sharpened bamboo rod to the POW's back. The emaciated prisoner, wearing only a loincloth and a bandage over his leg ulcer, is being forced to stand in the noonday sun, holding a heavy rock above his head. Of course he will soon waver, causing some amusement among his tormentors as he reacts to the bamboo piercing his skin. No doubt he will drop the rock before being signalled to do so, because he is too weak to hold it for long. This act will be an excuse for a beating, which a guard stands ready to do, leaning on a cudgel like a minor-league baseball player who waits his turn at bat. After the beating, as a gesture of appreciation for providing them with this noontime diversion, the Japanese will allow the prisoner to have a cigarette, before sending him back to work on the Railway.

No wonder Dickson enjoyed hearing the British general's description of having the Japanese major-general do, as he phrased it in his letter, "a strenuous course of 'exercise' in his bare feet very close to the point of a bayonet—just to let him know what the "exercise" he had given his former prisoners was like."

He was referring [not having quite heard the name correctly] to General Sir William J. Slim, who was very popular among the Australians, and later served as Governor-General to Australia. No doubt the general's talk to so many ex-POWs, gathered in Bangkok on their way home, was a well-planned event to assure them that those who were directly responsible for their suffering would not go unpunished. Like the carved artwork so often seen on court buildings, the general's speech was a welcome reminder that the scales of justice are still the best way to restore mental equilibrium for innocent victims of crime.

11

This Accursed Lack of Pence

September 16, 1945: Dickson displayed some rare peevishness as he struggled to keep up his morale, and wondered if he would *ever* hear from home—or get there!

Bankok, Thailand
September 16, 1945

My old darling,

In yesterday's letter I suggested that I might make an early visit to New Bankok. Funds not permitting, I have not done so yet. This accursed lack of pence hampers activities considerably, and according to latest reports there will be no pay for a week, when we receive 250 tikals or its equivalent in Singapore dollars, if we move before then. The tikal rate has jumped from 34 to 60 to the £1 sterling, but even with the increased amount it doesn't go far with prices at a high level. As in all of these countries, we are fair game for the local business people, large and small. Last evening, in search of cheap entertainment, Dixon and I walked across to Chinatown. Peering into the doorway of a Chinese theatre, we were invited in by the doorkeeper, so had an interesting hour or so for nothing. The colour scheme would have intrigued you. Almost every hue was represented on the stage and its surroundings. They should have clashed, but didn't. Costumes and headdresses glittered. The actresses were all young girls of the doll-like Chinese variety, while the male members of the cast were mainly long-bearded villains who posed and strutted and declaimed until retribution overtook them and the sword removed their heads. Leaving there, we drank iced coffee and ate fancy cakes at a restaurant with a European flavour. It was a typical sticky tropical night, and after wandering about watching the sights for a while we retraced our steps. Nearer home we dropped in an open air market cafe and sipped more iced coffee. Close at hand we found another Chinese theatre, and spent half an hour there. The show was comedy, which had the audience in a continuous simmer of laughter. And so home. Today I had a daylight dash about Bankok in a car with a Jap chauffeur in search of small change for a few hundred tikals of canteen profits to be distributed among the troops. This evening looks like free pictures at the Odeon theatre. Nothing came of my effort to crash into the news gathering, as the place is now teeming with correspondents. I hear there are two 'Aussie' men here, including a photographer. Have not yet contacted them. I don't know if you have seen the jungle battle dress we are fitted out in. It is 'jungle' green drill. Trousers are similar pattern to the Tommy khaki battle dress, with plenty of pockets about them. The shirt when not tucked into the trousers is a tunic, with four pockets and a belt of the same material. Boots are black, with short putters or gaiters. It's a good outfit and will be improved when the hats turn up. The old one is battered—just a bit! Tell Keith I was talking to Charlie Poulton to-day. Have also seen young Mac Kingham, and we have here also Bob Kevinan of Patchewollock.

Love till next time,

Pop

No letters from you yet, but hoping!

Since none of Dickson's letters mentions the check arrangement with local banks referred to by Cal Mitchell (see Chapter 7), it must be assumed that perhaps only a few commissioned officers had discovered this source of financial relief, or that the courtesy was extended only temporarily. Mitchell arrived in Bangkok before Dickson, and departed sooner for home. As late as September 29, Dickson reported that "the banks are not operating on exchange yet."

Most American ex-POWs were flown home before Bangkok's inflated prices became an issue. But for the Australian and British troops who had to wait for available ship transport, the euphoria of freedom became increasingly edged with a new form of confinement, dictated not by a guard but by an empty wallet.

So the hospitality of local people was much appreciated, and invitations to private homes became prized commodities. Best of all, such moments not only gave former prisoners something positive to write home about, but also assured loved ones that they were capable of sliding into normal social activities with some ease, after all they had been through.

Gordon Hamilton (who came home on the *Circassia* with Dickson) told his family about such a visit:

> The family that I met have been wonderfully good to me, and several others of us from this Camp. They are the kindest-hearted, most happy and hospitable people that you could wish to meet. They quite took us to their hearts and did everything they could to make our stay here as happy as possible. The family is: Mr. and Mrs. Serm. Saligupta, two daughters (the eldest seventeen), two younger sons, all from his first marriage, and a little daughter aged three. Then there are Mrs. Serm's cousin, a very fine woman, well educated, been to America (her sister married the present Premier of Siam, lately the Siamese Ambassador to America), his uncle and their adopted daughters, all aged about eighteen. In my last letter I told you we had been out there to dinner the previous night with two A.B.C. [Australian Broadcasting Company] men. Well, they so thoroughly enjoyed the night, that they decided to make a recording of the party to broadcast in Australia. So last night we all went out there again with recording apparatus, and did the whole thing again. You will probably hear it in a fortnight or so. I hope to be home by then!
>
> We had a grand time—lovely food, Siamese dancing and music, and the fun of making the recordings. Today they came out to lunch with us at the camp—I think that they enjoyed the fun, but not the food. We had tomato soup straight out of tins, and I must admit that it was rather strong; cocktail sausages in tomato sauce; sheep's tongue with tinned peas and carrots; finished with tinned peaches and evaporated milk. It was rather a funny mixture and must have been very peculiar to them, unused as they are to European food. Then they took us out on a shopping expedition, and we made our fond farewells.

An even greater disappointment than the continued lack of funds, perhaps, was Dickson's revelation that he had not been able to cut through red tape and resume his status as a working journalist. His hope of being allowed to contact the *Argus* or another news organization to receive such an assignment while still a member of the military ranks, had apparently been dashed by the sight of so many civilian correspondents, newly arrived from all over the world. The best he could do was to assist in the professional news-gathering (see Chapter 13).

For ex-POWs, maintaining morale in Bangkok was a matter of battling some frustrations; as prisoners, maintaining morale in the camps was a daily battle against despair, and finding ways to remember who they were.

During the grim days of October 1943, as the exhausted, rain-soaked prisoners struggled to complete the Railway, Colonel Williams made this entry in his diary: "They return [from a long shift] weary, hungry, but defiant, as one man demonstrates when he brazenly whistles a tune entering the camp. He is a real morale builder."[1]

Turning harassment by the Japanese into an act of absurdity was a more subtle form of defiance, and any opportunity was quickly seized. Cal Mitchell recalled one such occasion, at Kanburi camp: "One night, in the pouring rain, the Japs said there had to be another roll call. We were all in bunks, with clothes off. One man stood up and started to leave the hut naked. The others said, 'What are you doing, going out like that?' He said, 'Why should I get my clothes all wet, and have them soggy all night and into tomorrow?' We all decided that made a lot of sense, so 800 men went outside naked, and it was the Japs who got their clothes all wet."[2]

Another time: "One day we had to all line up and at 11 a.m. all face the north and bow and send our mental salutations to the Emperor on the occasion of his birthday. As we straightened up I heard the chap in front of me say, 'If that old—receives my message he'll burst into—flames!'"[3]

Birthdays, anniversaries and indeed, any special occasions were looked forward to, with determination—a milestone to strive for, a certainty to count on. Defiance was still in his voice, a lifetime later, when Pioneer Jack D'Argaville said: "We always knew we'd win, and we always said we'd be home by Christmas, by my birthday, by Easter. When that day would pass, we'd say, 'next year.'"[4] Many around him nodded in agreement.

Towards the end of the war, as the rumors became more persistent that the Japanese were about to capitulate, some POWs became openly defiant of the Japanese. American Ben Dunn was one:

> We were standing around a tent where some [Japanese] officers and non-coms were having a meeting. While we were waiting for them to put us to work, Henry 'Bull' Barbatti, a sailor [from the *USS Houston*], who was getting pretty cocky, decided he wanted a smoke and walked brashly in their tent and interrupted the meeting and asked for a cigarette. One of the officers gave him one and Barbattti said, 'No, I want three more for my friends.'
>
> Almost any other time, this boldness would have earned him a good

bashing, but this time, the officer simply gave him three more cigarettes. Barbatti came out grinning and distributed them among the three of us, but since I didn't smoke I gave mine back to him. He had earned it with his courage.

A few minutes later a guard came out of the tent and told us to move some 100 kilogram sacks of rice . . . I'm certain he knew that none of us could carry a 220 pound sack of rice, but he looked at me and told me to pick one up. Even when I had been in perfect physical condition, I could never have shouldered one without help.

Thinking how stupid the guard was to suggest such an impossible feat, and remembering how successful Barbatti had just been in his bold request for cigarettes, I couldn't resist replying, 'Pick it up and carry it yourself, you son-of-a-bitch!' I was positive he couldn't understand English because we hadn't heard any of those Japs say a word to us in English—just their gutteral Japanese.

As soon as I called him a son-of-a-bitch, he grabbed a bamboo pole, hit me in the head with it, and said in perfect English, 'Don't you ever call me a son-of-a-bitch!'[5]

If the struggle to keep spirits up was a daily task for POWs, it was equally so for their relatives back home—especially because of the sparse mail distribution. As Cal Mitchell put it, "The contact with our people, or lack of it, was one of the most difficult crosses to bear." [6] His sister-in-law, Eileen, remembered attending meetings of the Pioneer Battalion Relatives Association:

Jean [Cal's wife] and I used to go every Tuesday lunch time to the Battalion Women's Auxiliary meeting in the Railway Building [Melbourne] where wives and mothers gathered to share news and to chat. Being only a fiancee and not next of kin, I never held any office or did anything of note, but it was lovely to go and talk and listen. The mothers all seemed old and very gallant . . . The lack of all news was so appalling—hard to believe in this day of instant communication that it could happen. That fact speaks loudly of the utter disruption the war brought. I was absolutely thrilled when the first card came for me, at the end of 1943. There had been silence since March 1942 [when the unit was captured on Java]. The card was apparently written at the beginning of 1943—it had no date. Al had crossed out the printed words—sick, in hospital, etc., and left in 'well'. He said he was with three friends, Harry Bishop, Pemberton and Tranter. It was a good idea to mention names as we could then let other people know. The cards came at random and we all shared the joy of whoever had just got one—they came very seldom. Some men wrote things like: 'Tell this to the Marines', after saying they were well and happy.

Only three cards ever came for me. Much later, in January 1945, two came almost together. One was dated May of 1944. they were the same kind of printed cards. Al told me years later that at the time of writing one of them he was delirious with an attack of malaria. I have studied the cards to try to work out which one was written at that time [without success]. My memory of the women in the little club rooms is so much of the patient middle-aged mothers; some seemed very old. The wives I saw on different Tuesdays—I suppose everybody young had a job, but I suppose the mothers stayed [at the gathering] all day. I remember at least two Christmas parties for Pioneer children; all [of us] working together for a happy afternoon.[7]

In utter contrast to the deprivation of contact between POWs and their families, an American airman stationed in the mountains of Burma at Christmastime, 1944 not only had a typewriter at his disposal, but a mimeograph machine as well. He even had colored pencils to shade the Christmas newsletter he composed, to duplicate and send to a list of friends and relatives back in the States. William Palmer Goetz, of Buffalo, NY, composed his Christmas message on December 12, 1944, in full confidence that it would reach everyone in time to act on his request: "Be sure on Christmas Eve to step outdoors and lift your eyes to the Heavenly stars above. Find the Big Dipper—for on each star I will have planted a very warm and sincere wish for your good health, happiness and good fortune throughout 1945, and it will be just 12 hours before!"[8]

For thousands of prisoners confined a few hundred miles away from Airman Goetz, their only communication was to gaze at those same stars, silently send their prayers and wishes aloft, and hope that next Christmas would come for them.

12

'You Understand?'

Bankok
Siam
September 26, 1945

Dearest old Binks,

*Note that we are no longer in Thailand, the new Prime Minister having
announced that in future the country will go under its old name of Siam.
I was corrected at the Publicity Dept. yesterday where I went to collect a map
of the city, and referred to 'Thailand.' 'No Thailand', the clerk said. 'You
understand—Siam.' We've been talking that sort of language so long now that
it will be a pleasure to hear English unadulterated again. The expression, 'You
understand?' was a common one with our former hosts when enforcing their
point of view. One of the standing jokes was that, whether you replied yes you
did understand, or no you didn't, you received a wipe over the chops just the
same. 'You understand?' 'No.' Bang! 'Now you understand?' 'Yes.' Bang!
It usually didn't hurt much—just an open-hander—but was somewhat
lowering to the dignity. One of yesterday's pleasures was a civilised haircut in a
comfortable chair in a clean saloon, with electric hair clippers. Having cleaned
up the pay, I went out early, alone for a change, took a train to the other side of
the city (New Bankok), where I had some stripes sewn on my shirt, lunched,
and wandered about looking at things. On the way back I tried to buy some
pencils, but the Chinese business people are having a sit-down strike at present
and all they would say was 'No sell!' On the previous evening the curfew was
lifted, as there had been no shooting for a day or two, and we were allowed out
until 11 p.m. With another man I walked down to the Odeon theatre, having
to avoid certain thoroughfares that were picqueted, but with no street lights,
and all the Chinese shops in darkness, and hardly anyone about except a few*

scared-looking young Siamese soldiers, the prospect was rather gloomy. Last night rain came down heavier than I've ever known before, and to-day there are heavy monsoonal showers. Rather a bad day for drying my jungle greens, which I washed this morning. Capt. Winning, whom I'd not seen for eight months, came in to see me to-day. I am driving with him to-morrow. He and I have got on well together over the last few years. Of that more when I return. This evening I am driving with Felix von Kispal, born a Hungarian baron, now a naturalised Dutchman, who was a good friend in the leaner times. While confident that you have written, I have not yet received a post-war letter from you. A lot have received mail, but many others have missed out so far. Better luck in the next day or two perhaps.

Love from your old

Pop

Had a vaccination to-day!

As mentioned earlier, the constant bashings to which any POW might suddenly be subjected kept everyone's nerves on edge. Because many beatings seemed to happen for petty reasons, these incidents might be classified as "petty brutality", if only to separate them from more prolonged savagery which brought a prisoner close to death.

The incident Dickson describes, being slapped in the face for who-knows-what minor infraction of protocol, was quite a common form of torment; its main purpose probably being, as he says, 'somewhat lowering to the dignity'. What he *doesn't* mention is that, before his punishment began, he was made to kneel. Fellow Pioneer Bob Adolphson recalls: "Cec was so tall, [over 6'4"] that the Japs made him kneel for 'discipline', so they could reach his face to slap him around, or to give him a bashing."[1]

Australian POW artist Murray Griffin sketched an incident from memory, showing a kneeling Australian being beaten; his drawing hangs in the POW exhibit at the Australian War Memorial, Canberra (see illustration, p.121). Even though the Australian is on his knees, his head is still almost level with the caps of the two guards, who are taking turns thrashing him. As an added torment, he is being made to kneel on a freshly cut wedge of wood, which has just been hacked out from a Railway construction log. While the beating goes on, he has to hold a heavy metal pipe aloft, perhaps to remind him how weak

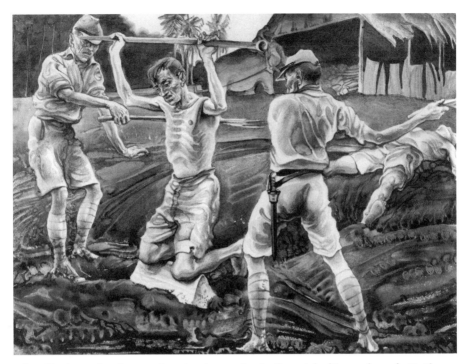

A tall prisoner has been made to kneel on a chunk of wood freshly cut from the Railway construction site, so that the two guards can more easily reach his body, to take turns beating him. He is made to hold a heavy pipe aloft. Soon he will collapse, unconscious, as his fellow POW in the background has done. (MURRAY GRIFFIN: *AN INCIDENT ON THE BURMA RAILWAY,* BRUSH AND BROWN INK WITH WASH OVER PENCIL, 35 X 50.8CM. AUSTRALIAN WAR MEMORIAL AWM 26525)

and emaciated he is. Soon he will simply collapse and fall prone, unconscious, as his fellow POW in the background has done.

Dickson's way of maintaining his dignity at moments like that was to stand up, dust off his knees, and go about his business as best he could. Long before their capture—in fact, shortly after they had enlisted as Pioneers back in Melbourne—Alan Mitchell labelled the tall, unflappable man from Geelong "Dignity". In a letter to his finacee Eileen, written from bivouac camp in the summer of 1940, Mitchell remarked that even when bedding down under the stars during field manoevres, Dickson insisted on wearing his hat.

Walter Summons claimed that Dickson "Had the ability to appear dignified under any conditions, and was one of the few who could invest a loin-cloth and wooden clogs with a little of the 'dignity of man'. He, and his brother, who was known as 'Gentleman John', because of his faultless manners, were a great pair to have in the same camp."[2]

Many years later, Gordon Hamilton still recalled : "He had an innate dignity of bearing and behaviour whatever the circumstance, and that is how I shall always remember him."[3]

And, after half a century, Leo Cornelius was still trying to figure out why Dickson joined the Pioneers: "How such a gentle, urbane person could have come to roost in a tough old battalion like ours has always seemed to me an absolute paradox."[4]

On one occasion, Dickson's friends remembered, he lost his cool—but that was because his brother, John, was being savagely beaten. Finally, Dickson couldn't stand watching any longer, and he tried to intervene (John was much shorter and smaller in build than Cecil; see photo). Of course, the guards then turned their attention to Cecil, and beat him, too.

Harry Bishop pointed out that "The Japanese appear to be very susceptible to alcohol, and periodically there would be trouble with guards and NCOs for this reason." Several ex-POWs have said that some of the worst sudden beatings were at the hands of Japanese or Korean guards who were drunk. Bishop continues: "I can remember when I had a run of ten bashings over ten weeks, all of which were to do with my duty as cook house *shohu* (officer). One was because a cook set fire to a chimney; another was when I was standing in front of the cookhouse—I saw a guard coming and moved to the back so I wouldn't have to salute him."[5]

Dickson may have joked at dinner parties about still enjoying rice, after consuming over 3800 consecutive meals of it; but surely in his mind there was the flashback of being on the brink of starvation for that whole period—and gratitude for the creative genius of cookhouse personnel like Harry Bishop and Harry Whelan. Getting a cookhouse going, and searching for food to supplement their dwindling rations was of vital importance. Whelan remembered working with Dickson:

> Both Cec and I had jobs in the quartermaster's store at Tamarkan camp, which was the camp near the two bridges. (The wooden one later became known in the movie as 'The Bridge Over the River Kwai').

The number in this camp was usually 2000–3000 men. But when the wooden bridge was washed away in a flood in early 1944, soon after it was completed, the Japs brought about another 2000-odd men in to quickly rebuild it. At one time we had about 5000 in the camp. In order to feed everybody we had four kitchens: one for the Dutch, one for naval personnel, one for officers, and one (the biggest) for everybody else.

We used to issue the rice direct to the kitchens; in other words, they at times had up to a week's stock of rice. The entitlement or ration was 500 grams of dry rice per man, per day. We did not always receive this because some of the bags had split or were holed, and did not contain 50 kilos. This was the cause of an argument with the Japs, who insisted that a bag was 50 kilos, although it may be only half full.

A daily record was kept of the numbers eating from each kitchen, and transfers of rice from one kitchen to another were constantly being made. In other words, the quartermaster's store controlled all stocks of food, although the stock may be in the hands of individual kitchens.

You will appreciate the fact that everyone was hungry, and every effort had to be made to ensure that everybody got his fair share and appeared to be getting his fair share. Hunger turns men into beasts, and I have seen fights develop if one man thought he was getting less than someone else. Doling out the cooked rice and the soup was always a source of much argument.

Eldon Schmidt [of the 131st Field Artillery, Texas National Guard] lent me his slide rule, in a leather case, with his monogram on it, to assist me in splitting up the vegetable ration. That's how exactly we tried to measure out everyone's fair share! I kept it all these years, hoping to find out his address and return it. [As a result of the research for this book, Whelan was put in touch with Crayton 'Quaty' Gordon, longtime secretary of the Lost Battalion Association, as the 131st came to be known. To his dismay, Whelan learned that Schmidt had recently died.]

The Japs had supplied us with a platform scale. The vegetables used to arrive each day by river barge, and be carried into the camp by POWs. I used to supervise the weighing, and being armed with the numbers eating from each kitchen, I would use the slide rule to work

*Here an Australian prisoner has photographed a team of fellow Australians
drawing water outside a cookhouse, Kanchanaburi, Thailand, 1944.
The water will be used for a 'stew', which will contain rice and whatever
vegetables, meat scraps, or bones the cooks have been able to acquire.*
(COURTESY OF C.J. MITCHELL, AWM P1502/04).

out the number of kilograms to go to each kitchen. I believe we were
supposed to get 400 grams of vegetables per man, per day, in addition
to the 500 grams of rice.

In Tamarkan, we also got a meat ration. I think it was 20 grams
per man per day. We never actually got any meat as such, usually just
enough to flavor the soup, [but] it made the soup more palatable.
Cecil used to supervise the killing and splitting up of the meat ration.
The killing was done in the camp by POW who had been butchers in
civil life. [Dickson often remarked in later years to his family, how
vividly he recalled trying to portion out the 'miserable carcass of some
half-starved yak'.]

The kitchens were built of bamboo, with roofs made up from atap
leaves, as were all other buildings in the camp.

The rice was cooked in 'kwalis'. A kwali was a cast iron dish about four feet across and one foot deep in the middle. A mud frame would be built up to support the kwali, with an opening in the mud frame about one foot wide to enable a wood fire to be built under the kwali. The only other cooking equipment we ever had were 44 gallon drums (British measure, about 20% larger than US measure). The soup, whatever it consisted of, was always cooked in these drums.

In Tamarkan, we were also supposed to get 20 grams of salt and 20 grams of sugar per man, per day. We did not always receive salt or sugar. We occasionally received some tea, but not often. Compared with what we had received in the jungle, while building the Railway, the rations in Tamarkan were quite reasonable. You were always hungry, but not starving.[6]

Some POWs who surely would have been starving, except for the constant attention of their fellow prisoners, were those confined to the camp 'hospital'. As mentioned earlier, the Japanese tended to cut off rations for "non-productive" POWs; Colonel Williams routinely notes in his diary how rations were cut back in order to provide some for the sick. Sometimes, "healthy" prisoners did without a meal entirely so the sick could be fed something.

If a particularly nourishing bit of food came their way, POW cooks always made sure it went to the sick first, so prisoners were always on the lookout for an enhanced opportunity to find such morsels, particularly if possessions did not have to be sold clandestinely to natives in order to acquire them.

Cal Mitchell provided one vignette which could be considered high comedy, if its underlying purpose were not so grave. An Australian, passing the Japanese kitchen, spotted a bullock liver, unguarded for the moment. Thinking of its exceptional nutritional value for sick men, he grabbed it, plopped it on his head, and covered the oozing innard with his hat. As the liver blood began running down his face, a Japanese officer came upon him, and immediately sent the Australian to the camp hospital for treatment of his "injury". So the liver got a direct trip to its destination, the hospital stew-pot.

The prisoners also supplemented their diet with literally anything that moved, which happened to slither within range. In later years, Dickson would joke to his family and friends: "In the jungle, I found that I *could* eat snake!"

Harry Bishop remembered some of the ways cooks found to supplement rations during the leanest days, while constructing the Railway:

An Australian prisoner has photographed another vital daily task at
Kanchanaburi, Thailand, 1944, as a crew of Australian prisoners chop
and saw wood for cooking fires. During the worst days of rain and constant
moves in 1943, the prisoners were sometimes unable to gather wood,
so no food could be cooked on those days.
(COURTESY OF C.J. MITCHELL, AWM P1502/01).

When my party, Java 5A, started in Burma we were getting cattle for
our beef ration and we had butchered them in the camp; rice and
vegetables were delivered by truck. Six months later the cattle we
were getting were so thin that they were dying in the yards before we
killed them. The Japs tried a whole range of alternatives as conditions
became worse (supplies couldn't be trucked in during wet season).
They slaughtered the cattle in Moulmein and packed it in boxes after
cooking it in a way to preserve it. They also got local dried fish,
including white bake and dried slices of a big fish. These were good,
but they were not enough.

Motor trucks began to buck up on the roads and they got Burmese
farmers with drays drawn by oxen to supply the camps. Very few got
back [to the camps] after the wet season set in. Apparently they were
susceptible to cholera. The end result was wagons abandoned along

the road and the oxen were turned loose. They could be seen in the forest by our wood cutters—always there were wood cutting parties. We had two butchers, one American, one Australian, who found that it was possible to catch the oxen and bring them in one at a time to butcher, close to the camp.

We also asked permission to collect edible plants to put in the stew. I simply picked leafy plants that were free of toxic tastes and didn't have too many fibres. It worked, but it only made a small difference to our stews. We could only get small parties to gather food, and there was a lot of walking between plants.

The Japanese engineers had a different approach. They took explosives and looked for pools along the only river in the area. They got fish and they had a few POWs with them to carry the fish back to camp. By chance I walked along the river with a jungle greens party next morning. There were still a lot of fish floating belly up, and sitting on a rock was a beautiful otter, which dived in when we came by. The fish were beginning to smell, so we left them for the otter.

However, we made arrangements that the next time the engineers went fishing, one of their carriers would join a party of jungle green-seekers and lead us to the site. It worked; there were quite a number of fish floating, and we cleaned them straight away and hurried them off to the kitchen.

I had that job for the whole period I was on the Railway, and this continued until the last six months of the war, when all the officers were concentrated at Kanburi and I had a row with the British. During much of the time, I shared cookhouse space with the 131st Texas Regiment and *USS Houston* survivors, and also with the Dutch.[7]

Bishop's resourcefulness extended beyond buying the bolt of military cloth in Java, and creative measures to supplement POW diets. He also seems to have figured out the Japanese hierarchy quite well:

This was part of the drill in the Japanese army: officers bash NCO; corporals, privates; and first-class privates, recruits. If this was accepted then there is less likelihood of them getting really nasty. The best outcome is to stand to attention until it is finished. I had one [Japanese] corporal tell me that I was a very good soldier when he finished slapping me. The worst thing to do was to dodge, or to fall down.

On the Railway the guards were Koreans but with Japanese officers and NCOs in charge of administration. However, there was little difference between them in the way they operated.[8]

That the prisoners could keep up their spirits despite constant harassment was a source of wonder and curiosity to many Japanese who witnessed it. Reflections on the POW attitude prompted Henry Shigeru Yagake to write an essay on the subject, which appeared in the January 1992 issue of *Rafu Shimpo,* a Japanese-language newspaper published in Los Angeles, California. Yagake described how, toward the end of the war, while at Takli airbase in northern Thailand, his curiosity got the best of him, and he initiated a dialogue with three POWs whose work he was supervising. One prisoner was an American, the second was British, and the third was a Malay, whom the Japanese called 'New York', 'London' and 'Calcutta', respectively:

> 'New York' was always very cheerful. So one day I just had to ask them the question that was utmost in my mind. because [we] were inculcated to believe in the *Senjin-kun* [Combatant's Code] of the Japanese Military, that said in part: 'One should not shame oneself by being taken alive as a prisoner; one should die instead and not shame his name for posterity of one thousand years.'
>   When I said to the POWs: 'the Japanese men think it is a great shame to be taken a prisoner. What are your thoughts on the subject?' The answer came back promptly. 'No. We fought to our best of ability in the front line until we were captured, so we don't feel ashamed at all.' I then understood why they were so sunny.[9]

Probably the most hated harassment was when POWs, especially after working long into the night on the Railway, were ordered to perform some service for the Japanese when they returned to camp—such as building a shower-house or trimming their captors' hair. This form of abuse might be classified in a category by itself, if a suitable name could be found for it.

Even the most unreasonable order, if refused, brought swift retribution. Ron Winning, who was so brutally tortured for over a month in Java, remembered many examples of 'lesser' brutality as well:

> The senior NCO sent for me and demanded that sick men in the camp be sent out to work. I refused, and he beat me with a heavy

wooden waddy, breaking one of my ribs. When I still refused the Jap
C.O. ordered all men in the huts be on the parade ground. He went
along the lines, pointing his cane to any one he considered fit to
work—even men carried out on bamboo stretchers were sent out.[10]

It would probably be safe to say that every ex-POW has memories of what
he saw and endured, very close to the surface. Sometimes a recollection, or flashback, is triggered by a phrase or gesture made at another time and place, as was
the case with Dickson when the clerk in Bangkok used a phrase, in broken English, which had so often been the prelude to a beating in the camp.

Too often, though, the memories bubble up at unwanted moments, like the
middle of the night. Many years later, Dickson confided to his second wife,
"When I was first in Bangkok, I drank a whole bottle of whiskey every night,
and slept like a baby. I never drank that way again".[11]

But like many of his friends, especially in his later years, Dickson relied on
sleeping pills, just in case a troublesome scene from the POW years haunted
his night.

Even so, he could never predict when some image would intrude on his
pleasant life. One such unwanted intrusion occurred during a visit by the Dicksons to the United States during the 1976 Bicentennial year. As part of the fes-
tivities, tall ships from all over the world had been invited to sail into New York
Harbor, and then up the Hudson River on Independence Day, July 4.

Knowing how much Cecil had enjoyed sailing during his younger days, Margaret's daughter and son-in-law, Susan and Ralph Gross, had arranged to take
the Dicksons on Ralph's sailboat up to Newport, Rhode Island, where the tall
ships were assembling for their parade down Long Island Sound, past the Stat-
ue of Liberty, and into the harbor. It was to be an overnight outing, and in def-
erence to the Dicksons' comfort, Susan and Ralph had booked a nice hotel room
with a waterfront view in Jamestown, just next to Newport.

During the night, many of the tall ships put into port, and as luck would
have it, the captain of a large sailing vessel from Japan dropped anchor directly in front of the Dicksons' window. The next morning, Cecil opened the
draperies to greet the sunlight, only to find the Rising Sun flag waving in front
of his nose.

Later, at breakfast, he confided to his family: "Of all the flags I would rather
not have slept in the shadow of, it was *that* one. It brought back a flood of memories, of my unwilling tenure as a guest of the Emperor."[12]

13

News From Home!

Septeember 29, 1945: Dickson was so full of news and happiness that, despite squeezing two sentences on each line and omitting paragraphs, he still used ten pages torn from an accounting ledger to complete this letter, At last he had received mail from his wife and sister—and funds wired from a bank officer to which, regrettably, he did not have access.

Chinese Chamber of Commerce
Bankok, Siam
September 29, 1945

My dear old girl,

Two very exciting days just past. After writing to you on the 26th your cable arrived—first post-war intimation that you were all right. For which three cheers! Then yesterday morning I received your letter of September 16, and one from Marie of the same date. Then in the afternoon I had the opportunity of saying a few words into a microphone, one of 30-odd who were allowed to send a verbal message home. The recordings are being flown to Australia, where it is expected they will be broadcast from national stations in about a week. It is possible that I might be in another broadcast, as the A.B.C. correspondent here has asked me to assist with a programme he is planning. I expect a ring from him this morning. If anything comes of it I shall certainly let you know the details. Facilities and conditions are not good enough here at present to broadcast direct, so the discs will probably be sent home, the same as with the personal messages. At this stage I was called away to receive a new 'hat'. It is one of the green berets that go with the jungle green battle dress. Very acceptable, as the old khaki fur felt, which was passed on to me early this year by Cal Mitchell, had outlived its period of usefulness. The last two days have been busy with pay again. It comes once a week at the rate of 60 tikals, which at 5d. Australian to the tikal goes like the wind. After balancing out {the accounting ledger} yesterday afternoon I took the surplus cash back to the field pay office away out the other side of Bankok by truck. It was quite an interesting run, taking me through parts I had not seen before. I was dropped eventually at the Oriental Hotel, where the surplus officers are quartered, and went out to dine with Ron Winning and an English M.O. {Medical Officer} who had spent most of his POW days as doctor in coolie camps. What appalling stories he had to tell. The Chinese strike continues, which means that it is difficult even to get a meal. But we did manage to dig up fried eggs and German sausage. Went on to a newly opened cabaret called the New World. It's quite an attractive place as these turnouts go, but as there had been some trouble over the band, and there was no music, it was rather flat. On our way back to our respective abodes we called at another cabaret, where dancing was in full swing, but the 11 o'clock curfew cut that rather short. As Ron had just come down from up-country where there wasn't much chance of spending, and I had personally paid the M.O. 490 tikals that afternoon, the evening cost me nothing! The banks here are not operating on exchange yet, so I do not hold out much hope of receiving any money in response to Mathers' cable. It would have been handy to buy a few things before leaving here. Latest information about the move is that at present the planes are being used to fly the 861 Australians out from Petburi, which I left on July 4. That should be complete by October 1, when movement from Bankok is expected to be accelerated. Some time in October should see me home. The evening before last spent with Kispal (aforementioned). He has been busy preparing reports on a number of Japanese offenders, with whom he had extensive contact. To-day he is leaving with a commission that is going up-country to investigate Japanese treatment of coolies. After the last war, in which he fought as an officer for the Hungarian army, he accompanied the commission which fixed the new boundaries of Hungary. Kev Nolan, whom I had not seen for two and a half years, and with whom I spent leave in Damascus and Tel Aviv, came in a day or two ago with an escort to a couple of Japanese who are 'on the list'. He is looking exceptionally well, his only imperfection being that one leg has not quite straightened out yet as a result of a bad ulcer he had behind the knee. It is very little handicap to him now and is expected to come good with treatment.

Well, it was great to receive your letter. Give my love, of course, to the family at 50 Canterbury Road and regards to all other friends. I'm looking

forward to making the acquaintance of the new grand-niece. Great thrills!
Good old Jay! Now whatever you do, old girl, don't run yourself thin over
the house-hunting business. I'm well practised in the art of living anywhere.
Being with the old Missus again will be sufficient, whatever it might be.
Incidentally, the chest swelled with pride at some remarks in Marie's letter
about a certain person's doings in the last four and a half years.

You'll be bored if I don't stop prattling. So cheerio, old darling, till next
time.

Much love,

Pop

Having been denied direct contact with loved ones for so long, Dickson absolutely revelled in the thought that, although not directly, his wife may actually hear his voice the following week—then surely she will have no doubt that he is all right, too!

Cal Mitchell also recorded a message from Bangkok, but he beat it home:

> I recall the radio messages being sent to our people from Bangkok in October 1945. In fact I sent one to Jean and my father. They were recorded on platters. When I arrived home on October 23rd, I asked if they had heard the message but no, they hadn't. About a fortnight after I got back, Jean received a message to say that if she listened to the radio at a certain time and date, she would be able to receive a message from her husband in Bangkok. At the appointed time we both sat and listened to me from Bangkok![1]

In one of his preprinted postcards from POW camp, Dickson apparently tried to signal his wife that some of the radio messages, broadcast monthly by relatives, were getting through. In the limited space at the bottom of the card, reserved for a few personal words, Dickson says: "Would be thrilled to receive message"—not 'letter' or 'card', but 'message', as in 'radio'. It must have been a real lift for the Relatives Association members gathered in the Melbourne Railway station meeting room, when Freda Dickson shared that bit of confirmation, albeit many months after it was written.

Although clandestine wireless radios were set up in almost every POW camp, most units were equipped only to pick up news broadcast by the BBC. Unfor-

Australian officers standing inside a hut, Kanchanaburi, Thailand, 1944,
photographed secretly by a fellow prisoner. Hollow bamboo poles sometimes
concealed radio wires. Hanging bags of belongings were often stolen by Japanese
or Korean guards while prisoners were out. The POW in the foreground, looking
at the camera, has managed to keep a table marked with the initials 'R.S.'.
(COURTESY OF C.J. MITCHELL, AWM P1502/04).

tunately, for quite some time messages from families were beamed to Java, since it was over a year before most relatives learned that their loved ones had been shipped to Burma and Thailand.

Cal Mitchell confirmed that the handful of Pioneers who remained on Java did receive several messages directed to them, but he did not recall hearing of any along the Railway, for Pioneers. One lucky exception seems to have been Ron Winning, who described how two men at a nearby camp risked their lives to bring him a message from his wife just before Christmas 1943:

> I was in a different group from the Pioneers, but two men risked their
> lives to contact me and give me the message . . . The work camps at
> this stage were fairly close together. They were not fenced. However,
> the Jap orders were that anyone caught outside [his assigned] camp

would be dealt with. The two men who brought me the message slipped out at night, and walked about five kilos to my camp.[2]

Several POWs have described how wireless sets were hidden. A favorite spot was the lower section of a water bottle, in which a false bottom had been placed; one such contraption is on display in the POW exhibit at the Australian War Memorial. Bamboo poles which supported the huts were a handy conduit for wires. A strict security system was devised, to pass information by word of mouth, and POWs made it a point to visit the sick first with news of an Allied victory, to boost their spirits and give them the will to live.

According to Mitchell, one of the more ingenious methods of hearing regular newscasts was hit upon in Java by a British aviator, who managed to keep his helmet intact when captured. He never took it off, because the earphones inside were still working fine. He was able to acquire an iron bed, to which a wire could easily be grounded. Mitchell could still visualize the Englishman, nodding and smiling a greeting at the Japanese guards inspecting the hut, as he sat and listened intently to the latest BBC news summary.

Of course, keeping a wireless operating without a ready supply of batteries was a challenge, and by war's end many "nightingales", as the sets were called, had stopped "singing." However, resourceful POWs often took advantage of the presence of Japanese motor vehicles parked in the camps; many a truck parked for the night was the victim of a quick battery switch, and puzzled drivers would wonder the next morning how the battery had run down so much overnight.

Gordon Hamilton told his family with evident pride that "Despite danger, two British officers have kept a set going [in his camp] throughout, and the effect on the Japanese when they produced the set after capitulation was ludicrous. We had just moved camp, been subject to a stringent search; but the set travelled packed up with the Jap camp commander's personal electric equipment! Such a joke."[3]

But in the same letter, Hamilton mentioned that two British officers caught operating a wireless in 1943 "Were beaten to death in the most brutal manner." Although quite a few pieces of wireless equipment were found during the 'blitz' searches of POW belongings, it could not always be established to whom they belonged. Various punishments were meted out, of course, but the incident to which Hamilton referred occurred at Kanchanaburi in late 1943, and was even remembered by certain Japanese for its severity.

Iinterpreter Takashi Nagase recalled that the equipment was discovered in a surprise inspection:

When all suspects were brought to the Military Police, they had already been beaten up badly. Most suffered broken bones and were gasping for breath. One prisoner had been beaten to death in camp. This well-known case was called the 'Shortwave Incident.' After the war ended, the officers and noncommissioned officers . . . who had been involved in the affair were indicted as B and C class war criminals. Some of them were condemned to death.[4]

Nagase's role in helping to secure data for war crimes, and the lasting effect these memories have had on him, will be discussed in the next chapter.

Toward the end of his letter, Dickson cheerily mentioned that his friend Kevin Nolan's bent leg "is expected to come good with treatment." but the restoration to reasonably good health was a long path for many POWs, and for most, it was never complete.

Nolan detailed the onset of his leg trouble, and its impact on his immediate postwar plans:

It was in Niki camp that I began to develop the ulcer to which Cec referred in his letter. After a nightmare trip by train to Kanchanaburi we were expected to walk to Tamarkan, where a large number of Pioneers were gathered. Nothing would stop me from reuniting with some of my old mates, some of whom I hadn't seen for a year or so. The uselessness of one leg, combined with a recurrence of malaria contracted on the train on the way down, allowed me to walk about half a mile before collapsing. Two burly Dutchmen carried me back to Kanburi, where I spent three and a half agonising months before being transferred to a new 'hospital' camp at Nakom Paton, where I remained as a hut commander until that magical day in August 1945 . . . Like Wally Summons, I had to endure the seemingly endless medical examinations, and a two month sojurn in a 'Thomas splint' getting the offending leg 95% straightened.' [This treatment forced temporary postponement of his wedding plans.][5]

Summons, who died in 1990, was among the most severely ill of POW survivors. Harry Bishop recalled:

Wally Summons had a bad run on the Railway and was sent back to a hospital camp in 1943. Later on he was transferred to the camps in

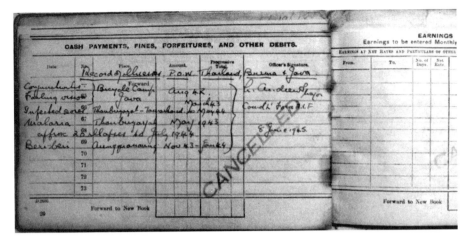

*Cecil Dickson's pay book, showing the list of known illnesses he contracted
during captivity, written on pages which should have beeen a record
of his daily pay as a soldier—blank for three and a half years.*
(PHOTOGRAPHED FROM ORIGINAL COURTESY OF MRS. T.C. DICKSON)

southern Thailand, where Australians were concentrated over a period
in 1944. Wally had recovered a lot in the previous year, but he was far
from fit and he was held in hospital for a couple of years after he got
home.[6]

Despite Dickson's upbeat assertion, in an earlier letter, that his brother John
was "in fine fettle", the younger Dickson spent considerable time in the hospital once he arrived in Australia. He recovered remarkably well, but suffered
increasingly severe arthritis as he got older, and when he underwent emergency
surgery in October 1991, surgeons speculated that scar tissue they discovered
could well have dated back to ulcers developed as a POW.

The illnesses Gordon Hamilton described in his first letter home was probably quite a representative one:

Our captivity is something we are fast trying to forget. I have not
space to tell you any details, but as you can guess, we had a very thin
time, especially for the fifteen months after leaving Java. Burma was a
hell hole. Fortunately we were brought down to Thailand at the end
of '43 and conditions improved considerably. I survived dengue, and

bacillary dysentery in Batavia September '42, and in Burma got malaria and amoebic dysentery. Went down to 6 stone 6 [about 85 pounds] in August '43 but pulled round . . . We will all be rather a bad bargain for a while though. Mentally we have become very slow and stagnant, and have developed queer habits and outlook—hope that diet and environment will soon correct that, but the past three and a half years must have left its mark. It is only when we come in contact with outside people that we realize our peculiarities.[7]

Eileen Mitchell said that although she and her husband enjoyed a full and active life raising their family, "Alan was never really well again, though—often back in hospital with an anxiety state, a strange heart-beat and amoebic dysentery for years and years. [But] he was never embittered."[8]

The recurrence of strange tropical illnesses, sometimes unfamiliar to, and therefore unrecognized by local physicians, plagued just about all ex-POWs, and shortened the lifespan of many. Ernest Gordon observed during his ministry at Paisley Abbey in the immediate postwar years, that a disturbingly high number of ex-POWs died within 10 years of their release from captivity, due to lack of proper medical treatment for illnesses contracted in the POW years. He credits his own vigorous recovery to a physician in Leith, Scotland, who established a wing for tropical diseases in the local hospital, and took it upon himself to become educated about the proper treatment for these illnesses. Most important for Gordon, this physician offered treatment to ex-military personnel. Gordon felt that the Socialist British government took very little interest in the individual health of ex-POWs. "They seemed *angry* at us", he mused, and showed a rare flash of pique as he remembered the offhand attitude of one "rank-conscious" British military physician. When asked what he meant by "rank-conscious", The Reverend Dr. Gordon replied: "Oh, you know, 'Yes-sir, no-sir, three-bags-full-sir.'"[9]

Gordon estimated that about 10 per cent of ex-POWs returned to very good health following their release, and about 10 per cent remained in somewhat precarious shape, suffering from repeated neurological breakdowns, kidney failure, increasing blindness and limited use of limbs due to severe arthritis. Skin cancer was a common ailment for many, including himself and Dickson.

Sir Edward 'Weary' Dunlop agreed with Gordon that a premature death rate among ex-POWs may have seemed disturbingly high, but he points out that a survey taken some ten years after the war purported to show roughly the same death rate among ex-POWs as in the general population. However, he commented:

This study [was] flawed in that the comparison should have been with a controlled group of young men selected as fit for war service. However, the death rate at that stage [approximately 1955] was not alarming . . . Nevertheless, an early survey, which I obtained, did reveal quite a lot of residual disease and disability . . . As regards Australian Prisoners of War, in rough round figures of 22,000 POWs, 8,000 died in prison camps due to disease, starvation, or drowning at sea. A few were executed. Of 14,000 who were recovered, recent Veterans Affairs [figures] state 5,300 still surviving. I suppose one could conclude that of the selected men fit for service, those who survived were very tough men.[10]

Because physicians like Dunlop and Lieutenant Colonel Albert Coates had been in charge of large numbers of POWs, they became effective spokesmen to underscore the need for immediate follow-up treatment, having kept detailed records of their efforts to provide care despite the lack of medicines. And as mentioned earlier, Colonel Williams spent nearly ten weeks between September and December 1945, providing authorities with a complete medical record of each Pioneer. He also kept notations about each POW, regardless of nationality, who passed through his camp.

So when over 14,000 ex-POWs returned to their homeland, they and their relatives made a powerful lobby group indeed. And if the government faltered in its response, the Returned and Services League and the newly forming Ex-POW Association of Australia were there to prod the bureaucrats along!

As a result, Australian ex-POWs have probably received more enlightened, comprehensive and lasting health care than those of any other nation. The War Veteran's Villages, designed and supported by the Returned and Services League, are unique in the world. They provide security, camaraderie, subsidized housing and healthcare, in a most attractive setting; they serve as a model of how to say "thank you" in a very practical way.

In terms of aftercare, American ex-POWs fell somewhere in between British Socialist government indifference and Australian personalized attention, provided by both government and private groups. Like the Reverend Dr. Gordon, many American ex-POWs lamented the difficulties some of their friends have had in trying to deal with postwar life: higher than average rates of alcoholism and suicide, and lingering health problems. Although the United States does have a Veterans Administration system which operates hospitals and clinics throughout the nation, the burden of discovery primarily rests with the individual, in terms of identifying his needs and getting treatment. Many American ex-POWs who survived Pacific War captivity have reported that it has taken them 50 years or more to receive the full disability payments for which they qualified the minute they returned to American soil.

As was true among Australian and British POWs, the Americans had several medical personnel in their number, among them a surgeon, Commander William A. Epstein, assigned to the *USS Houston.* According to Otto Schwarz of the *USS Houston* Survivors Association, a personnel profile of each survivor was kept by a yeoman from the *Houston,* which he turned over to the Department of the Navy at war's end. A year later, the yeoman happened to discover his records stuffed in a Navy office desk drawer, virtually discarded. He retrieved them, and gave the files to Schwarz as a memento. Schwarz still had those records when he died in August 2006.

14

Another Anniversary Apart

October 2, 1945: It was the Dickson's nineteenth wedding anniversary, and although he did not mention it, Cecil's 43rd birthday was to come in just four days.

Chinese Chamber of Commerce
Bankok
Siam
October 2, 1945

Dearest old Binks,

That most important anniversary has come round again, and here I am still in Bankok. The business of getting started seems a bit slow, but it would appear now that within a week at the outside I should be on the way, and the journey should not take long. With ordinary luck, say, home by the end of October. Meanwhile the time is passing pleasantly enough. In the evenings there is not much to do but sit about in cafes, which are innumerable, except on nights when there is something special on, such as a performance by the ex-POW party two nights ago, and to-night another dance at the Alliance Française, which I might attend. The alternative to going out is being eaten by mosquitos in camp, where they abound. Incidentally, I sleep under a mosquito net again. Although I had not been using one, I had been remarkably free from malaria. Only one attack (three months ago) in 16 months. Previous to that I had had a consistent run of attacks for more than a year. Yesterday I took the day off. Met Ron Winning at the Oriental in the morning, called on a friend at Diethelm & Co., a large Swiss importing house, then visited the Royal Palace which is open to the public in the day time. The young King has not yet returned from Switzerland, where he has been receiving his education.

The palace buildings are very ornate in the Siamese fashion, but unfortunately the most interesting part, the shrine, was closed. We then drank iced coffee in the lounge of the Ratanakosin Hotel, where we met again Simpson, the A.B.C. correspondent, and a bunch of Dutch officers known to us both. One, Lieut. Bom, a very pleasant fellow, invited us to join his party for lunch to celebrate his wife's birthday. The result was the best meal I have had in Bankok. After strolling the hot streets for a while we drank more iced coffee, then separated. I immediately ran into Kispal, with whom I drank more iced coffee while listening to his experiences at identification parades, where he has been helping to single out offenders among Jap prisoners. Having been an interpreter, he has had close contact with many of them and knows their form. The colonels and what not who have wielded the power of dictators in prison camp administration, are now performing the manual work that we have been doing for them—their clothing being one pair of shorts and no footwear. They do not walk about the gaol—all movements are done on the double! Have received cables from Panden Orbost & Keith Pearson. The mail position here as far as inward letters are concerned gives no cause for cheers. I have had only the one letter from you and one from Marie so far.

Much love old darling

Pop

Japanese interpreter Takashi Nagase, like Kispal, was put in close contact with the hierarchy at several camp locations, especially when prisoners were being interrogated. In fact, it is chilling to note that as soon as Java fell to the Japanese, Nagase was sent there "in order to collect information", as he puts it. Thus he may have been in one of the rooms where Pioneer Captains Winning and Handasyde, or the Commanding Officer, Colonel Williams, were being so brutally interrogated for 30 days non-stop.

And, as previously noted, Nagase was familiar with the details surrounding the wireless radio incident, discovery of which brought about the immediate death of two British officers. He was at Kanchanaburi and Ban Pong for over a year, beginning in August 1943.

Although he was a soldier of lower rank, the necessity to be present during prolonged torture of POWs deeply affected Nagase, and flashbacks have haunted him through all the years since. He candidly admits that Westerners are always puzzled by his rationalization that absolute obedience to orders was required, because the directive may have come from the Emperor himself. Japanese soldiers, he says, were told in no uncertain terms that if they disobeyed orders, they would face court-martial. But perhaps worse still, their families and all relatives would face reprisal, because the soldier's disobedience would immediately be reported to his home town. His family would then be ostracized, and suddenly find themselves unemployable. Ruefully, he acknowledges: "No matter how earnestly I tried to explain this to Westerners, I have never been successful in convincing them. This might be because of the environment in which they were brought up and educated. The respect for fundamental human rights seems to be rooted in the minds of people in the West. I have never seen any Western reporters look satisfied with my explanation."[1]

The only time such strict obedience to orders worked to the advantage of POWs was when the Emperor issued the direct order, over the radio, for all Japanese military personnel to lay down their arms. One of the points Colonel Williams was able to prove, by documentation, at the Class A War Crimes Trials in Tokyo was that the general treatment of POWs was carried out on direct orders from the highest level.[2]

After the capitulation, Nagase was at the Japanese Army War Termination headquarters in Nakhon Pathom, trying to control his panic at rumors that Japanese soldiers were about to be put to work on the Railway, as reprisal, under the same conditions they had imposed on POWs. Apparently word of the regimen being undergone by camp commandants, described by Dickson in this letter, had reached Nagase's ears—and had become embroidered with the threads of fear.

He was also terrified that an ex-POW who had been tortured would recognize him as having been involved in these procedures, and turn him in as a war criminal. So it was with considerable apprehension that he learned, on September 22, 1945, that he was to accompany members of the Allied War Graves Commission on a seven-week trip through Burma (which was not yet fully secured), to recover the remains of POWs, in order that they might be reburied in official war cemeteries in Thailand and Burma. An equally important purpose of the expedition, Nagase was to discover, would be to gather evidence for War Crimes Tribunals. Composed entirely of ex-POWs who had worked on the Railway, the expedition was headed by British Captain Bruce and Australian Captain White. Non-commissioned officers and soldiers were all Australians.

Nagase was as frightened to be among this delegation of thirteen ex-POWs as he was to be entering the domain of the legendary fierce tigers who roamed the Burma countryside. His fears did not abate when the two captains point-edly reminded him that their sketch maps of gravesites had been confiscated during searches of their personal belongings. Nagase had participated in some of these searches, posing as an "inspector", to gain tidbits of information about the prisoners.

On September 25, the party arrived at a spot near Thanbyuzayat. Captain White had a compass, and seemed to know just how many paces he needed to take, to find what he was searching for. Then he found it: part of a rotted wood-en cross, and another, and another, as the party made the Japanese clear the graveyard overgrown with two and a half years of thick jungle foliage.

As the party moved by railway, progressing in its search, advance word of its arrival resulted in the appearance of already-cleared graveyards, because the Japanese had removed foliage from known spots. On September 28, the group arrived at one such cleared POW cemetery, in the Apalon district of Burma. Captain White paced over and over again in a certain direction, holding his compass. He knew just where to order the Japanese to start digging. Nagase tells why this spot was special:

Teams of two or three Japanese continued digging very deep by turns. The depth was nearly two meters, but the captain did not order them to stop. The other officers were looking at the hole, holding their breath . . . Soon a rotten blanket covering a body came in sight. The color of the blanket was hardly distinguishable from that of the dirt . . . white leg bones poked out of the dirt.

'The other way round. Dig again on the head side', ordered the officer. Soon the hoe made a sound over the chest of the body.

'That's it.'

The Captain ordered them to stop, and he jumped into the hole. He pushed dirt aside. A reddish, rotten 20 liter petroleum can came in sight. The can had lain over the body for two and a half years. The body was quietly awaiting the War Graves Commission in the depth of the weird jungle. I stood there in silence.

Captain White came out of the grave with the can in his hand and put it on the ground like a precious thing. He ordered a Japanese soldier to break open the can. With a blow of the hoe, coal tar splashed in all directions . . .

The Captain ran up to the can, thrust his hand in the coal tar and took out a small round tin. It was a sealed container of fifty navy-cut cigarettes . . . Cold silence continued between the Allies and the Japanese.

What they explained to me later was: 'He suffered from malaria and was unable to walk any longer during the march to the back regions. He asked the Japanese for permission to leave the march, in vain. He ended up dying in the jungle.'

What he had on his chest for the period of two and a half years was a sheet of paper which said the names and ranks of the Japanese commander, a medical doctor, an interpreter and a soldier in charge who were responsible for his death, as well as the marching conditions and his wage statement [soldier's pay book—see illustration]

'We were not allowed to carry any documents with us. We did not have any other means than what you saw just now. The evidence lay hidden with the body for future reference.'[3]

Nagase goes on to quote Captain White as further explaining:

'It is necessary that we show [the Japanese] what justice really is . . . There would not have been this many deaths if the Japanese had been a little more humane. When there was an epidemic of cholera, they did not even give us any lime to spray over the latrines. Of course, the Japanese had enough. I suspect there were very few Japanese who died of cholera. The disease is easy to prevent. We could only watch our comrades die in great pain. Things were no different with tropical ulcers. With a little mercury medicine, most patients could have been cured easily. Many of them had to have their limbs cut off [in order to live]'[4]

Nagase was profoundly impressed that the prisoner who died, as well as his friends, had complete faith that his remains *would* be found one day, and that those responsible for his death would be brought to justice. It took him another 30 years of meditation to realize that this faith was centered in firm convictions about the nature of God.

The withholding of medicine, particularly when it had been delivered to POW camp locations in Red Cross parcels, was just about in a class by itself as a war crime, and seems especially anachronistic. Article 108 of the third Geneva Convention, which governs the rights of prisoners of war, dictates that among other things, prisoners must be able to receive and send mail, and to receive one relief parcel monthly. Although the Japanese Government apparently endorsed the general principles set forth in the Conventions, when it came time to ratify this particular Article, Japan declined to do so. No doubt this article made little sense, in 1929, to a nation so dominated by its military elite, whose units were thoroughly trained to believe that captivity was too dishonorable to consider. Perhaps the assumption was made that soldiers of other nations would surely feel the same way. In other words, Article 108 just didn't fit into their thinking. But an often overlooked fact is that the Diet *did* ratify the convention pertaining to the Red Cross; thus Japan was obliged to honor that Convention, which it did not do, for the most part.

Although the Japanese government did honor Article 108 to the extent of assisting in the delivery of Red Cross parcels to POW campsites, either their public Japanese statements did not mirror written instructions to camp officers; or local commandants were less zealous in following orders than some would have us believe. The result was that lifesaving food, medication and clothing intended for prisoners was either stolen by Japanese camp personnel, or allowed to rot, unused.

At the War Crimes Trials in Singapore, Australian physician Colonel Albert Coates testified that Red Cross medicine and supplies were actually known to be on hand at Nakhon Pathom camp, and that failure of the local commander to distribute them caused the death of many men who would otherwise have survived.[5]

Benjamin Dunn obtained a list from the office of the United States Provost Marshal General of the items contained in Red Cross parcels which were being sent for *weekly* distribution to prisoners: 16 oz. milk powder, 8 oz. processed cheese, 6 oz. liver paste, 12 oz. corned beef, 16 oz. oleomargarine, 12 oz. pork luncheon meat, 8 oz. salmon, 4 oz. sardines, 8 oz. sugar, 12 oz. prunes, 4 oz. concentrated orange juice, 1 oz. coffee, 4 oz. chocolate, 1 oz. salt and pepper mixed, 3 packages cigarettes, 7 oz. biscuit, and 4 oz. soap. Dunn commented:

> If these foods were ever sent to the prisoners of the Japanese in Burma
> and Thailand, the Japanese must have used them. One time in Burma
> we were given a can of butter or cheese to divide among six men.
> They were old and rank and ordinarily would not have been eaten,
> but under the circumstances we were glad to get what little we did.

That was the only commodity of Red Cross supplies ever issued by the Japs in any camp in which I was interned on the Railroad or in Java, Burma or Thailand.[7]

According to a report prepared in 1943 by the Liaison and Research Branch, American Prisoner of War Information Bureau, 50 per cent of the Red Cross supplies sent to Thailand were known to have been kept by the Japanese, and very few reached their destination. Red Cross parcels were usually distributed through the Swiss Consulate in Bangkok. The consul there requested receipts signed by POWs; at first the Japanese complied, but soon informed him that they would not continue to do so. An additional problem for international relief agencies was that the stated policy of the Thai Government indicated it did not recognize the existence of Allied POWs within its borders.

The report also says that "despite repreated requests by 'neutral authorities' (including the Red Cross) the Japanese have categorically refused neutral visits to prisoners 'on the reason of military purpose'"—the main reason being that the building of the Burma Railway was supposed to be a secret project, as well as the fact that they were violating the Geneva conventions by using prisoners of war to construct it.

Corroborating Ernest Gordon's view, the report quotes the Swiss consul as having seen Japanese officers inspecting POW camps at Nonpladuk, where prisoners of healthy appearance had been placed near the railway line for propaganda purposes.[8]

Most unfortunately for the more than 650 American POWs on the Railway, this 1943 report lists just three Americans known to be prisoners in Thailand. It was not until a few Pioneers and other lucky 'Japan Party' survivors were questioned near Brisbane in October 1944, that the world learned about the *USS Houston* survivors, Texas 131st Field Artillery, and other American military personnel who were prisoners there, too.

Cal Mitchell remembered being aware that Red Cross supplies were delivered, through the Swiss, to Tamarkan. They were big cartons, containing medical supplies, clothing, food—even phonographs. Almost everything was kept by the Japanese, he said.

In the Battalion History, Dickson recorded the one occasion at Tamarkan when Red Cross medical supplies were distributed, in May 1944. The shipment included valuable drugs and surgical dressings, he noted, which "Saved the lives of many very sick men."[9] One can only guess at how many more very sick men might have recovered and returned home, had they received the many parcels so carefully packed for them.

Although the indifference of the Japanese to pleas for available medical supplies and food was a source of anger and heartbreak to prisoners, the basis of this attitude can be traced to the Imperial military training code, which teaches that the deprivation of food is an especially good test of how "hardened" one is. The lack of calories is ignored, and the correlation of noruishment to strength is not recognized. Even civilians were expected to accept this teaching; during the war, propaganda on Japanese radio told people in air raid shelters that calisthenics would make hungry people strong and vigorous again.[10]

In view of such daily hardship on the Railway, it is easy to see how acts of kindness, when they occurred, were appreciated. One of the most famous expressions of appreciation took place at the Tokyo War Crimes Trials, when a British officer, David Boyle, testified *on behalf of* Teruo Saito, who was adjutant to the Commandant at a POW camp, and who had been sentenced to death, along with the Commandant. Boyle confirmed that Saito had done everything in his power to ameliorate conditions for POWs, and as a result of Boyle's statement, Saito was spared.[11]

Saito was probably just as astounded at Boyle's appearance as Takashi Nagase was to witness Captain White and several other Australians in September 1945, rushing to greet a Japanese lance corporal at Niki railroad station, with smiles and handshakes. They presented him with cigarettes and some precious tins of food; then Capt. White explained to Nagase: "[The corporal] was very kind to us. He often gave us cigarettes and told us jokes . . . in those days, our only pleasure was to go out [on a work party] with him."[12]

The scene witnessed by Nagase is somewhat reminiscent of the gesture of gratitude displayed by Bill Mayne and fellow POWs in Japan, toward the elderly civilian who had been kind to them in the factory (see Chapter 8).

Gordon Jamieson recounted the story told by a fellow member of the Ex-POW Association of Australia, an airman who was captured in Java:

His Commandant was a very harsh person, a high-ranking naval person who was demoted to his position [as a POW camp commandant] due to the loss of his ship. He was very harsh until he heard of the event, following the [Japanese] midget sub attack on Sydney Harbour on the 31st of May, 1942. The Australian Government honoured the dead Japanese sub-mariners with a

Military funeral and sent their ashes back to Japan in the midst of war. The story is that the Commandant, on hearing this news, paraded the POWs and informed them of the gesture of the Australian Government, and from that time, he became lenient in his behaviour towards them. Unfortunately, this was short-lived due to the [fact that] most of the inmates [were] shipped for work on the Burma-Thai Railway, where they met with very harsh conditions.[13]

As time went on, POWs noticed that the Japanese were capable of great brutality and indifference to their own ranks, as well as to prisoners. Never was this more apparent than toward the end of the war, when the Japanese military units were in disarray; and with capitulation imminent, POWs were being moved about as well. Trainloads of POWs would be alongside trainloads of sick and wounded Japanese soldiers, to whom no apparent care had been given. Several ex-POWs described scenes like the one Ron Winning remembered: "Towards the end of the war, all POWs were transferred to camps north of Bangkok. Our train was stopped by a bombed bridge and a trainload of wounded Japs pulled in alongside us. They had no food and begged water from us to drink. They had been over a month coming from Burma. Five corpses were pulled out in the morning."[14]

Ernest Gordon told about encountering a similar scene, possibly even the same trainload:

The wounded men looked at us forlornly as they sat with their heads resting against the carriages, waiting fatalistically for death. They were the refuse of war; there was nowhere to go and no one to care for them. These were the enemy, more cowed and defeated than we had ever been.

Without a word, most of the officers in my section unbuckled their packs, took out part of their ration and a rag or two, and, with water canteens in their hands went over to the Japanese train to help them. Our guards tried to prevent us, bawling, 'No goodka! No goodka!' But we ignored them and knelt by the side of the enemy to give them food and water, to clean and bind up their wounds, to smile and say a kind word. Grateful cries of 'Aragatto!' ('Thank you!') followed when we left.[15]

In view of how Korean guards were remembered for their brutality, Harry Whelan's anecdote is all the more remarkable:

> The Japanese disarmed and refused to feed a number of Korean members of the Japanese army, who had acted as guards in prison camps. They were desperate, as the local Thai population would have nothing to do with them. The Koreans appealed to Sergeant-Major Edkins [at Tamuan camp] for help. He offered to put them under the protection of the British Crown, provided they were prepared to work and to cause no trouble. They accepted with gratitude and shared our rations.[16]

And perhaps most remarkable of all is Kevin Nolan's story about kindness toward a particular guard who had been known for his viciousness to POWs:

> Most of the guards we had along the line had nicknames, some of which were 'Gold Tooth' (had a gold-capped tooth); 'Silver Tooth' (two prominent amalgam fillings); 'the Boy Bastard' (baby-faced); and 'The B.B.C.' (Boy Bastard's Cobber, or pal). These were four of the most vicious specimens.
>
> Late in the war [again, possibly in that same trainload described above] Silver Tooth was found among a trainload of sick and wounded Japs and Koreans. He was very emaciated, sick with dysentery, and malaria to the point where he could barely stand. Sgt. Hal Saddler, who had good reason to hate him, with aid of a friend, lifted him off the train, cleaned him by a roadside pool, gave him a banana and settled him back on the train. This was one of several cases of men not seeking 'a tooth for a tooth', refusing to sink to the level of the opposition.[17]

But the guard Cecil Dickson remembered best was one who found a subtle and very meaningful way to lift the POWs' spirits, during the darkest days of Railway work. A guard would have direct responsibility for a certain number of prisoners along the line; the same guard might be assigned to one work party every few days. Dickson and his friends noticed that whenever this particular guard was in charge of their group, he was especially easy on them, making sure they had regular breaks, and time for a cigarette or a sip of water.

Communication was strictly forbidden by the supervising engineers, and a guard could be punished just as severely as a POW for breaking this rule. One day, however, the guard, without making eye contact with any of the POWs, began whistling a tune, softly. After he repeated the refrain a couple of times, several Dutch, Australian, British and American POWs looked up at one another, exchanging glances of recognition. The tune the guard was whistling had been written especially for the 1937 International Boy Scout Jamboree, for which 28,000 Scouts from 54 countries, including Japan, had gathered—in the Netherlands! Apparently the guard was among them, and he correctly guessed, from their ages, that some of the POWs might have been there, too. His reminder of international brotherhood gave that handful of prisoners a bucket full of hope to carry back to camp on that day.[18]

15

Free to Shake
the Shackles

O ctober 3, 1945: In what was to be his final letter from a Southeast Asian address, Dickson allowed himself a wonderful thought: he may celebrate his birthday, in just three days, by leaving for home! He even celebrated the thought of not having to skimp on paper any more, by indenting paragraphs.

This letter opens with an abbreviation of the Crusader's forward cry: "D.V.W.P. [Divine Will Providing]. We prevail."

Chinese Chamber of Commerce
Bankok, Siam
October 3, 1945

Dear old Binks,

D.V.W.P. I look like celebrating October 6 by leaving Bankok for home. According to Major Kerr, the camp commandant, that date will see the closing down of this 'camp' and we shall then be free to shake off the shackles of the East. Singapore is about 6 hours by air from here. What the rate of progress will be after arriving there remains to be seen. If by air, which I believe is a possibility, it will be a matter of days; if by boat a couple of weeks—say three at the most. So it looks as if, whichever way we travel, this is the month! Our 19th anniversary passed uneventfully until the evening, when I went to the Alliance Française dance. Despite the worries of Madame ——, President of the Alliance, it was a great success. The beginning was unpromising. About 7:30 rain began, and continued for 2 hours. A few minutes after the rain set in, the electric light failed, and remained blacked out for an hour. The bus to bring the English nurses and VAD's {auxiliary volunteers} had disappeared, and Madame's two chief assistants were nowhere to be found. When we left here by truck she was

153

here in her car. When we reached the Alliance she was at the top of the stairs receiving the guests. She flew about like a streak of lightning, never sitting in the one place for more than three seconds. Then everything came good. I believe that Madame even influenced the ending of the rain and the restoration of the city's electricity supply. She is the English wife of a Frenchman, and has done a tremendous amount for the ex-P.Ws. One of her greatest achievements last night was to get yours Truly to dance, twice.

Was just called to the telephone. Ron Winning reporting that he was leaving for the aerodrome. Our daily useful {servant} placed my boots in position and gave them the final polish, and off I went round to the Oriental to say good-bye and relieve Ron of his final few hundred ticals, which would be of no use to him once he left here. A later word from the C.O. re: the move is that we leave here for the aerodrome at 11 a.m. on the 5th and fly to Singapore on the 6th. That, he says, makes us too late for the next ship, which is due to leave there on the 6th. So the last party, 75 of us, he says, will fly straight on to Australia. We'll see!

To return to the dance—despite Madame's whirlwind personality, the undoubted pièce de résistance of the evening was Lady Louis Mountbatten's chief-of-staff, who is here carrying on the good work while Lady L. is in Batavia. She is 6 feet high, about 30, and a good looker. The RSM {Regimental Sergeant Major} here (Sunny Lay), Peter Cutter (Pioneer Sgt.) and I had half an hour's chat with her after the guests departed. She has been all over the place with Lady L., including Russia. One result of the talk was that a consignment of Cadbury's chocolate has already reached here and been distributed.

I do not remember mentioning that I went to 7 o'clock Communion last Sunday morning at Christ Church, Sathorn Road. The inside differed not the least from a parish church at home, about the size of Christ Church, Hawthorn, except that instead of gothic windows in the side walls there were gothic doors, all of which stood wide open, letting in the fresh morning air. A plate inside the church records the fact that the site was given by King Chulalongkorn on condition that it should be used by all Protestant Christians, irrespective of nationality or creed.

Well, old girl, this might be the last letter from overseas, and furthermore I might even beat it home. You can guess how I have been looking forward to and longing for the great day. Now it's coming close I can't realise it. The sight of the old Missus again will do the trick!

Cheerio

Pop

Article 108 of the third Geneva Convention provides that a prisoner is to have "Whatever spiritual assistance he desires." It appears that the Japanese started out with a willingness to allow services of worship on a regular basis in Java, but soon found an excuse to ban them. The excuse was that POWs were being uncooperative about following instructions to sign a pledge saying, among other things, that they would not attempt to escape. Even after the commanding officers reluctantly ordered troops to do so (on American Independence Day, July 4, 1942), the privilege was not restored.

Cal Mitchell wryly reflected on the result of this ban: "If ever the churches want to have maximum attendance, they should declare churches out of bounds on Sunday." He noted that on the Sunday following the Japanese announcement that henceforth church parades would be prohibited, "Instead of about 100 turning up as usual, hundreds turned up; many of them no doubt had never attended church voluntarily in their lives."1

The chaplain to the Pioneer Battalion, the Reverend Frank Kellow, an Anglican priest, was captured with the unit on Java, and remained with them all during construction of the Railway. He is always referred to as 'Padre', and his presence among POWs of all units meant a great deal, as many accounts attest.

Mitchell chronicles the various efforts to meet spiritual needs in the camps—always at the whim of whoever happened to be their commandant at a particular site:

In so far as regular services go, whenever we were in a settled camp, services would be held, but on the Railway of course only brief Communion services could be arranged. It basically depended on the Japanese commander at the time. On the Burma side of the Railway there were a number of chaplains, with the exception of the Group 5 force, which my brother Alan was in. This was the force commanded by Colonel [Blucher] Tharp who commanded the American [131st Texas] Artillery unity in Java. They had a very bad time. Their doctor, Captain Lumpkin died and they had a particularly vicious Japanese commander. There was no chaplain with the force. We had two brothers whose name was Hovenden; Bernie, who was a sergeant with our force, and his brother whose Christian name escapes me. They were Methodists, I think, not that this mattered at all, since all services were ecumenical. Bernie's brother, after working on the Railway would, when he returned to camp, perform the duties of the chaplain with hospital visiting, burials and other acts of Christian charity. These acts were of course a great strain on him, and he eventually died.

After we had finished the Railway we moved to Tamarkan. Services were held weekly, but when the movement of officers from the other ranks took place in early 1945, the officers were moved to Kanburi where the commandant was a sadistic psychopath. Any group of more than six people standing together was making plans to escape [in his view] and were punished. This led to clandestine meetings for services. Before we reached Kanburi, we had lost Frank [Padre Kellow], who had been selected to go on one of the Japan Parties. We were fortunate to have other good men including our two Royal Australian Navy chaplains.

[Generally] no religious services were permitted in the camps.

This would depend on a general direction by the Japanese Camp commandant, or the passing whim of one of the guards who, possibly becoming bored, would decide on some action to either silence the tedium, or just to show his superiority.

I am only too happy to tell you more about Padre Kellow, whom I looked upon as a good friend. Frank was a very fine man, who had until he injured his knee, been a top sportsman, playing football and cricket at high levels. Frank was second wicket keeper for Victoria, (somewhat akin to the catcher on a baseball team.)

He had a little parish in a tiny country town in the northeast of Victoria. The name of the town was Corryong. He enlisted from there.

When Frank was posted as chaplain to our unit in 1940, he was dubbed 'Pearly Gates' by some of the irreverent young officers, and to us he remained 'Pearly' from then on. I think he rather enjoyed it. It became so commonly used that when Jean [Mrs. Mitchell] first met Bettye [Mrs. Kellow], she said, 'How are you, Mrs. Gates?'

On the Railway, Frank was a tower of strength. In the early days, Frank built a small chapel, open air, rails to sit on and a Communion rail. However, after our move to the actual rail laying force, there were no more chapels built. Frank spent his time going out with the work force initially, until the number of sick in the camp took up his full time. He ministered to the sick and he buried the dead.

One task he took upon himself to do was the erection of crosses on the graves. These were made of quite solid wood, to try and make sure they would not rot away. He carved the names on the crosses when possible and when time permitted.

Whenever possible he gave communion to small groups. I recall in the 131 Kilo camp there was a thicket. Frank waited in the thicket with a small silver chalice which he carried, and we went in one at a time, to avoid suspicion. My memory does not recall the wine! But the bread was pieces of burnt rice. The wine was probably a mixture of burnt rice and hot water, which produced something we called coffee. Naturally, Frank's chalice held cold coffee.

Frank was very direct, and could never be described as a 'Holy Joe'! He had volunteered to go with the Japan Parties, but in view of the horrible loss of life to those parties [from torpedoes], his group was still in Saigon when the war ended. After the war Frank served as the chaplain [Anglican] at the Heidelberg Repatriation Hospital.

Frank baptised both our children; he also performed the marriage ceremony for my brother Alan's wedding. [He] never missed a reunion until near the end of his life, when he became very crippled. He died around 1982.

It has given me much pleasure to write about him.[2]

Driver Thomas Fagan, who did not survive captivity, kept a detailed diary, which was kept by his friends, and given to his family after liberation. On October 2, 1943, he wrote:

I must pay homage to our respective Padres. It is not only what they say and how they say it, but what they do. They give as much physical help as they do spiritual. They are universally appreciated. They hold services in the various huts and it matters little whether one is a Church of England, a Catholic or Methodist, or whatever. The denomination is of little concern. We all join in and pray not only for ourselves, mainly for our loved ones waiting back home.[3]

Earlier that same year, on June 10, 1943, Fagan wrote: "Many exist, I am sure, purely on the power of prayer and a determination to make it, no matter what they may have to suffer to be alive when this war is over. I, for one, have my faith and my religion."[4]

One of the most memorable settings for being reminded of the strength which one's faith provides, was described to Benjamin Dunn by another American ex-POW, Gene Stevens, a survivor from the *USS Houston.* Stevens told of an incident which happened in the jungle of Thailand:

It was on one of those forced marches at night, during the rainy season,

and most of the men were sick, hungry, tired and almost without hope.
As the men were being prodded by the Japs after a rest period to
continue with their march, the place was as quiet as a tomb, when
a Scotsman began singing a hymn, 'The Old Rugged Cross', in a
beautiful voice. Everyone stood perfectly still, and the only sound we
could hear was the hymn. Tears ran down my cheeks, and the men
near me were crying. I have never heard anyone sing 'The Old Rugged
Cross' like that Scotsman did. I'll never forget that as long as I live.[5]

Although not labelled as such, it was the ministry of one man to another
which made the most enduring memories. Gordon Hamilton remembered the
special ministries of Cecil Dickson and fellow Pioneers: "Without the compan-
ionship and encouragement of Cec, together with Pearse McCarthy and Wally
Summons, who visited me in the 'Death House' at the 30 Kilo camp, I do not
think I would have survived those very dark days of 1943. One or the other of
them visited every day, and I cannot say how sustaining they were."[6]

Ernest Gordon told of lying in a similar "Death House," and being ministered
to by fellow POWs, some of whom he had not known before—and whose caring
and coaxing gave Gordon a renewed will to live, when he had all but lost it.[7]

And Ronald Searle credits "A bunch of cheerful Australians and two Dutch
officers, all of whom were still in rather a mess themselves", with nursing him
back to health in the hospital hut at Kanchanaburi. "They nursed me, spent
their money on eggs and extras from the natives for me, washed me and, of all
unlikely things, procured some sulphur drugs from somewhere for me. Anything was possible for the Australians—even the impossible. They saved my life
and got me back on my bare feet again."[8]

Whether they were conscious of it or not, these men were practicing the one
new commandment of their faith "That you love one another as I have loved
you."[9] In so doing, they gave the Japanese an image that some would never forget. Henry Shigeru Yagake, the former Japanese Air Force officer who finally
asked POWs about their cheerful outlook (see Chapter 12), reflected further on
how much he admired their spirit: "They displayed not a scintilla of bitterness
nor poor spirit", he wrote. "They encouraged each other to act happy even when
they faced difficulties, were sad, mortified, or felt down and out. I noticed all
that. They had splendid character. They did not acquire that trait from some
others, but had learned [it] personally from trying to stay alive."[10]

That so many succeeded, is a tribute to all.

16

We're Well On the Way!

O ctober 24, 1945: It was 11 a.m. on a beautiful Sunday morning aboard the troopship *Circassia,* 1200 miles from the Equator, and steaming for home at last. Apparently the *Circassia* waited for Dickson and his party of 75 to reach Singapore; this is the last ship out, laden with recovered POWs, combat troops and civilians. Only a hospital ship arrived in Australia later than this one.

Despite his constant laments in his previous fifteen letters about how long it was taking for him to arrange passage home, Dickson's brother John revealed in a 1994 conversation that Cecil actually relinquished his place on some earlier transports in order to remain in Bangkok, hoping to help write journalism's biggest story of the year: the recovery of Japan's captives.

Possibly unbeknownst to one another, Dickson and his good friends Ron Winning and Gordon Hamilton, along with 514 other recovered POWs, were on the same ship. No doubt Winning and Hamilton were billeted with other officers; Dickson good-naturedly points out in his letter that he and other sergeants were "bumped" from their quarters by civilians, so they were crowded in with the troops. But he cheerfully notes that there is a pleasant group at his table at mealtime.

Dickson used real ink, and tissue-thin airmail stationery emblazoned with the Salvation Army shield, the six-sided Australian Comforts Fund star, and the inverted triangle of the YMCA. In the upper right-hand corner, he sketched a map, showing how the ship had rounded the northern tip of Sumatra and crossed the Equator, headed first for (he believed) Fremantle, then Melbourne, and finally Sydney. He expected to post this letter at the first stop (which turned out to be Perth), and did so; the carefully-preserved envelope shows that it passed through the Melbourne post office on October 31 at 9: 30 p.m.

His jaunty mood is reflected in the way Dickson refers to the Pioneers as 'The 2/2 Famous Famous', and he is happy to be with others of his unit as they sail closer to what he terms, only half in jest, as 'This new country.'

159

Not only did he have to re-open the envelope to postscript the very important estimated date of arrival in Melbourne—but he completely forgot to mention the name of the ship (causing much microfilm searching by a certain researcher, several decades later).

Dear old Binks,

That's where we are at 11 a.m. Sunday, 24 Oct. So we're well on the way. Expect to berth at Fremantle sometime in the dark of Tuesday night, & there I shall put this on the airmail—if they have such modern innovations in this new country we're rapidly approaching. Well—not so very rapidly, but not bad—15 knots, or 400 miles (approx.) a day. I don't expect to feel really excited about it until I actually sight you on the wharf at Port Melbourne, or Victoria dock, or wherever it will be. We embarked about 10 a.m. on Monday, 15th, and, contrary to expectations, sailed the same day about 3: 30 p.m. Turned north-west up Malacca Strait (between Java and Sumatra), where at Oosthaven, on 15 Feb. 1942, we nearly landed to defend Palambay aerodrome, but were too late and returned to the ship. On Wednesday morning we rounded the top of Sumatra and headed for home. The weather has been very good—fair breeze and easy swell—and as the result of a good run we are actually some hours ahead of schedule. We are carrying a number of civilians, who are occupying the space that would otherwise have been allotted to the sergeants, who therefore are living & eating on the troop decks with the men. I am in a small mess of 7, a good crew, including a fellow sgt. of the 2/2 Famous Famous, (Arthur Gordon), a sailor (ex 'Perth') and the rest Malay volunteers. Quite uneventful.

Very much love to you old darling.

Pop

P.S. After sealing down the envelope it occurred to me that I had omitted one of the most important items. We are due to arrive in Melbourne about Wednesday, 31st Oct. Won't it be fun!

Ron Winning remembered some shipboard details before the *Circassia* reached Melbourne:

It was a very relaxing trip to Perth; weather good, and the knowledge that we would soon be home was wonderful. We reached Perth, and were able to phone our families. After a day in Perth we sailed again. However, there was a tragedy. One of the men [see below] phoned home and was told his wife had formed a liaison with another man. After we sailed, he slipped over the side. He wasn't missed for awhile. The ship hove to, but [the] search was hopeless. After all he had been through![1]

In a front-page article in its Monday, November 5, 1945 edition, the Melbourne *Sun* refers to the incident mentioned by Winning, but apparently the ex-POW's friends were not quite so forthcoming with newspaper reporters at the time. The story says: "When only two days from home after being a prisoner of war for more than four years, Private F.B. Coughlin, married, of Kew, was missing from the *Circassia*. The ship stopped and a vain search carried out for more than an hour in the dusk. Friends of Pte. Coughlin said he had been suffering from malaria and the effects of ill-treatment by the Japanese."[2]

Possibly because of the delay in searching for the missing man, the *Circassia* sat in Port Melbourne Harbor during the night of November 2, and did not dock until the following morning. Tom O'Brien remembers how "We sat up all night, looking at the lights of home. No one slept."[3]

Ex-POWs on deck of Highland Brigade *bound for Australia, October 1945. Mitchell brothers Cal* (hatless, balding head, arrow, right) *and Alan* (arrow, near centre background) *are coming home together at last.*
(COURTESY OF C.J. MITCHELL)

The next morning, Ron Winning said, "We sailed through the Heads into Port Phillip Bay and were welcomed by an escort of small ships and yachts."

Cal Mitchell, who arrived October 23 on the *Highland Brigade,* noted the universal welcome troopships received in Australia: "As the ship came up Port Phillip Bay, we saw the words 'Welcome Home' printed in huge letters on the roof of the sheds of the wharf."

The *Sun's account* added this detail: "As the *Circassia* berthed in front of the [British battleship] *King George V,* two banners were seen on the rail. One bore the inscription: 'Salute to [General H. Gordon] Bennett'; and alongside it, one showing a bowler hat with the words: 'A Soldier's Reward.' Sailors on the battleship turned out on deck to welcome the returning prisoners."

Each shipload was met on the wharf by a fleet of buses and driven through Melbourne. According to the *Sun,* the route took them via Bay Street, City Road, Swanston, Queensberry and Elizabeth Streets, Flemington Road and Racecourse Road, to the Agricultural Hall Showgrounds, where relatives had been assembled to greet them. The itinerary was announced because citizens were encouraged to greet each shipload of troops as they returned.

And indeed they did. Mitchell remembered one incident: "As we were being driven through the city, through crowds of cheering people, our bus stopped outside of Town Hall and I vividly recall a very well dressed lady wearing quite magnificent silver earrings running from the crowd and with tears streaming down her face, [she] gave me a beautiful kiss. Perhaps she had lost someone. I was leaning out the window at the time.I found my people and it was a wonderful moment. Cars or taxis were provided to take us home."[4]

Possibly Mitchell's face, with his jaunty smile and thin moustache, reminded the woman in the crowd of a loved one who had not returned; and when she spotted Mitchell, she determined to give out the welcome-home kiss she had saved for so long.

Eileen Mitchell's reunion with her fiancé, Cal's brother Alan, reads as well as any romance novel:

> Of course, the day of home-coming, was perhaps the most wonderful day of my life—though we were married six days after. We had planned in our letters from Bangkok the way we would meet. He hoped we would be all alone. I pictured he would get off a train and walk towards me, and I would hurry to him.
>
> What actually happened was that hundreds of soldiers were unloaded from buses at the Showgrounds in Flemington and we all

milled about in confusion till we bumped into the one we were
seeking. The first moment was his huge dark eyes and gaunt face.

We had such a frantic six days before our wedding that the memory
of what he felt is a blur. He must have felt strange and unreal, but
seemed his own delightful, thoughtful self that I took everything
for granted.

I know I failed to grasp what he had suffered and the horrors he
had been through. Jim was born in August '46 and the two little
girls quickly, so that our life was a rush.

There was a school of thought that the men should not be
reminded of their experiences. I am glad that I understood things
better as the years went by.[5]

The stages of Kevin Nolan's journey home could not be outdone by Hollywood:

When I finally got to Singapore, I was given a cake of soap, a big
fluffy towel and directed to a battery of hot showers. Whilst
luxuriating under the hot water, my delight turned to ecstacy when
over the Public Address system came the voice of a prewar favorite of
mine, John Charles Thomas, singing 'the Lord's Prayer.' My reaction
was to think to myself: 'This has *got* to be heaven.'

Later that day, after much searching, I located four letters from my
beloved. She had waited all those years. The war was over and life was
about to begin!

I embarked from Singapore on the *Moreton Bay,* headed for
Fremantle, where one of the joys of leave was the allowance of a direct
phone link to Victoria. I got through to Marj, and we spoke to each
other for the first time in four and a half years—and all we could
manage to exchange were banalities such as: 'How are you, Darling?
Yes, I'm fine thanks. You are well? That's good. No really, I'm in good
shape. See you soon.' Couldn't think of anything intelligent to say! A
few days later, we were reunited on the 31st of October, 1945, and
had no trouble carrying on from where we had left off, so long ago.
We married and settled on a mixed farm in western Victoria and
raised, among other things, four very nice children.[6]

As mentioned earlier, Dickson did not recognize his wife for several minutes
after she first approached him. For Tom O'Brien, the memory of reunion with
his loved ones was still an overwhelming reminder of all the family years he lost:

"I had been away five years [including the time in Syria]—and this lovely young woman came up and threw her arms around me. I didn't know who she was. It was my younger sister. She had been a child when I left, just about 13 years old. While I was gone, she had grown into a young woman. I recognized my older sister, of course—but I didn't even recognize my own sister." He turned away, unable to finish the sentence.[7]

As for Dickson, all his hints, requests and reminders in letters home during the previous two months paid off. Freda came to meet him unaccompanied by other relatives, and the quiet cottage in Queenscliff she had booked for an extended stay, was not the scene of family reunions for several weeks.

Time enough to again hear English spoken all day in complete sentences, and in a recognized accent; to slip into a familiar jacket and select a favorite necktie; to sit outdoors in comfortable shade with a minimum of winged pests; to savor favorite brands each day, from toothpaste to tea; to gaze at the stars each night, without longing; to share silence with a beloved; to make your own plans, and know that tomorrow will come.

Freda and Cecil Dickson, ca. 1946, planting a tree in their yard as they resume life together. (PHOTO COURTESY OF SUSAN GROSS)

17

Lost and Found

*C*ould anything more have been done to ease the suffering of POWs on the Railway? And why were the Japanese so brutal to their white captives?

In terms of the day-to-day treatment of prisoners on the Railway by the Japanese and their Korean conscripts, as to whether anything might have been done to ease their suffering, the sad answer is: probably not, given the mind-set and training of camp staff.

At the very end of his book, *Crosses and Tigers,* Japanese military police interpreter Takashi Nagase says, "No Japanese soldiers were taught about the treatment of prisoners."[1] He goes on to quote Japanese camp staff personnel who were convicted of war crimes as grumbling about this lack of instruction from their superiors.

A documentary shown on American television in the summer of 1992 suggests that the mind-set within Japan, regarding prisoners—has not changed much in the last 60 years. On the ABC program, '20/20', viewers were shocked to see scenes of Japanese civilian prisoners being routinely subjected to terrific beatings, while in jail awaiting trial. The reason given: just being suspected of criminal behavior in Japan is taken very, very seriously, and is cause for punishment, regardless of the disposition of the case.

Similarly, TV and newspaper accounts of stories about rigorous enforcement of rules in Japanese schools are a disturbing echo of prison camp life, where the punishment far exceeded the degree of infraction. Shock waves reverberated throughout Japan and the world in July 1990, when a high school girl was crushed by an iron gate being slammed shut by a teacher, as the final 8:30 a.m. bell was sounding.[2]

And the following year, debate was renewed in Japan over, as the *New York Times* phrased it, "The near-obsession of some school authorities in enforcing rules", in an article describing how two teenagers, at a private institution for troubled children, were put to death after being caught smoking in violation of school rules. The youngsters, a 14-year-old boy and a 16-year-old girl, were placed in a windowless shed, similar to the 'hot box' used for discipline in some prison camps. After 45 hours in temperatures as high as 122°, the children died. The school's principal was arrested, but no mention was made in the article, or in a subsequent CBS News story on the incident, of what action, if any, the children's parents planned to take.[3]

Such incidents tend, of course, to reinforce the belief echoed by many ex-POWs in interviews and correspondence, who say: "I just don't trust them".

Reinforcing that lack of trust has been the 1997 revelation that the governments of the United States, the United Kingdom and The Netherlands did, indeed, try to do more to ease the suffering of their citizens in Japanese captivity, in the form of a very secret relief fund, initially targeting especially the Railway POWs, to be administered through the many Southeast Asian branches of the Swiss National Bank. In 1997, three years after the first edition of this book was published, the United States National Security Agency declassified several hundred Japanese military and diplomatic messages which had been intercepted by Allied intelligence specialists during World War II. Among those messages was a November 13, 1944 cable from Japan's Foreign Minister, Mamoru Shigemitsu, to his envoy in Saigon, detailing exactly how the fund had been set up, and urging that disbursements be made without delay. This writer was the first to report not only the existence of the fund, but more importantly, what happened to the money, and why the millions their governments contributed for food, medicine and clothing never reached the suffering military and civilian captives throughout the Japanese Empire.

In short, the government of Japan broke its written agreement with the Swiss government (which was to administer the fund through its bank). Instead, the Japanese government ordered its official bank to hoard the money and not release it. And in a move which even the Nazis did not dare to make, the Japanese government cut off communication between Swiss Red Cross workers and their headquarters in Geneva, in early 1944. For the remainder of the war, the ICRC had no idea of how few supplies were reaching the captives, or even where its workers were—or whether they were safe. Many were not: as its war effort worsened, the Japanese military began to accuse Swiss workers of being spies for the Allies. Some were jailed; one Swiss woman died in a Tokyo prison. In the most extreme instance, the ICRC delegate to Borneo, Dr. Matthaus Vischer, was imprisoned, with his wife; both were tortured and beheaded in December 1943, along with their three children.

When the remainder of this huge relief fund, which eventually totalled 98 million Swiss francs, was discovered postwar (some two million Swiss francs were unaccounted for), the Japanese government apparently got off with a slap on the wrist. In a provision under Article 19 of the 1951 Treaty of Peace between the Allied governments and Japan, the balance of the funds was turned over to the International Committee of the Red Cross, for distribution on a pro-rata basis to those Allied nations whose military personnel had suffered in Japanese captivity, for their postwar comfort. The British government retrieved most of its contributed funds in July 1952, but did not distribute them to its ex-POWs (causing considerable outrage in 1997, when the facts became known). The United States, which had contributed $6.2 million (worth about $55 million in 2007 dollars), declined to take its share, for reasons which remain unclear. [For a detailed account of the secret relief fund and its disbursement, see Holmes, *Unjust Enrichment,* Chapter 11].

The fund was not turned over to the ICRC until 1955, and it took a further three years before the agency was able to begin distribution, owing primarily to delay by the government of India in providing an estimate of how many military personnel from that nation were affected. Australia, Great Britain, the United States and The Netherlands were able to provide figures rather promptly, due to more efficient record-keeping.

Nevertheless, the delay in payments, and the paucity in final amounts of distribution, caused extreme frustration to Colonel Williams, who was at that time President of the New South Wales Ex-Prisoner of War Association. Finally, in early 1958, it was announced that each former prisoner of the Japanese would receive a grand total of £ 86 [a little over $100 US equivalent], and the Government of Australia stated: "It is not expected that further funds will become available to enable additional payments to be made."

A vexing footnote to this most egregious act of the Japanese wartime government—is that at the suggestion of the ICRC, civilians who had suffered in Japanese captivity were not included in the disbursement of these funds because, Red Cross officials pointed out, military personnel had verifiable identification (serial) numbers, while civilians did not. So the thousands of Australian, British, Dutch and American civilians who had watched so many family members starve and die in Japanese captivity, got not a penny postwar—even though some of the relief money was originally earmarked by their governments for their benefit.[4]

Sitting in Margaret Dickson's living room in 1991 at the War Veterans's Village in Narrabeen, New South Wales, Harry Whelan reflected softly: "They'd do the same thing, if they had the chance." Gazing out the window, he added: "Let's hope they don't get the chance." Then, with a laugh which may have come easily to someone in his ninth decade, Whelan slapped his knee and exclaimed: "At least not in our lifetime, eh, Margaret?"

Whelan and his fellow ex-POWs might be surprised to learn that many Japanese agreed with them. Intense pressure was put on Japan by the United Nations, led by the United States, to contribute not only more money, but troops as well, to the peacekeeping forces in the Persian Gulf War during 1990–91. But the Japanese government, in keeping with its Constitution, steadfastly refused to deploy troops overseas at that time, while heated public debate took place.

Continuing diplomatic and political pressure by other world powers resulted in a reluctant 1992 agreement by the Japanese Diet [Parliament] to allow military personnel to serve under United Nations command, with a special vote necessary for each deployment. But a member of the Japanese Diet [Parliament], Masao Kunihiro, may have spoken for many Japanese, other Asian nations, and ex-POWs as well, when he told some Americans: "I know the day will come when you will regret it."[5] Similar reluctant votes occurred in the Diet when Japan agreed, under United States pressure, to send a token military force to Iraq in 2003.

Jay N. Woodworth, a New York banker who has made over 60 business trips to Japan and other Asian countries in recent years, reports that many Japanese have stressed to him that the continued presence of United States troops on their soil provides them with security against a resurgence of military power in their nation. Moreover, he agreed with Takashi Nagase that the Yasukuni Shrine, where Imperial War Minister Hideki Tojo is buried along with many other military leaders—is a disturbing reminder of the militarism which is still just below the surface in Japan.[6] Continuing visits by high Japanese officials to the shrine has exacerbated that perception, and causes ongoing resentment, particularly within nations like China and Korea which still harbor smoldering resentment about Japanese occupation of their nations during the 1930s and 1940s, prompting the often asked question:

Can the Japanese move toward a national understanding of their full role in World War II? And will remorse ever be part of the national psyche, as it is in Germany?

The Reverend Yuri Ando, pastor of the United Japanese Church of Westchester, an interdenominational Christian congregation which meets in Scarsdale, just north of New York City, sums up what she sees as the prevailing current sentiment among her countrymen: "When you have a victim mentality, you have no room in your heart to see the sorrows of those who suffered at the hands of the Japanese."[7]

Pastor Ando commented: "My parents lost their childhood", and said her mother still had nightmares about walking to work and crouching against a wall during air raids. Her father, who volunteered to be a language teacher in the Philippines rather than serve in the Japanese army, was nevertheless terrified to surrender to US troops when ordered to do so in August 1945. He had seen how the Japanese treated civilian prisoners, and he was sure American soldiers would do the same, so he fled into the hills. After living on snakes and lizards, and contracting malaria (a familiar scenario to Railway POWs), he finally turned himself in, and was astounded to be given chocolate and cigarettes, as well as spiritual comfort by a US Army chaplain, with whom he still kept in touch, half a century later.

Born in 1954, Pastor Ando said that in Japan, history classes are taught as a chronology, without comment. In fact, "It is not considered polite to interrupt the teacher", added Reiko Sasso, who was educated in Japan a generation earlier than Pastor Ando, and who for several years headed the library at the Japan Society in New York City. Even today, if children ask many questions in class, this is often reason for censure and a parental conference.

Pastor Ando remembered history textbook stories about how the Japanese people suffered during the war, but students usually are not told about prisoners, civilian or military, being taken by the Japanese. Her recollections were substantiated by Ryushi Hara, and his mother, Yasuko. Ryushi was born in Melbourne in 1972, and started school there. He completed elementary and junior high school in Japan (where he was strongly chastised for speaking English), before moving with his family to Scarsdale, New York, completing high school there, and continuing his education at a United States university. Yasuko Hara remembered learning "a little" about World War II, but "It was only a few paragraphs at the end of the textbook." The subject would not be discussed unless the teacher found time to bring it up. By the time her son was in junior high school, he said, the students learned a little more about the war, primarily the important military engagements such as the naval battles of the Coral Sea and

Midway. But, Ryushi confirmed, no mention of Bataan, Corregidor, the Burma Railway, or civilian internees.[8]

Pastor Ando summarized what had until recently been the view of the Japanese Ministry of Education: "If we show that shameful part of our history, then our children will not respect our country." She observed that "Japanese take many things personally, so they would feel personally shamed to learn of the atrocities committed by their troops during World War II."

But the efforts of Michiko Asano of the College Women's Association of Japan, and others concerned with education in that country—have begun to pay off. Up until 1992, a typical textbook in Japan read: "We must not forget that Japan caused inconvenience to neighboring Asian countries in the past." After strong urgings by the Ministry of Education, publishers distributed new textbooks beginning in April 1993 which have altered that same passage to read: "We must not forget that Japan caused unbearable suffering to neighboring nations in the past."[9] Depending on which Japanese officials are in power, the effort to confront Japan's wartime past is a continuing work in progress—or regress.

With the publication of this book, close-up photographs taken secretly, showing emaciated Allied POWs in Japanese camps, are being generally circulated for the first time, and have become part of the permanent POW exhibit at the Australian War Memorial in Canberra. Although some photos like the ones in these pages were shown as evidence in War Crimes Trials in Tokyo, Singapore and other tribunals immediately after World War II, they were not widely distributed, and most have remained in military archives, or in the hands of private collectors or former POWs like Cal Mitchell. For many years it may not have seemed appropriate to release these photos for general viewing; after all, most are taken at quite close range, so that many faces are recognizable. Some POWs shown here did not return. Only those who survived can easily say to children or grandchildren: "Look how skinny I was then!" But for a parent, wife or sweetheart whose loved one is buried in Burma or Thailand, these pictures will never be easy to look at. So Cal Mitchell waited a long time to pass these photographs along; no doubt for many of the same reasons Sir Edward 'Weary' Dunlop expressed in the preface to his *War Diaries* [published in 1986]: "I have shrunk from publishing these diaries for over 40 years. It seemed that they might add further suffering to those bereaved, and add to controversy and hatred."[10]

But eventually the need for an accurate record of history takes precedence over other considerations; and to his credit, Mitchell recognized this. Since nearly all those pictured are Australians, and since a book was being written centering on members of his battalion, he decided to hand them to the author as soon as her plane landed at the airport in Melbourne, in October 1991.

None of the photos in these pages have been retouched or altered in any way. What you see is what was there, in the jungles of Burma and Thailand during those awful years of internment, under what Cecil Dickson referred to so often as "unspeakable" conditions. These photos speak of those conditions as no words can. Some others, such as those taken by Colonel Williams, showing himself and other officers after 30 days of nonstop torture, might have spoken even louder. But those additional prints did not survive being in what the Battalion Commanding Officer called "unexpected places".

There is little question that without the constant reminders afforded by oft-printed photos of Nazi concentration camp inmates, the German public might never have built up the sense of collective shame they have been made to feel about what went on under their very noses, in some cases—or what they turned away from seeing. As a result, a "Never again!" determination still pervades the German conscience, despite increasingly bold neo-Nazi activity in recent times.

But apparently until now the Japanese have had no pictorial reminders of POW internment, in their own country or at other locations. So the textbook alterations mentioned above represent what for many schoolchildren will be a first step in developing a collective awareness and sensitivity to the reasons many Westerners and other Asians still feel such resentment, hostility and bitterness towards them.

Perhaps by the time these children are old enough to travel as tourists to the Australian War Memorial, they will actually visit the POW exhibit there, in contrast to the two busloads of young Japanese seen by this writer, arriving at the War Memorial just fifteen minutes before closing time, and emerging just twelve minutes later to re-board their buses (They stopped to use the lavatories.) It is partly this kind of insensitivity on the part of his countrymen who travel abroad which prompted Takashi Nagase to warn that "Hatred and resentment towards the Japanese are more fierce than the Japanese imagine."[11]

To his family, Cecil Dickson did not display a lingering resentment of the Japanese. When he did mention some aspect of camp conditions, he was likely to add that in the worst locations, "the Japanese had no better."But few of his friends were so sanguine; perhaps in private conversations with them, Dickson acknowledged feelings he was otherwise reluctant to express.

Ron Winning wrote: "I share with Colonel Williams and Cec Dickson an abiding hatred of the Japs."[12]. Leo Cornelius added: "I do not share or understand forgiveness for wanton cruelty and in fact bestiality."[13]

"I do find thinking or talking of our experiences at the hands of the Japanese quite distressing", Gordon Hamilton admitted.[14] Harry Bishop decided that "When you get into the eighties, it's time to relax a bit."[15]

Cal Mitchell picked up on the theme struck by Takashi Nagasi when he observed: "The Japanese are not only buying up [United States] assets; they are busy doing the same thing here [in Australia], although they seem to be very surprised at the ex-servicemen's reaction."[16]

Increasingly, when old World War II wounds are re-opened in their presence, Japanese government officials respond with acknowledgment of their government's involvement, but this is usually a personal, rather than an official government apology. Financial aid to the victims is usually offered by private entities, offending the victims even more.

The United States Government, by an act of Congress in 1988, apologized for the internment of 120,000 Japanese in the US during World War II, and authorized a payment of $20,000.00 to each survivor. The American public was led to believe that Japanese families were uprooted from their homes and gathered into common barracks at "relocation camps" [primarily in remote desert locations of Arizona, Texas and California] because they posed a "security risk" on the Pacific Coast, after Pearl Harbor was attacked. This explanation was plausible, especially to many Americans living along the Atlantic Coast, because German agents had been infiltrating the civilian population there all during the 1930s and early 1940s, with considerable success; numerous U-boat [submarine] sightings were being reported, and even some landings had begun to occur. So the large Japanese population, especially concentrated as it was in California, often near military installations and aircraft factories, was a sudden cause for alarm. By mid-February 1942, President Franklin D. Roosevelt had signed an Executive Order to remove "all persons" from the vicinity of military zones. Although many people were in such zones, only those of Japanese descent were moved—despite the fact that over two thirds were United States citizens by birth. [Japanese immigrants were not allowed to apply for United States citizenship until 1952.]

The official explanation of "national security" for these forced relocations has been perpetuated for over half a century, although the *New York Times,* in a 1992 editorial, termed the policy a "mistaken belief".[17] In retrospect, it is hard to imagine, for those not living on the West Coast of the United States in the first six months of the Pacific War, the daily fear which gripped residents of California, Oregon and Washington as Japanese submarines shelled oil fields in Riverside, California; flashlights could be seen signalling ships at sea from the hillsides of La Jolla; and half the Japanese fleet was heading for our West Coast in June 1942, until it was stopped at the epic Battle of Midway.

However in her meticulously-researched book, *Years of Infamy: The Untold Story of America's Concentration Camps,* published in 1976, Michi Nishiura Weglyn details a different and bizarre reason for the internment of herself, her family and so many others. It was done, she documents, in order to amass hostages to exchange for sick and wounded US military prisoners, as well as the many American civilians who were being held in Japanese -occupied territories. As of June 1942, Ms. Weglyn discovered, the US had precisely one Japanese POW in custody, an airman captured in Pearl Harbor when his plane ditched in shallow water.

So the roundup began, and even third-generation Japanese nationals from as far away as Peru were brought to detention centers in the southwestern United States. Over the next 20 months, nearly 3000 Japanese were exchanged for a comparable number of Americans. But in late 1943, a demonstration over poor living conditions took place at the Tule Lake detention center in California, and it was put down with force. Two Japanese died, and several more were wounded. In protest, Tokyo abruptly halted the exchange of prisoners—ironically, in November 1943, just after the Burma-Thailand Railway had been completed under far worse living conditions, and with such an appalling loss of American and other POW lives—but these details were unknown to the world at that time.

Despite its act of atonement, the US Government under-funded this compensation program, and four years later, many Japanese-Americans were still awaiting their checks.

But four years represents lightning speed, compared to the runaround Australian ex-POWs got from their government following World War II. Citing War Financial Regulations entitling them to a subsistence allowance when the military could not provide meals for them, ex-POWs requested that they be paid three shillings a day for all the meals they literally missed while prisoners of the Japanese. However, a September 26, 1950 government report contains the astounding conclusions that, among other findings, conditions to which Australians were subjected while prisoners was beyond the government's con-

Above: *Pioneers assembling for their first postwar Anzac Day parade, Melbourne, April 1946. Nearly all are ex-POWs. Below left: Pioneers marching, Anzac Day, Melbourne, April 1990. Below centre: Colonel J.M. Williams ready to lead the march, Anzac Day, April 1989.* (PHOTOS COURTESY 2/2 AUSTRALIAN PIONEER BATTALION ASSOCIATION)

trol; and besides, the government had lost the services of its soldiers during their captivity![18]

Worse still, the Australian government ultimately decided that rather than pay direct compensation to its ex-POWs, as the US had done,($1.00 a day for"missed meals" in captivity; and a further $1.50 a day for "pain, suffering and forced labor") payments should be distributed through the International Red Cross, lest the government appear to be setting a 'monetary premium' for soldiers remaining prisoner during future wars![19]

To add insult to injury, the government rejected the requests for subsistence pay or additional compensation for those interned by the Japanese; while acknowledging that conditions for these men had been notably more harsh than any those encountered by prisoners in Europe and the Mideast. Payment would be made, the government determined, from reparation funds from the Japanese government, turned over to the International Committee of the Red Cross (along with the remainder of the secret Allied relief fund); the cash value of Japanese assets frozen in foreign countries; and, finally, proceeds from the sale of the Railway by the Thai government.

After the 1997 revelations about the existence and disbursement of the secret relief fund, the governments of Canada, the United Kingdom, Australia, New Zealand, The Netherlands and the Isle of Man passed legislation granting an *ex gratia* payment of between $20,000 and $24,000 to each surviving ex-POW, in recognition that the Japanese government was not likely to do so in their remaining lifetimes—and also in recognition that in the immediate postwar years, Allied governments whose nationals had suffered in Japanese captivity did not do enough for them. Similar efforts have been made in the United States Congress, but have been thwarted. The Japanese government pays a Washington lobbying firm $60,000 per month just to deal with World War II issues, which may explain why in 2003 and again in 2006, both houses of Congress authorized payments to Pacific War ex-POWs, only to have those authorizations deleted by the House-Senate Conference Committee, reportedly at the request of the White House.

It would be the understatement of the century to say that no payment could begin to compensate prisoners of any nationality for their suffering; for prisoners of the Railway, their best compensation is the triumph which each day since August 16, 1945 has represented. Although each had ample entitlement to revenge, most recognized that in order to have a future, one must let go of the past. For many, their first act of power was choosing *not* to seek revenge. The

moment that each ex-prisoner was able to turn his back on his former tormentors, to dismiss them from his sight, he took back the power over his own life—
which had been denied to him for so long. And each time that a flashback from
captivity fills his mind, he is a prisoner again, if only for a few minutes.

Cecil Dickson took great pride in telling members of his family how he had
greeted a Japanese businessman at the London office of J.B. Were & Co. in the
mid-1950s, only to discover that he was looking into the face of an especially
unpleasant former commandant of one POW camp. Dickson was able to be civil
to the Japanese, and conclude business with the man in a highly professional
manner, to his own everlasting satisfaction and, perhaps, relief.

Not all ex-POWs have had the opportunity to confront their past so directly; and some found, to their dismay, that even a lifetime later they could not do
so with Dickson's aplomb. One former prisoner of the Japanese, a physician who
became a prominent throat specialist in New York City, confided to a friend
that he had always avoided Japanese patients. One day in the late 1980s, he
decided that forty years was surely long enough to get over hs feelings, and he
agreed to see a Japanese businessman who had been referred by a colleague. As
he began to examine the patient, the physician suddenly realized that he was
choking the Japanese who, incidentally, was a total stranger. Chagrined, the
physician released his hold on the patient's throat, turned away, and asked the
man to please put on his shirt and leave the office.

Reflecting on Cecil Dickson's bearing, former United States Navy Chaplain
Peter D. MacLean remarked: "I knew that I was in the presence of someone
who had been to Hell, but Cecil lived very much in the present. By the time I
met him, in the late 1970s, whatever hatred there was in him, had been left
somewhere."[20]

What remained, like gold purified by fire, was a joy in, and reverence for,
life—and the brotherhood shared with his closest friends, most of whom were
fellow Pioneers. Because theirs was mostly a home-town unit, drawing recruits
from the environs of either Melbourne of Sydney, many Pioneers already shared
a familiarity which the crucibles of combat and captivity strengthened into lifelong friendships. The 2/2 Pioneer Battalion Association is still one of the most
active in Australia, now swelling its ranks with second and third-generation
members. All seem to embody the motto of the Ex-POW Association of Australia, in which many are active: "We Honour our Dead By Caring For Our
Living."

The Battalion's commanding officer, by constantly challenging the treatment of his men by the Japanese, earned the title of "No. 1 bad man, Australian" from his captors, and by all accounts he paid dearly for that distinction. Colonel Williams is acknowledged to have been more harshly treated, and with greater frequency, than any other prisoner. Often, after arguing unsuccessfully with Japanese camp officials over the conditions imposed upon the men under his command, Colonel Williams would enforce his own rigorous sanitation measures, driving his exhausted troops to scrub, burn and dig when they arrived at some filthy campsite just vacated by coolie laborers. Some men in his unit deeply resented him for this, until they discovered, after the war, that the Pioneers had just about the lowest death rate on the Railway: of 865 who became POWs, 607 managed to survive. American Railway POWs also had a "good" survival rate: of 668 Americans captured on Java from the *USS Houston*, Texas 131st Field Artillery and California 26th Field Artillery units, 535 survived to come home again.

It would be hard to measure how many lives were sustained with fellowship, or how many final moments were comforted by it, when there was nothing else to give. I had an opportunity to see this spirit at work on one of the final days of my visit to Australia in October 1991, a little over three years after Cecil died. His brother John lay gravely ill in a Melbourne hospital, after two emergency surgeries. Sadly, I realized my long-anticipated meeting with the younger Dickson would not take place after all, and I reluctantly gathered my things together to leave for Sydney and New York. Cal Mitchell was stopping by my hotel for a few minutes; we would sit in the sunlit breakfast room while he identified when and where each captivity photograph had been taken. Typically, Mitchell balanced the grim reality of each scene with a few light anecdotes of camp life, as if the see-saw in his mind could remain level, and not ever quite crash to the ground. He looked at his watch, and as I carefully replaced each photo in the manila envelope, he stood, picked up his hat, and said quietly: "It's my turn to go and sit with John for awhile this morning. You see, in the camps, no one ever died alone."[21]

And then he was off, stepping briskly into the fine Spring morning, making sure the tradition would continue.

Roster of Pioneer Battalion Members

Listed below are the names of 212 Australian Pioneer Battalion members who were ordered to surrender to the Japanese, beginning 8 March 1942, or who were subsequently captured.

Each asterisk indicates a man who died in captivity while trying so hard to live, often knowing his friends were nearby—always knowing he would not be forgotten. All deserve our remembrance and our gratitude for the example they set.

Abbott, Pte E.*
Acheson, Pre A.A.
Adams, Pte D.K.
Adolphson, Pte F.A.*
Adolphson, Pte R.G.
Aggett, Pte T.A.
Aiken, Pte F.C.
Alexander, Pte J.W.
Allardice, L/Cpl M.D.
AlIchin, L/Cpl C.E.*
Allen, Pte E.
Allen, Pte F.A.
Allen, Pte K.E.*
Allen, Lieut R.W.
Allingham, Pte J.F.C.
Altman, Pte J.F.C.
Amoore, Pte J.
Anderson, L/Cpl A.
Anderson, Pte A.W.J.
Anderson, Cpl D.R.
Anderson, Pte W.
Anning, Pte C.C.
Archibald, Pte G.S.
Armstrong, Pte E.B.
Armstrong, Pte W.*
Ashford, Cpl H.*

Atkin, Pte H.
Atkinson, Pte N.H.*
Baade, Pte S.A.
Bacon, Pte F.J.
Bailey, Cpl L.W.
Bailey, Pte M.*
Baines, Pte W.T.
Baker, Pte A.E.
Baker, Pte S.R.
Banfield, Pte A.G.*
Barber, Pte B.*
Barden, Pte W.J.E.
Barker, Pte C.R.
Barlow, Pte JjJ.
Barnes, Pte AJ.
Barnes, Pte F.G.*
Barnes, Pte J.C.
Barnett, Pte E.N.
Barnstable, Pte F.J.
Barrett, L/Cpl K.T.
Barrett, L/Cpl W.J.
Barry, Pte S.R.*
Bateson, L/Cpl N.*
Batten, Pte L.E.*
Batten, Pte W.J.
Battye, Cpl D.H.

Baylis, Pte J.W.
Beadle, Pte AJ.*
Beaument, Pte A.C.
Beecham, Ptc C.E.
Belchambers, Pte P.G.
Bell, Pte CJ.
Benfield, Pte J.M.
Bennett, Pre W.H.
Bergin, Pte E.F.
Beverly, Pte C.W.S.
Biesse, Pte R.C.*
Birkitt-Vipont, Pre S.A.
Bishop, Capt A.H.
Bishop, Pte H.C.S.
Bishop, Pte H.R.
Bishop, Pte W.T.
Black, Sgt H.
Blake, Pte A.E.*
Blake, Pte W.
Bland, pre B.G.
Blyton, Pte H.W.
Bock, Pte E.W.*
Bond, Cpl J.C.*
Boreham, Pte H.E.*
Bould, Pre K.A.*
Bourke, Pte L.J.

Bourne, Pte W.E.*
Bover, Cpl C.F.
Box, Pte RJ.*
Boyd, Pte W.
Boyd, Pte H.W.
Boyes, Pte H.C.*
Brackley, Pte W.E.A.
Bradley, Pte J.J.
Brady, Pre C.*
Bramfitt, Pte A.E.
Bredin, Pte G.H.
Britt, L/Sgt C.W.
Broadhurst, Pte T.B.
Brodribb, Pte J.E.E.*
Broes, Pte J.
Broome, Pte A.L.*
Brown, Pte A.M.*
Brown, Pte L.C.*
Brown, Pte L.D.
Brown, Pte L.G.
Bruce, Cpl J.H.
Buchanan, Pte E.A.D.
Buckland, Pte A.B.
Budge, Pre W.G.*
Buerckner, Pte E.F.
Bulmer, Pre C.F.
Burke, Pte F.J.
Burkitt, Pte AJ.E.
Burns, Pte A.*
Butler, Pre A.F.*
Butler, Pre L.V.*
Cain, Pte K.K.
Cameron, Pte A.
Cameron, Pte I.D.*
Cameron, Pte J.J.*
Camm, L/Cpl A.S.
Camm, Pre R.*
Campbell, Pte D.
Campbell, Capt E.
Campbell, Capt I.A.
Came, Pte W.*
Carpenter, Pte C.A.
Carroll, Pte FJ.
Carroll, Pte G.P.
Carroll, Pte PJ.

Carter, Sgt S.G.
Casey, Pte F.
Cassidy, Pte S.N.
Cavanagh, Pte C.*
Cattanach, Pte SJ.
Chandler, Pte S.P.
Cheeseman, Pte W.H.
Chick, Pte A.V.*
Childs, Pte R.W.
Chivers, Sgt F.A.*
Chivers, Pre H.C.
Christie, Pte CJ.
Christie, Pte D.E.*
Clark, Pte F.
Clark, Pte F.D.
Clark, Pte W.M.*
Clarkson, Pte F.
Cleary, Pte R.
Clement, Pte J.T.L.
Clements, Pte E.G.*
Clifford, Pte V.
Close, Pte V.T.*
Coatsworth, L/Cpl G.E.
Coe, Pte J.C.G.
Collins, Pte H.
Comptom, Pte S.A.W.
Connan, S/Sgt A.D.*
Connell, Pte D.W.*
Connell, Pte W.E.
Connelly, Pte N.A.
Connors, Pte F.
Connors, Pte S.J.*
Cook, Pte P.C.
Cook, Pte W.R.*
Cookson, Pte W.R.
Coombe, Pte J.
Cooper, Pte C.W.*
Cooper, Pte GJ.*
Conder, Pte E.G.C.
Condon, Pte D.AJ.
Cornelius, L/Sgt L.G.
Corrie, Sgt E.C.W.
Cosson, Pte E.G.
Coughlin, Pte F.B.
Coulsell, L/Cpl C.B.

Coulson, Pre G.C.
Courtney, Cpl E.R.
Cousins, Pte A.H.
Cowden, Cpl M.B.
Cowley, Pte H.
Craig, Pte WJ.
Cramsie, Pte B.
Cravcn, Pte D.F.
Cream, Ptc G.T.J.
Croft, Sgt T.M.
Cross, Pte R.C.
Crozier, Pte T.J.
Cunningham, Pte W.F.
Curry, Pte MJ.
Cutter, Sgt A.R.
Dale, Pte J.S.
Daly, Maj E.A.
D'Argaville, Pte J.
Dart, Pte S.W.
David, Pte H.
Davidson, Pte A.L.*
Davidson, Pte N.A.
Davis, Pte H.H.
Dawson, Pte A.W.
Dean, Cpl W.*
Delaney, Pte R.
Dellaca, Pte J.T.*
Denholm, Pte D.G.
Dewsburry, Pte A. deF.*
Dibb, Pte H.L.*
Dickinson, Pte R.W.*
Dickson, Pte D.H.
Dickson, Cpl J.B.
Dickson, S/Sgt T.C.
Dixon, Pte J.
Dixon, Pte J.H.
Dobson, Cpl G.K.*
Doherty, Pte A.
Doig, Pte A.C.*
Donald, Pte J.
Donnelly, Pte R.A.
Donovan, Pte N.R.*
Dosser, Pte H.
Douglass, Pte N.*
Dowie, Pte J.W.*

Down, Pte R.V.*
Downes, WO W.
Drew, Pte C.E.*
Drury, Cpl A.L.
Duggan, Cpl . J.C.
Dunn, Cpl B.
Durkin, Pte J.E.*
Dyer, Pte LJ.
Dyson, Pte F.A.*
East, Pte W.*
Easton, Pte H.W.
Esther, Pte A.
Edmondson, Pte F.E.
Edward, Pte A.H.*
Edwards, Pte F.G.
Eley, Pte I.S.*
Ellis, Pte S.
Enever, Pte KJ.
English, Pte D.W.*
Eva, Sgt C.S.*
Evans Pte A.L.
Evans, Pte G.P.
Evans, Pte J.R.
Fallon, Pte H.V.*
Fallows, Pte W.J.*
Farlow, Pte F.L.
Farnell, Pte J.C.
Fearn, Pte D.A.
Feehily, Pte A.A.
Fell, Cpl K.V.*
Fenwick, Pte H.G.
Field, Pte A.F.E.
Finch, Cpl W.
Firth, Pte J.F.
Fisher, Pte A.
Fisher, Pte L.K.
Fitches, Cpl AJ.
Fitzclarenee, Pte J.
Fitzgerald, Cpl E.T.
Fitzgerald, Pte J.
Foote, Pte M.
Forbes, Pte W.
Foreman, Pte B.H.
Forrest, Pte G.
Foster, Cpl F.F.

Fowler, Pte G.W.
Fraser, Pte F.V.*
Fraser, Pte S.
Free, Pte H.S.
Freebody, Pte 1.
French, Pte J. StG.
French, Pte RJ.*
Fuller, Pte B.A.*
Gannaway, Pte W.D.*
Gapes, Pte L.C.*
Garvie, Pte W.L.
Garvin, Cpl J.S.*
Gathercole, Pte M.V.
Gaut, Cpl T.G.
Gay, Cpl M.V.*
Gazzard, Pte B.W.
Gee, Pte G.A.*
George, Pte T.
Gill, Pte R.
Girdlestone, Pte R.H.
Gist, Pte H.E.
Gladstone, Pte D.S.*
Glazner, Pte R.W.
Glover, Pte J.F.
Glynn, Pte F.W.
Goding, CaptJ.R.
Goodman, Pte R.G.
Goodman, Cpl G.J.P.*
Goon, Pte E.
Gooney, Sgt P.J.
Gordon, Sgt A.W.
Gordon, Pte J.V.
Gordon, Cpl PJ.
Gore, Pte W.T.
Goss, Pte L.T.*
Gottschutzke, Cpl A.V.*
Graham, Cpl A.*
Grandland, Pte L.J.*
Grant, Pte A.A.
Grant, Pte B.R.
Grant, Pte E.*
Gratten, Pte G.A.
Gray, Pte N.A.
Green, Pte L.J.
Greenham, Sgt R.A.

Greenhatch, Pte M.W.
Greening, Pte R.J.
Gregson, Pte H. McD.
Griffith, Pte J.
Griffith, Pte A.
Grigg, WO E.C.
Grumley, Pte E.T.
Grundy, Pte H.A.*
Gunning, L/Cpl G.W.
Guy, L/Sgt J.
Haig, Pte A J.
Haines, Pte L.L.
Haines, Pte C.W.*
Haldane, Pte S.E.
Hall, Pte F.J.
Hall, Pte G..R.*
Hamilton, Lieut C.G.
Hamilton, Pte K.H.
Hamilton, Pte T.A.V.
Hamley, Pte C.
Hamley, Cpl D.J.*
Haniling, Pte L.C.*
Hammond, Pte G.
Hampton, Pte RJ.*
Handasyde, Capt S.J.
Hands, Pte R.*
Hanrahan, Pte M.J.*
Hansen, Pte E.J.
Harbridge, Pte G.
Hardstaff, Pte TJ.*
Harper, Pte RjJ.
Harrington, Pte J.J.
Harris, Pte C.H.*
Harrison, Pte E.W.
Harrison, Pte H.
Harvey, Pte R.H.
Hattley, Pte W.A.R.
Hay, Pte C.E.*
Haydon, Sgt J.P.
Hayes, Pte V.A.
Hayhoe, Pte S.H.
Hayles, Pte W.T.
Haynes, Pte H.G.
Head, Cpl F.E.*
Heard, Pte S.

Helfier, Pte J.L.
Henderson, Pte E.*
Henderson, L/Sgt J.S.
Hendy, Pte G.E.
Herbert, Pte T.J.
Herbert, Pte O.A.
Heron, Pte 0.
Hicks, Pte J.A.*
Hill, Pte R.R.
Hillas, L/Cpl G.L.*
Hills, Pte H.R.*
Hindrickson, Pte C.H.*
Hoban, Pte D.*
Hock, Pte L.J.
Hocking, Cpl J.R.
Hocking, Pte P.A.
Holden, Pte HJ.
Holdsworth, Pte K.W.
Holmes, Pre S.J.
Holt, Pte A.F.
Hook, Pte A.H.
Hooper, Pte E.E.
Hooper, Pte G.M.
Hooper, Pte G.R.*
Hopkins, Pte J.G.
Hopkins, Sgt R.C.
Horsburgh, Pte A.C.*
Horskins, Pte A.C.
Horton, Pte C.
Hose, Pte D.C.
Hough, L/Sgt E.A.B.
Houston, Lieut R.G.
Hovenden, Sgt J.B.
Hovenden, Pte R.S.*
Howard, Pte C.N.*
Howarth, Pte R.T.
Hoyle, Sgt P.A.
Hughes, Pte J.*
Hughes, L/Cpl L.G.
Hughes, Pte R.E.*
Hunt, Pte F.
Hunt, Pte H.B.
Hunt, Pte R.S.
Hunter, Pte M.C.
Hutchinson, Pte A.

Hutchinson, Pte R.
Hutchinson, Pte V.S.
Hutton, Pte L.G.
Iles, Pte R.J.
Ilsley, Cpl A.C.W.
Irwin, Pte J.R.*
Jackman, Pte G.C.
Jackman, Pte J.H.
Jackson, Pte D.
Jackson, Pte G.S.
Jackson, Pte P.F.
Jean, Pte H.C.
Jeffery, Pte L.
Jellett, Pte .I.S.
Jenkins, Sgt C.L.
Jenkins, Pte C.S.
Jensen, Ptc C.*
Jewell, Pte C.H.
Johnson, Pte L.H.*
Jolinstoll, Pte H.E.*
Johnston, Pte P.J.
Johnstone, Cpl G.L.
Johnstone, Pte H.M.
Johnstone, Pte J.J.*
Jones, Pte A.A.L.
Jones, Pte G.S.*
Jones, Sgt L.
Jones, Pte R.J.
Juers, Pte H.M.
Junek, Pte B.
Kellow, Chaplain F.
Kelly, Pte G.A.
Kennedy, Pte P.J.
Kimber, Pte J.*
King, Pte A.E.
King, Pte B.J.
King, Pte G.H.
King, Pte H.G.E.
King, Pte J.L.
Kinnear, L/Sgt L. McD.*
Kirby, Cpl J.
Klicke, Pte A.R.*
Knape, Pte A.S.
Knape, Pte J.E.G.
Knight, Pte A.

Knight, Pte H.W.
Knudsen, Pte H.S.N.
Krygger, Pte R.G.
Kuno, Pte R.A.
Lamb, Lieut G.H.*
Lambert, Pte C.*
Langer, Pte F.B.
Lawley, Pte J.A.
Lawrence, Pte F.H.*
Lay, Pte F.W.
Leach, Pte A.W.*
Leahy, Pte A.H.
Lebas, Pte K.A.*
Lechmere, Pte A.R.*
Ledwidge, Pte L.AJ.*
Lee, Pte C.J.
Leigh, Pte A.G.
Lennard, Pte R.*
Letchford, Pte J.T.*
Lewis, L/Cpl W.A.
Limbrick, Pte L.G.*
Lindrea, Pte R.T.
Linklater, Pte S.R.
Linnane, Pte V.P.P.*
Litchfield, Pte EX.
Lloyd, Pte W.E.*
Lock, Pte W.E.
Long, Pte F.M.*
Lorimer, Pte G. McL.
Lott, Pte C.R.
Lowe, L/Cp1 G.H.
Lowe, Pte H.E.*
Lowe, Pte W.H.
Lupton, Pte L.*
Lynch, Pte R.T.*
Lynn, Cpl K.H.*
Lyon, Pte E.
Magnuson, Pte C.H.
Magrath, Pte R.H.
Maher, Pte W.R.
Mailes, Cpl C.V.
Malady, Pte L.
Malone, Pte T.L.
Manning, Pte C J.
Mansfield, Pte J.

Mansfield, Pte J.F.*
Marks, Pte R.E.*
Marquis, Pte A.
Marquis, L/Cpl G.F.
Marr, Pte C.D.
Marr, Pte W.
Marsh, Pte A.D.
Marshall, Pte J.*
Marshall, LieutJ.H.
Marson, Pte E.
Marston, Pte R.N.*
Martin, Pte A.
Martin, L/Cpl A.E.
Martin, Pte A.W.
Masterman-Smith, Sgt B.
Matheson, Pte M.D.
Mathews, Pte E.W.
Mathewson, Pte J.W.*
Matthews, Pte C.H.
Matthews, Pte H.L.
Matthews, Pte N. McK.*
Mawby, Pte R.H.
May, Pte H.
Mayne, Pte W.E.J.
Maynard, Pte T.P.
Meagher, Maj E.R.
Medcraft, Pte A.
Meddings, Cpl F.R.
Meers, Pte J.
Melbourne, Pte L.
Melhuish, Pte R.L.
Menzel, Cpl J.C.
Mermod, Pte J.W.*
Merritt, Pte R.*
Merton, Cpl L.F.
Miley, Pte L.T.
Millar, Pte E.S.C.
Miller, Pte CJ.
Miller, S/Sgt F.C.
Miller, L/Cpl J.M.*
Miller, Pte N.L.
Milliken, Pte D.*
Minns, Pte E.K.
Mitchell, Lieut A.A.
Mitchell, Pte A.W.*

Mitchell, Lieut C.J.
Mitchell, Pte J.S.
Moore, Pte A.
Moore, L/Cp1 T.A.*
Morgan, Pte E.C.
Morris, Pte A.J.*
Morris, Pte C.L.
Morton, L/Cpl E.
Moss, Pte J.C.*
Mucklow, Sgt C.W.*
Mulholland, Pte P.J.
Mumford, Pte W.*
Munro, Pte C.
Munro, Pte J.H.
Munro, Pte W.S.
Murnane, Pte J.A.
Murphy, Pte J.C.*
Murphy, Pte T.R.*
Murphy, L/Cpl W.P.
Murray, Pte R.M.
Murray, Pte T.L.
Murrihy, Pte M.J.
MacGregor, Pte J.M.
MacMillan, Pte W.*
MacPherson, Pte N.O.
McArdle, Pte J.P.
McCann, Pte K.
McCarthy, Pte H.C.
McCarthy, Pte J.*
McCarthy, Pte T.W.*
McCarthy, WO W.R.P.
McClelland, Pte D.
McConnell, Pte A.E.
McCrae, Pte V.L.J.
McDermott, Pte J.D.*
McDiarmid, Pte N.F.
McDonald, Pte J.*
McDonald, Cpl N.L.
McDonough, Pte V.G.
McGillien, Pte E.G.
McGovern, Pte J.R.*
McGrath, Pte A.T.
McGrath, Cpl F.X.*
McGuigan, Cpl J.K.
McInnes, Pte F.

McIntosh, Pte H.T.A.
McIntosh, L/Sgt P.
McIntyre, Pte L.S.
McKay, L/Cpl L.W.
McKenzie, Pte D.
McKenzie, Cpl K.V.
McKinnis, Cpl R.*
McLean, WO A.
McLean, Pte WJ.
McLennan, Pte K.W.*
McLennan, Pte WJ.
McLeod, Pte R.M.
McNally, Pte L.R.
McNeil, Pte A.
McPhee, Pte AJ.
McPherson, Pte H.T.
Nankivell, Pte H.R.
Nason, Capt C.H.T.
Nelson, Pte C.R.
Nicholls, Pte A.S.
Nicholls, Pte J.
Nicolson, Capt I.D.
Nightingale, Pte J.K.*
Noble, Pte A.W.J.*
Noble, Pte C.J.*
Nolan, Sgt K.
Nolan, Pte L.R.
Noonan, L/Cpl H.W.
Norton, Pte M.
Nugent, Pte J.D.S.*
Nutt, Cpl W.G.
Nybo, Pte P.W.
Oats, Pte C.H.
O'Brien, S/Sgt T.
O'Brien, Pte T.R.
O'Connor, Pte J.H.*
O'Donnell, Pte B.A.*
O'Keeffe, Pte E.V.*
Oldham, Pte G.F.*
Oldham, Pte H.J.
Oliphant, Pte T.
O'Loughlin, Pte T.
O'Loughlin, Pte V.
O'Neil, Pte T.E.
O'Rourke, Pte P.J.

Osbourne, Pte B.S.*
Osmond, Pte A.W.
O'Sullivan, Pte J.J.*
Page, Pte E.C.*
Paine, Pte F.
Pallss, S/Sgt J.E.
Pannowitz, Pte N.O.
Parker, Pte J.H.*
Parker, Pte J.R.*
Parrett, Pte R.
Pattison, Pte F.C.
Payne, Pte A.C.*
Peady, Pte S.
Pearce, Pte L.T.
Pearson, Pte F.C.
Peck, Pte H.J.T.
Peck, Pte M.E.
Peeler, WO W.
Pell, Pte L.*
Pemberton, Lieut J.M.
Penaluna, Pte J.S.
Peter, Pte C.T.*
Peters, Pte V.*
Peterson, Pte C.W.*
Phillips, Pte C.W.
Phillips, WO F.V.
Phillips, Pte R.J.*
Plain, Cpl T.W.*
Pople, Pte W.H.*
Poulton, Cpl C.H.
Powell, Pte L.
Power, Pte K.L.
Prescott, Pte H.J.
Prior, Pte A.N.*
Pritchard, L/Cpl G.
Prydderch, Pte S.*
Pugh, L/Cpl H.B.A.
Pugh, Pte A.*
Pugsley, Pte H.C.
Quinn, Cpl A.J.
Quinn, Pte J.W.
Radcliffe, Pte K.E.*
Rampling, Pte R.W.*
Ramsey, Pre H.G.
Ransome, Pte E.G.

Rayment, Pte K.C.*
Rea, Pte E.A.
Rees, Pte L.W.
Reese, Pte L.R.*
Reilly, Sgt W.J.
Renton, Pte K.C.
Reshke, Pte B.
Rex, WO R.
Reynolds, Pte G.H.
Rhook, Pte W.D.
Rice, Pte R.C.
Richards, Cpl A.J.
Richards, Pte E.
Richards, Cpl F.A.
Richards, Lieut G.W.
Richards, Pte J.T.*
Richardson, Pte W.H.*
Richter, Pte W.A.*
Ridley, Pte T.A.
Rielly, Pte J.
Rielly, Pte W.G.
Ritchie, L/Sgt J.G.
Rivett, Pte L.
Rixon, Pre S.K.
Roberts, Pte D.*
Roberts, Pte H.G.
Roberts, Cpl J. McA.
Robertson, Cpl H.S.*
Robertson, Sgt J.H.
Robertson, Pte K.C.
Robertson, Pte T.*
Robinson, Pte F.R.*
Robinson, Pte J.C.*
Robinson, L/Cpl T.*
Rodd, Pte S.J.J.*
Rodie, Lieut A.F.D.
Rohead, Pte N.
Rolston, Pte J.
Rose, Pte V.
Ross, Capt A.H.J.
Ross, Pre G.
Rossiter, Lieut F.M.
Rowe, Pte A.W.
Rowe, Pre E.A.
Ruddle, Cpl J.W.

Rumble, Pte AJ.
Rumble, Pte J.
Ryan, Pte J.
Ryan, Pte J.J.
Ryan, Sgt W.A.G.*
Sadler, Sgt H.R.K.
Sargent, Pre F.J.
Sarkies, Pre R.G.
Saw, Pte G.E.R.*
Schultz, Pte A.J.*
Scharmahan, L/Sgt E.*
Scott, Pre T.*
Shannon, Cpl T.A.*
Sharman, Pte L.V.
Sharock, Pte W.J.
Shepherd, Pre W.J.
Sheridan, Pte J.A.*
Sherritt, Pte D.
Shraden, Pte A.C.*
Simpkins, L/Cpl W.A.
Sinclair, Pre C.H.
Sipthorpe, Pte A.
Skipper, Pte J.C.
Smith, Pte A.C.
Smith, Pte C.W.
Smith, Pte G.
Smith, Pte H.J.*
 (VX40057)
Smith, Pte H.J.
Smith, Pte J.W.P.*
Smith, L/Sgt L.J.*
Smith, Sgt N.L.
Smith, Pte P.C.*
Smith, Pte P.H.
Smith, Pte R.*
Smith, Pre T.G.*
Smith, Pte W.T.
Smythe, Pte E.J.
Somers, S/Sgt R.P.
Somerville, Pte A.C.*
Sorley, Pte H.
Spence, Pte A.T.*
Spence, Cpl W.L.*
Spikpn, Pte T.*
Sprague, Pre C.G.

Spriggs, Cpl W.

Spriggs, Pte J.J.

Stafford, Cpl T.J.

Stammers, Pte W.G.*

Staples, Pte W.C.

Steel, Sgt J.H.*

Stephenson, Pte J.

Stevenson, Pte F.

Stewart, Pte E.D.

Stewart, Sgt H.K.

Stilley, Pte G.*

Stockton, Pte F.

Stockton, Pte T.H.

Stokes, Sgt A.

Stokes, Pte F.E.

Stokes, Pte S.F.

Strahan, Pte LJ.

Stratton, Pte G.F.

Stuart, Pte A.*

Sunderland, Pte N.

Sullivan, Pte W.B.*

Sullivan, Pte T.A.

Summons, Lieut W.I.

Sutherland, Pte J.

Swanson, Pte K.J.

Tait, Pte A.J.

Taylor, Pte A.

Taylor, Pte D.E.

Taylor, Pte D.G.

Taylor, Pte H.

Taylor, Sgt L.F.

Templeman, Lieut J.H.

Thomas, Pte H.I.

Thomas, Pte H.R.

Thomas, L/Cpl T.C.

Thompson, Pte C.G.

Thompson, Pte H.W.*

Thompson, Pte R,A.*

Thompson, Pte R.E.

Thompson, Pte F.S.

Thomson, Pte W.J.

Thorn, Cpl C.

Thorn, Pte L.*

Thornton, Pte D.J.S.*

Tilney, Lieut W.W.

Timms, Pte B.J.

Timms, Pte D.W.

Todd, Cpl G.B.*

Tolliday, Pte L.R.

Tomison, Pte A.G.

Tomlin, Pte G.B.

Toogood, Pte R.W.*

Toomey, Pte J.J.H.

Topfer, Lieut G.H.G.

Tottenham, Pte N.C.

Towers, Pte A.W.

Tranter, Lieut N.G.H.

Tregea, Pte P.J.

Trewin, Cpl R.L.

Tubb, Lieut F.H.

Tuck, Pte W.G.

Tully, Pte A.J.*

Tully, Pte F.W.

Turner, Pte G.H.

Tyrrell, Cpl A.*

Upton, Pte H.P.

Vale, Pte F.P.

Vandervord, Pte A.S.

Vardy, L/Sgt M.*

Veal, Pte E.S.

Veitch, Pte A.E.

Verrall, Pte F.C.

Vickery, Pte C.

Vincent, Pte R.W.

Waddell, Pte H.A.*

Waddell, Pte R.F.

Waite, Pte W.J.*

Walker, Cpl H.E.

Walker, Pte W.D.

Wallis, Pte F.J.

Walters, Lieut J.H.

Warren, Cpl F.E.*

Watkins, Pte W.R.

Watson, Pte J.*

Watson, Pte K.B.

Waugh, Pte A.L.*

Waugh, Pte J.T.

Webb, Pte P.J.

Webster, Lieut G.N.

Webster, Pte T.H.

Weir, Pte J.A.*

Westbrook, Pte H.

Westgarth, Sgt A.T.

White, Sgt C.N.

White, L/Cpl F.S.

White, Pte J.J.

Whitfeld, L/Sgt L.E.*

Whitmore, Pte R.

Whytcross, Pte L.W.

Wild, Sgt L.J.

Wilkie, Pte S.R.

Wilkinson, Pte M.W.

Wilkinson, Pte R.W.

Willard, Cpl J.A.*

Willey, Pte H.A.*

Williams, Pte B.

Williams, Pte J.

Williams, Lieut Col J.M.

Williams, Pte L.J.

Williams, Pte M.A.

Williams, Pte P.H.

Williams, Pte R.N.

Williams, Pte R.T.

Williamson, Pte K.M.*

Willoughby, Pte M.

Wills, Pte A.

Wilson, L/Cpl A.W.

Wilson, Pte K.V.

Wind, Pte K.K.

Windebank, Pte N.S.

Winning, Capt R.F.H.

Wood, Pte P.J.

Wood, Pte W.A.*

Woodhead, Pte J.A.*

Woods, Pte P.J.G.*

Wornes, Pte R.S.

Worrall, Pte E.W.*

WorraH, Pte N.E.

Wrathall, Pte D.*

Wright, Pte G.

Wright, Pte V.J.

Wust, Pte V.G.*

Wyatt, Pte A.A.

Yorston, Cpl J.W.

Youens, Pte H.L.

Young, Sgt K.L.

Notes

Chapter 2

1. B. Dunn, *Bamboo Express,* p. 170.
2. Conversation with the author, Melbourne, October 1991.
3. Sir E.E. Dunlop, *War Memoirs,* p. xxviii.
4. D.M. Horner, *High Command,* Allen & Unwin, Sydney, 1982, p. 443.
5. *The New York Times,* February 28, 1992, p. 1.
6. *Australian National Dictionary,* Oxford University Press, Melbourne, p. 492.
7. B.Dunn, *Bamboo Express,* p. 171.
8. Walter Summons, *Twice Their Prisoner,* Oxford University Press, Melbourne, 1946, p. 63.
9. *Story of the 2/2 Australian Pioneer Battalion,* (privately printed), Melbourne, 1953. p. 136.
10. Australian War Memorial Document # AWM 52, item 8/6/2.
11. W.Summons, *Twice Their Prisoner,* foreword, p. 13.
12. A.H. Bishop, letter to the author, April 30, 1992
13. *Bn. History,* p. 139.
14. *ibid.*
15. R. Benedict, *Chrysanthemum and Sword,* p. 241.
16. Conversation with the author, February 16, 1992
17. Benedict, *The Chrysanthemum and the Sword, pp. 190 ff.*
18. *Holy Bible, The Book of Genesis, Chapter 45.*
19. Dunlop, *The War Diaries of Weary Dunlop.* p. xxiii.
20. *The New York Times,* April 1, 1992, p. 1.
21. *Bn. History,* p. 143.
22. Leslie Hall, *The Queen of Hearts,* unpublished manuscript, p. 259.
23. *Bn. History,* p. 145.
24. Leslie Hall, *The Blue Haze, p. 62.*
25. Letter to the author, December 2, 1992.
26. *Bn. History,* p. 145.
27. B. Dunn, *The Bamboo Express,* p. 31.
28. Letter to the author, December 2, 1992.
29. Letter to the author, November 10, 1992.
30. Letter to the author, January 24, 1992.
31. Letter to the author, October 8, 1992.
32. Conversation with the author, Melbourne, October 29, 1991.

33. Conversation with the author, Jell's Park, Melbourne, October 27, 1991.

34. *Bn. History,* p. 146.

35. A.H. Bishop, 'A Voyage With the Jap in South East Asia', unpublished article, pp. 14–17.

36. *Bn. History,* p. 155.

37. United States Government, Department of State File # 740.0015, Pacific War/290, RG 59, National Archives. First researched by Michi Weglyn for her book, *Years of Infamy* (see bibliography)

Chapter 3

1. Kevin Nolan, letter to the author, August 21, 1992.

2. L. Hall, *Blue Haze,* pp. 296–7.

3. Ernest Gordon, conversation with the author, August 19, 1991.

4. Ronald Searle, *To the Kwai- and Back,* New York, The Atlantic Monthly Press, 1986, p. 104.

5. L. Hall, *Blue Haze,* p. 208.

6. J. and C. Blair, *Return/Kwai,* p. 15.

7 L. Hall, *Haze,* p. 129.

8. Lavinia Warner and John Sandilands, *Women Beyond the Wire,* Leister, F.A. Thorpe Publishing LTD, 1982, p. 358.

9. L. Hall, *Blue Haze,* p. 208.

10. Takashi Nagase, *Crosses and Tigers,* Bangkok, The Post Publishing Co., LTD, 1990, p. 13.

11. L. Hall, *Blue Haze,* p. 191.

12. R. Searle, *To The Kwai,* p. 10.

13. L. Hall, *Blue Haze,* p. 146.

14. Holy Bible, King James version, Second Epistle of Paul the Apostle to the Thessalonians, Chapter 10, verse 3.

15. R. Benedict, *Chrysanthemum/Sword,* p. 37.

16. Sir Edward Dunlop, letter to the author, November 9, 1992.

17. L. Hall, *Blue Haze,* p. 300.

18. Hank Nelson, Prisoners of War: Australians Under Nippon, Sydney, Australian Broadcasting Company, 1985.

19. Conversations with the author, Melbourne, October 1991.

Chapter 4

1. *Battalion History,* p. 166.

2. From an interwvew with the author at Dr. Gordon's summer home, Amagansett, NY USA, August 29, 1991.

3. Letter to the author, January 8, 1993.

4. From an interview with the author, Melbourne, October 29, 1991.

5. From a conversation at Narrabeen, NSW, October 23, 1991.

6. From a letter to the author, November 9, 1992.

7. Nagase, *Crosses and Tigers,* p. 18.

8. Ernest Gordon, *Miracle on the River Kwai,* William Collins & Co., Glasgow, 1963, p. 169.

9. Letter to the author, April 30, 1991.

Chapter 5

1. Hall, "The Queen of Hearts", unpublished manuscript, 1991
2. Hall, *The Blue Haze,* p. 300.
3. ibid., p. 141
4. Nagase, *Crosses and Tigers,* p. 30
5. ibid., pp. 30–31.
6. Letter to the author, January 26, 1992.
7. Hall, "The Queen of Hearts", p. 269
8. Dunn, *The Bamboo Express,* pp. 167–168.
9. Letter to the author, August 21, 1992
10. Letters to the author, February, April, July 1992
11. Letter to the author, June 12 1992.

Chapter 6

1. G. Hamilton, letter to his family, September 8, 1945.
2. H. Whelan, letter to the author, January 26, 1992.
3. Letter to the author, August 3, 1992.

Chapter 7

1. Letter to the author, February 16, 1991.
2. Dunn, *the Bamboo Express,* p. 27
3. Hall, *The Blue Haze,* quoting excerpt from diary of Col. Williams, p. 315.
4. ibid.
5. Dunn., op. cit., p. 180.
6. ibid., p. 125.
7. Hall, op. cit., p. 310

Chapter 8

1. Peter N. Davies, *The Man Behind The Bridge: Colonel Toosey and the River kwai,* Athlone, London/Atlantic Highlands, NJ, 1991, p. 177.
2. Conversation with the author, Melbourne, October 27, 1991.
3. Conversation with the author, Narrabeen, NSW, October 25, 1991.
4. Hall, *The Blue Haze,* pp. 133–134.
5. ibid., p. 286.
6. Warner and Sandilands, *Women Beyond the Wire,* p. 171.
7. Blair, *Return From the River Kwai,* p. 16.
8. Conversation with the author, Shelter Island, NY, May 26, 1992.
9. Letter to the author, September 10, 1992.
10 Warner and Sandilands, *op. cit.,* p. 146.

Chapter 9

1. Letter to the author, June 6, 1992.
2. Warner and Sandilands, *Women Beyond the Wire,* p. 23.

3. Letter to the author, October 23, 1992.

4. Letter to the author, June 12, 1992.

5. Letter to the author, October 23, 1992.

6. Dunn, *The Bamboo Express,* p. 187, and conference with the author, November 10, 1992.

7. H. Nelson, "Prisoners of War", Australian Broadcasting Company, 1985, p. 45.

8. Hall, *The Blue Haze,* p. 135.

9. Benedict, *the Chrysanthemum and the Sword,* p. 159.

10. ibid., p. 210.

11. Colonel Harold Doud, "How the Japanese Army fights", *Infantry Journal,* 1942, pp. 54–55. First quoted by Benedict, op. cit., p. 181.

12. Letter to the author, October 7, 1992.

13. Conversation with the author, Melbourne, October 28, 1991.

14. Letter to the author, October 3, 1992.

Chapter 10

1. Hall, *the Blue Haze,* diary excerpts, p. 307.

2. ibid., p. 255, Fagan diary entry for October 2, 1943.

3. Searle, *To the Kwai—and Back,* p. 114, Imperioal war Museum, London, #P91.

Chapter 11

1. Hall, *the Blue Haze,* p. 294; Williams diary entry, October 6, 1943.

2. Letter to the author, February 16, 1991.

3. Letter to the author, April 30, 1991.

4. Conversation at a Pioneer Battalion Association gathering, Jell's Park, melbourne, October 27, 1991.

5. Dunn, *The Bamboo Express,* pp. 164–165.

6. Letter to the author, April 30, 1991.

7. Letters to the author, August 25 and November 12, 1992.

8. Letter to the author, March 19,1992.

Chapter 12

1. Conversation with the author, Jell's Park, Melbourne, October 27, 1991.

2. Summons, *Twice Their Prisoner,* p. 174.

3. Letter to Dickson's widow, after his death, August 8, 1991.

4. Letter to the author, January 8, 1993.

5. Letter to the author, July 16, 1992.

6. Letter to the author, July 11, 1992.

7. Letter to the author, July 16, 1992.

8. ibid.

9. Essay from the *Rafu Shimpo,* January 1992 edition. Quoted with permission of the essayist, Henry Shigeru Yagake. Translated from the Japanese by Reiko Uyeshima.

10. Letter to the author, July 6, 1992.

11. Conversation with the author, Narrabeen, NSW, October 19, 1991.

12. Recollection by Ralph Gross, September 18, 1992.

Chapter 13

1. Conversation with the author, Melbourne, October 28, 1991.

2. Letter to the author, July 16, 1992.

3. G. Hamilton, letter to his family, September 8, 1945.

4. Nagase, *Crosses and Tigers,* p. 15.

5. Letter to the author, August 21, 1992.

6. Letter to the author, July 16, 1992.

7. Letters to his family, September 1 and 8, 1945.

8. Letter to the author, August 25, 1992.

9. Conversation with the author, Amagansett, NY, August 27, 1990.

10. Letter to the author, April 3, 1992.

Chapter 14

1. Nagase, *Crosses and Tigers,* p. 17.

2. Letter to the author, July 12, 1992.

3. Nagase, *Crosses and Tigers,* p. 39–41.

4. ibid., p. 42

5. Nelson, *Prisoners of War,* p. 147.

6. Article in the Melbourne *Herald,* May 22, 1946, p. 1.

7. Dunn, *The Bamboo Express,* p. 188.

8. Captain James Norwood and Captain emily Shek, "Prisoner of War Camps in Areas other than the Four Principal Islands of Japan", Liaison and Research Branch, American Prisoner of War Information Bureau, 1943. Declassified July 31, 1946. Document courtesy of Otto Schwarz, President, *Uss Houston* Survivors Association.

9. *Battalion History,* p. 172.

10. Benedict, *the Chrystanthemuym and the Sword,* p. 182.

11. Peter N. Davies, *the Man Behind the Bridge,* Athlone, London, 1991, p. 58.

12. Nagase, *Crosses and Tigers,* p. 46.

13. Letter to the author, July 29, 1992.

14. Letter to the author, July 6, 1992.

15. Gordon, *Miracle on the River Kwai,* pp. 162–163.

16. Letter to the author, January 26, 1992.

17. Letter to the author, August 21, 1992.

18. Conversation with the author, Shelter Island, NY, May 1979.

Chapter 15

1. Letter to the author, December 4, 1992.

2. Letters to the author, October 29 and December 4, 1992.

3. Hall, *The Blue Haze,* p. 257. Extract from the diary of thomas Fagan.

4. ibid., p. 221.

5. Dunn, *the Bamboo Express,* pp. 181–182.

6. Letter to the author, March 17, 1992.

7. Gordon, *Miracle on the River Kwai,* pp. 73 ff.

8. Searle, *To the Kwai—and Back,* p. 128.

9. Holy Bible, Gospel according to John, chapter 13, verse 35.

10. Letter to the author, June 30, 1992, commenting on his essay in the *Rafu Shimpo,* January 1, 1992.

Chapter 16

1. Letter to the author, April 3, 1992.

2. Melbourne *Sun,* November 5, 1945, p. 1.

3. Conversation with the author, Jell's Park, Melbourne, October 27, 1991.

4. Letter to the author, February 16, 1991.

5. Letter to the author, August 25, 1992.

6. Letter to the author, July 16, 1992.

7. Conversation with the author, Jell's Park, Melbourne, October 27, 1991.

Chapter 17

1. Nagase, *Crosses and Tigers,* p. 75.

2, The *Washington Post,* July 15, 1990, p. 22.

3. The *New York Times,* August 4, 1991, p. 1.

4. For a detailed discussion of the secret Allied relief fund and its postwar disbursement, see Holmes, *Unjust Enrichment,* Chapter 11.

5. The *New York Times,* June 16, 1992, p. 15.

6. Conversation with the author, October 19, 1992; T. Nagase, *Crosses and Tigers,* p. 76.

7. Conversation with the author, October 13, 1992.

8. Conversation with the author, Scarsdale, New York, January 8, 1992.

9. The *New York Times,* November 22, 1992, "the Week in Review", p. 5.

10. Dunlop, *War Diaries,* preface, p. xxi.

11. Nagase, *Crosses and Tigers,* p. 61.

12. Letter to the author, July 6, 1992.

13. Letter to the author, January 8, 1993.

14. Letter to the author, March 17, 1992.

15. Letter to the author, April 30, 1992.

16. Letter to the author, April 30, 1991.

17. The *New York Times,* July 7, 1992, p. 1.

18. Excerpts from *Barbed Wire and Bamboo,* official organ of the New South Wales Ex-Prisoners of War Association, December 1950 issue, pp. 4ff.

19. ibid., February 1958 issue, p. 11.

20. Conversation with the author, November 18, 1992.

21. Conversation with the author, October 28, 1991.

Bibliography

Aitken, E.F. /Dickson, T.C.: *The Story of the 2/2nd Australian Pioneer Battalion,* 1953, privately printed, Melbourne.

Arneil, Stan: *One Man's Battle,* 1983, Sun Books PTY LTD, South Melbourne.

Australian National Dictionary, 1988, Oxford University Press, Melbourne.

Benedict, Ruth: *The Chrysantemum and the Sword: Patterns of Japanese Culture,,* 1967, Meridian Books, New York. [first published 1946.]

Blair, Joan & Clay, Jr.: *Return From The River Kwai,* 1954, Vanguard Press, New York.

Bowden, Tim: *The Photographer of Changi: George Aspinall's Record of Captivity,* 1984, William Collins Pty LTD, Sydney.

Boulle, Pierre: *The Bridge Over The River Kwai,* 1954, The Vanguard Press, New York.

Boyle, James: *Railroad To Burma,* 1990, Allen & Unwin, Sydney.

Braddon, Russell: *The Naked Island,* 1952, Werner Laurie, London.

Clarke, Hugh V.: *A Life For Every Sleeper,* 1986, Allen & Unwin, Sydney.

Davies, Peter N.: *The Man Behind The Bridge: Col. Toosey and the River Kwai,* 1991, Athlone Press, London.

Dunlop, E. E.: *The War Diaries of Weary Dunlop,* 1990, Penguin Books, Ringwood.

Dunn, Benjamin: *The Bamboo Express,* 1979, privately printed.

Gordon, Ernest: *Miracle on the River Kwai,* 1963, William Collins Sons & Co., Glasgow.

Hall, Leslie G.: *The Blue Haze,* 1985, privately printed.

Holmes, Linda Goetz: *Unjust Enrichment: How Japanese Companies Built Postwar Fortunes Using American POWs,* 2001, Stackpole Books, Mechanicsburg, PA.

Horner, D.M.: *High Command,* 1982, Allen & Unwin, Sydney.

Lord Russell of Liverpool: *The Knights of Bushido: A Short History of Japanese War Crimes,* 1958, Cassell & Co. LTD, London.

191

Nagase, Takashi: *Crosses and Tigers,* 1990, The Post Publishing Co., Bangkok.

Nelson, Hank: *Prisoners of War: Australians Under Nippon,* 1985, Australian Broadcasting Company.

Rivett, Rohan: *Behind Bamboo,* 1946, Angus & Robertson, Melbourne.

Searle, Ronald: *To the Kwai—and Back: War Drawings, 1939–1945, 1986, The Atlantic Monthly Press, New York.*

Summons, Walter: Twice Their Prisoner, *1946, Oxford University Press, Melbourne.*

Wall, Don: Heroes at Sea, *1991, privately printed.*

Warner, Lavinia & Sandilands, J.: Women Beyond the Wire, *1982, F.A. Thorpe Publishing, LTD, Leister.*

Weglyn, Michi N.: Years of Infamy: The Untold Story of American Concentration Camps, *1976, William Morrow & Co., New York.*

Newspapers and Periodicals

The *Argus,* Melbourne, various 1945 editions.

The *Sun,*, Melbourne, various 1945 editions.

Yagake, H. Shigeru, essay in The *Rafu Shimpo,* Los Angeles, CA, January 1992 edition.

Bhimaya, K.M.: ' Leadership in Captivity: A Case Study of Kwai Prison Camp', article in *Journal of the United Services Institution of India,* January-March 1986 edition.

The *New York Times,* various editions.

Archives

Australian War Memorial Research Centre, Canberra.

Boy Scouts of America, International Division, Irvine, TX.

The Herald and Weekly Times Archives, Melbourne.

The National Archives, College Park, MD.

U.S. Library of Congress Archives, Washington, DC.

Unpublished Manuscripts

Bishop, A.H.: 'A Voyage With The Jap in South East Asia' 1991.

Hall, Leslie G.: 'The Queen of Hearts', 1991.

Index

For sales, editorial information, subsidiary rights information
or a catalog, please write or phone or e-mail
Brick Tower Press
1230 Park Avenue
New York, NY 10128, US
Sales: 1-800-68-BRICK
Tel: 212-427-7139 Fax: 212-860-8852
www.BrickTowerPress.com
email: bricktower@aol.com.

For sales in the United States, please contact
National Book Network
nbnbooks.com
Orders: 800-462-6420
Fax: 800-338-4550
custserv@nbnbooks.com

For sales in the UK and Europe please contact our distributor,
Gazelle Book Services
Falcon House, Queens Square
Lancaster, LA1 1RN, UK
Tel: (01524) 68765 Fax: (01524) 63232
email: gazelle4go@aol.com.

For Australian and New Zealand sales please contact
Bookwise International
174 Cormack Road, Wingfield, 5013, South Australia
Tel: 61 (0) 419 340056 Fax: 61 (0)8 8268 1010
email: karen.emmerson@bookwise.com.au